# Cacti, Agaves, and Yuccas
## of California and Nevada

# Cacti, Agaves, and Yuccas of California and Nevada

Text and Photos by
Stephen Ingram

Cachuma Press
Los Olivos, California

Copyright © Cachuma Press 2008

Second printing with revisions, June 2017

All rights reserved. No part of this book may be reproduced in any form or by any electronic or mechanical device without written permission of the publisher. Requests for permission to make copies of any part of the work should be mailed to: Cachuma Press, P.O. Box 560, Los Olivos, CA 93441. For more information on purchasing Cachuma Press titles, visit us at: www.cachumapress.com

Photos: Unless otherwise noted, all photos copyright © Stephen Ingram
E.O. Murman art: copyright © Margo Murman
Susan Bazell art: copyright © Susan Bazell

Editors: Marjorie Popper and John Evarts
Graphic Design, Production, and Proofreading: Katey O'Neill
Cartography: Sue Irwin and Dan Van Dorn
Printing: Tien Wah Press, Malaysia

Library of Congress Cataloging-in-Publication Data

Ingram, Stephen, 1961-
  Cacti, agaves, and yuccas of California and Nevada / text and photos by Stephen Ingram. -- 1st ed.
    p. cm.
  Includes bibliographical references and index.
  ISBN 978-0-9789971-0-6 (pbk.) -- ISBN 978-0-9789971-1-3 (hardcover)
  1. Cactus--California. 2. Agaves--California. 3. Yucca--California. 4. Cactus--Nevada.
  5. Agaves--Nevada. 6. Yucca--Nevada. I. Title.

QK495.C11I64 2008
583'.5609794--dc22

2008001199

*Front cover: Mojave mound cactus.*
*Back cover: (from top) Mojave prickly-pear and Engelmann hedgehog; Shaw agave; chaparral yucca.*
*Page i: (clockwise from upper left) little prickly-pear; Shaw agave; short-joint beavertail; Mojave yucca.*
*Page ii–iii: Joshua trees.*
*Page iv: (above) beavertail cactus. Artwork by E.O. Murman*

# Contents

Preface . . . . . . . . . . . . . . . . . . . . . . . . . . . . . . . . . . . . . . . . . . . . . . . . . . . . . . . . . . . . . . . . . . . . vii

Acknowledgments . . . . . . . . . . . . . . . . . . . . . . . . . . . . . . . . . . . . . . . . . . . . . . . . . . . . . . . . . viii

Introduction . . . . . . . . . . . . . . . . . . . . . . . . . . . . . . . . . . . . . . . . . . . . . . . . . . . . . . . . . . . . . . . 1

Chapter One: Evolution, Classification, and Botanical Characteristics . . . . . . . . . . . . . . . . . 3

Chapter Two: Ecology and Habitats of Cacti, Agaves, and Yuccas . . . . . . . . . . . . . . . . . . . 15

Chapter Three: Species Profiles . . . . . . . . . . . . . . . . . . . . . . . . . . . . . . . . . . . . . . . . . . . . . . 25
    Cactaceae . . . . . . . . . . . . . . . . . . . . . . . . . . . . . . . . . . . . . . . . . . . . . . . . . . . . . . . . . . . . 27
    Agavaceae . . . . . . . . . . . . . . . . . . . . . . . . . . . . . . . . . . . . . . . . . . . . . . . . . . . . . . . . . . . .149
Nolinas, Ocotillo, and Non-Native Species . . . . . . . . . . . . . . . . . . . . . . . . . . . . . . . . . . . . .181

Chapter Four: Conservation and Cultivation . . . . . . . . . . . . . . . . . . . . . . . . . . . . . . . . . . .191

Chapter Five: Exploring the Cactus Country of California and Nevada . . . . . . . . . . . . . . .203

Appendices
    A: Cactus, Agave, and Yucca Species of California and Nevada . . . . . . . . . . . . . . . . . .214
    B: Major Vegetation Types and Habitats for Cacti, Agaves, and Yuccas . . . . . . . . . . . .216
    C: Scientific Names for Non-featured Species . . . . . . . . . . . . . . . . . . . . . . . . . . . . . . .219
    D: Cholla Species Comparison . . . . . . . . . . . . . . . . . . . . . . . . . . . . . . . . . . . . . . . . . . .220
    E: Prickly-pear Species Comparison . . . . . . . . . . . . . . . . . . . . . . . . . . . . . . . . . . . . . .222
    F: Species Rarity Status . . . . . . . . . . . . . . . . . . . . . . . . . . . . . . . . . . . . . . . . . . . . . . . .224
    G: Education, Conservation, and Cultivation Resources . . . . . . . . . . . . . . . . . . . . . . .225
    H: Species List For Selected Public Lands in California and Nevada . . . . . . . . . . . . .226

Key to the Genera . . . . . . . . . . . . . . . . . . . . . . . . . . . . . . . . . . . . . . . . . . . . . . . . . . . . . . . .232

Glossary . . . . . . . . . . . . . . . . . . . . . . . . . . . . . . . . . . . . . . . . . . . . . . . . . . . . . . . . . . . . . . . .234

Bibliography . . . . . . . . . . . . . . . . . . . . . . . . . . . . . . . . . . . . . . . . . . . . . . . . . . . . . . . . . . . .236

Index . . . . . . . . . . . . . . . . . . . . . . . . . . . . . . . . . . . . . . . . . . . . . . . . . . . . . . . . . . . . . . . . . .244

*A mountain cactus in full bloom perches high on an alpine ridge in Nevada's Schell Creek Range. [White Pine Co.]*

# Preface

My attention to California cactus was rekindled in the spring of 1998 when a group of friends from the California Native Plant Society and I drove along the Bradshaw Trail to find, among other botanical treasures, Munz cholla. This locally common cholla—I had just learned—occurred only in this general area south of the Chuckwalla Mountains, and it was the first cactus I knew from California that I could stand next to and look up at. We also searched unsuccessfully for lone saguaros rumored to survive in the nearby Palo Verde Mountains, but we saw no other cacti that impressed me as much as the tall, gangly cholla named for California botanist Philip Munz. I have long been interested in plant adaptations and the biogeography of plants, and the beauty of cacti, agaves, and yuccas have inspired my photography for many years. In 2004, when Cachuma Press gave me the opportunity to research and photograph our native spiny succulents for a new book, I was excited to begin the journey.

Although my travels of over 30,000 miles across California and Nevada to observe and photograph these plants clearly lacked many of the challenges that faced 18th- and 19th-century naturalists, this fieldwork gave me enormous respect for earlier botanists who traveled some of these same roads and whose research has been instrumental for this and other books written about these plants. The cacti, agaves, and yuccas native to California and Nevada have been collected, studied, described, and written about for over 160 years. Yet many of these species are still poorly known, and some have been described only recently.

From the discovery of new cactus, agave, and yucca species by the first botanist-explorers who ventured into the western frontier to the discovery of the evolutionary relationships of these species using DNA sequences, botanical research continues to change and enlighten our views of these plants. In this book I relate some of the interesting history, biology, and ecology to come from studies of these successful succulents. Hopefully, *Cacti, Agaves, and Yuccas of California and Nevada* will fill the gap between highly technical publications that may not appeal to a general audience and field guides that don't allow room to discuss the natural history of their botanical subjects.

*Some hybrid cacti, like this cross between two prickly-pears, are still unnamed. [Joshua Tree N.P.]*

Our understanding of cacti, agaves, and yuccas may be more complete than it was 50 years ago, but their place in the environment is now more threatened than ever. Illegal collecting, habitat degradation due to the proliferation of exotic, invasive plants, and habitat loss due to the expanding human footprint continue to chip away at the long-term viability of some of these species. My hope with this book is to give readers a deeper picture of these plants and perhaps an increased awareness of their ecological relationships and environments. Only if our cacti, agaves, yuccas, and other native plants are better appreciated will they be conserved.

## ACKNOWLEDGEMENTS

This book would not have been possible without the generous help of many people. I especially want to thank Jon Rebman, Curator of Botany at the San Diego Natural History Museum, for sharing his time, cactus insight, and for his thorough review and helpful comments. I am very grateful to the other technical reviewers who gave generously of their time and offered many useful comments, including Patrick Leary, Botanist at Community College of Southern Nevada; Allan Schoenherr, Professor of Ecology at Fullerton College; and Arnold Tiehm of the Nevada Native Plant Society. Jim D. Morefield, Botanist for the Nevada Natural Heritage Program, also provided critical reviews and helped enormously with assistance on finding some of Nevada's rare cacti.

I also want to thank Carol Bornstein of the Santa Barbara Botanic Garden, Stephen McCabe of the University of California Santa Cruz Arboretum, and Mark Porter of Rancho Santa Ana Botanic Garden for their important reviews and help with several sections of the manuscript.

This book benefited greatly from the reviews of local land managers and botanists, and I want to thank them for their time and energy: Kim O'Connor and Andrea Compton at Cabrillo National Monument; Darren Smith at Torrey Pines State Reserve; Mark Jorgensen, Superintendent of Anza-Borrego Desert State Park; Cristina Mills and Jim Andre at Mojave National Preserve; Tasha La Doux at Joshua Tree National Park; Dianne Bangle and Jim Holland at Lake Mead National Recreation Area; and Athena Sparks at Red Rock Canyon Interpretive Association.

For their enormous help providing herbarium collection data, specimens, and their insight, I thank Elizabeth Makings at Arizona State University, Judy Gibson at San Diego Natural History Museum, Steve Boyd and Sula Vanderplank at Rancho Santa Ana Botanic Garden, Steve Junak and Dieter Wilken at Santa Barbara Botanic Garden, Margriet Wetherwax at the University and Jepson Herbaria at University of California, Berkeley, Andy Sanders at University of California, Riverside, Kathryn Birgy and Wes Niles at the Wesley E. Niles Herbarium, University of Nevada, Las Vegas, and Christy Malone and Arnold Tiehm at University of Nevada, Reno.

Numerous friends and colleagues also contributed significantly to this book project by sharing location information for uncommon species, loaning books and journals, sending reprints, identifying insects from photos, answering my persistent questions, making suggestions, and willingly providing their help. These people include: Jim Andre, Marc Baker, Roxanne Bittman, Larry Blakely, Rick Burgess, Annie and Rick Cashner, Ellen Cypher, Sarah DeGroot, Jim Dice, John Dicus, Mark Dimmitt, John Dittli, Erin Dreyfus, Teri Drezner, Erika Edwards, Julie Evens, John Game, Arthur Gibson, Sara Good-Avila, Anne Halford, Bruce Hanson, Steve Hartman, Scott Hetzler, Glenn Huntington, John Johnson, Steve Larson, Kristi Lazar, Tasha La Doux, Michael Loik, Jack Longino, Pam MacKay, Judy MacKenzie, Sally Manning, Malcolm McLeod, Diane Mitchell, Sia and Emil Morehardt, Londie Garcia Padelsky, Bruce Parfitt, Frank Parker, Olle Pellmyr, Ralph Philbrick, Diana Pietrasanta, Jerry Powell, Cathy Rose, Margareta Sequin, Frank Starkey, Melody and John Taft, Tim Thomas, Rob Wallace, Greg Warrick, Mike Williams, Darrell Wong, Wally Woolfendon, and Jerry Zatorski. Thank you all for your time and generosity.

I'd also like to thank my family, Carola, Dave, John, Jane, and Jack Ingram, for their support and for providing housing in strategic locations.

I want to thank Katey O'Neill for her excellent proofreading, design, and book production skills, and Sue Irwin for her talent and patience making the range maps.

I also owe a big debt of gratitude to John Evarts and Marjorie Popper of Cachuma Press for their fine editing and organizational skills, for having faith in my abilities, and for being so great to work with.

Finally, I want to thank my wife, Karen Ferrell-Ingram, for her numerous helpful reviews and suggestions, encouragement, and constant support and love.

—Stephen Ingram, October 2007

## ABOUT THE PHOTOGRAPHS

All of the photos in this book, except for those credited to other photographers, were made with Nikon F3 and F4s 35 mm, Pentax 645NII medium format, and Fuji GX617 panorama film cameras; a Nikon D200 digital camera; and assorted lenses. No filters were used for the macro photos, but other filters employed included a warming circular polarizer, an 81A warming filter, and several different graduated split neutral density filters. A diffuser was used for many of the close-up images to decrease contrast. The non-digital photographs were exposed on Fujichrome Velvia 50 and Velvia 100 films.

## ABOUT THE PAINTINGS

The 15 genera of Cactaceae and Agavaceae that occur in California and Nevada are introduced in Chapter Three, and each is represented by a full-page watercolor illustration of one of the species in the genus. Twelve of these paintings are by Eugene O. Murman and three are by Susan Bazell. Most of these paintings are published here for the first time.

**Eugene O. Murman** (1874–1962) was born in Russia and emigrated to the United States in 1905. After a successful career as a designer, he turned his talents to painting. In collaboration with his second wife, Rosaleen, he embarked on an ambitious undertaking to paint the flora of California. During the 1940s and 1950s he completed more than 500 watercolors, which are remarkable for their artistic beauty and botanical accuracy. (Forty-nine of his paintings are featured in the Cachuma Press title *Conifers of California*, by Ronald M. Lanner.) The Murman Collection is archived at the History and Special Collections Division of the Louise M. Darling Biomedical Library at the University of California, Los Angeles. The reproduction of Murman's work in this book has been made possible by the permission of Margo Murman and the Murman family, whose cooperation and generosity are greatly appreciated. Thanks also to Teresa G. Johnson at the Louise M. Darling Biomedical Library for her valued assistance.

**Susan Bazell** (1940–2012) was an accomplished botanical illustrator. Her artwork has been featured in several publications, including *Life of an Oak, Plants of the East Bay Parks,* and *Conifers of California*. For this book, she painted three species of Cactaceae, and she also produced the black and white illustration of cactus stems and flowers on page 29. Bazell utilized herbarium specimens from the University and Jepson Herbaria, University of California, Berkeley for two of her paintings. We thank them for granting permission to use those specimens for her illustrations and acknowledge Andrew Doran for his help.

Top: *The photographer catches morning light in the Tierra Blanca Mountains. [Anza-Borrego Desert S.P.]*
Bottom: *E.O. Murman poses by healthy specimens of giant saguaro. [Courtesy of the Murman Collection, UCLA.]*

*Grand Canyon cottontop and Mojave yucca are an integral part of this vegetation near the Virgin Mountains. [Clark Co.]*

*An Engelmann hedgehog (front) and a Mojave prickly-pear bloom in unison. [Providence Mountains S.R.A.]*

# Introduction

Cacti, agaves, and yuccas please the eye and intrigue the mind. With their luscious flowers and strange growth forms, they stand out from most plants and attract legions of admirers. For many people, they are the most bizarre and fascinating plants of the American West. Although the cactus family and the agave family—which includes yuccas—are not closely related, we associate the species from these two families with each other because they so often occur in the same habitats and share similar physiological attributes that help them survive in arid climates.

Most people recognize a cactus when they see or, inadvertently, feel one. Their bright, colorful, short-lived flowers that bloom on succulent, spine-covered stems are enough to inspire "cactophilia" or "cactomania" among plant-lovers. Cacti are also renowned for their ability to thrive in the desiccating heat of the desert. For centuries, humans have utilized cacti for many purposes: as sources of food and drink, drugs for medicine and religious ceremonies, dyes, fences and other structural materials, tools for fishing and hunting, and numerous other uses. Like the cacti, agaves and yuccas have long been admired for their distinctive growth forms, dramatic flowers, and utility. They have been a source of food, sweet drinks, alcoholic beverages, soap, and fiber.

California and Nevada contain a rich selection of representatives from the cactus and agave families, and more than 60 species or varieties are found in the two states. The Mojave and Great Basin deserts, as well as California's subdivision of the Sonoran Desert—also known as the Colorado Desert—provide habitat for most of the cacti, agaves, and yuccas from California and Nevada. Although each state claims a few of its own endemic species from the cactus and agave families, there is significant overlap in the species occurring within their combined borders; one-half of the species found in California also grow in Nevada, and over two-thirds that grow in Nevada also occur in California.

What is perhaps less appreciated than the beauty and boldness of cacti, agaves, and yuccas

*Harriman yucca is the smallest of the five yucca species found in California and Nevada. [Cathedral Gorge S.P.]*

is their successful colonization of a wide range of environments. In California, they are found from the cool, foggy Channel Islands and coastal bluffs of San Diego County to the low, hot Colorado River Basin and north to the canyons of the Eastern Sierra. In Nevada, they range from the red-rock country of the eastern Mojave Desert, north through numerous limestone ranges and into the remote, high desert of northwestern Humboldt County. Their diversity in form, and their physiological adaptations, have enabled them to thrive in both equable and harsh climates. Enchanting yet tough, cacti, agaves, and yuccas are captivating succulents that offer a unique view into the world of the plant kingdom.

*A lack of fossil evidence obscures the evolutionary history of Cactaceae and Agavaceae. [Desert N.W.R.]*

CHAPTER ONE

# Evolution, Classification, and Botanical Characteristics

*Nature insists that something shall fight heat and drouth even here, and so she designs strange growths that live a starved life, and bring forth after their kind with much labor. Hardiest of the hardy are these plants and just as fierce in their way as the wild-cat. You cannot touch them for the claw. They have no idea of dying without a struggle. You will find every one of them admirably fitted to endure.*
—John C. Van Dyke, *The Desert,* 1901

## Evolutionary History of Cactus and Agave Relatives

Plant fossils and fossilized pollen have provided excellent evidence to paleontologists about the evolution of many plant families. When it comes to studying the cactus and agave families, scientists have a limited fossil record to analyze because the soft plant parts of cacti, agaves, and yuccas tend to decompose before they become fossils. In addition, fossils form when organisms are buried, and cacti, agaves, and yuccas don't occupy wet habitats where sedimentation is likely. Radiocarbon dating of cactus spines and seed fossils excavated from packrat middens has revealed that some of these cactus plant parts are at least 24,000 years old. This is useful information for determining past distribution of cactus populations relative to climate change, but a fossil record covering millions of years is needed to clearly elucidate the evolutionary history of a plant group. Therefore, botanists have had to rely on several other fields of scientific study, such as biogeography or phytogeography (the study of global plant distribution), plant chemistry, morphology, and—most recently—molecular genetics to discern the evolutionary path of the cactus and agave families.

## Cactaceae

The cactus family, Cactaceae, includes about 1800 species in 125 genera and is found from central Canada to Patagonia in southern Argentina. The lone exception to this New World, or Western Hemisphere, distribution is the epiphytic (tree-dwelling) *Rhipsalis baccifera,* a recent bird-dispersed immigrant found in western Africa as well as on Madagascar and other Indian Ocean islands.

*Cacti grow in diverse habitats; here a coastal prickly-pear thrives on a sea bluff. [Torrey Pines S.R.]*

The story of the origins and distribution of Cactaceae began long ago and far away, in a place called Pangea. The drifting together of continental plates created this "super-continent," but continued plate movement began to break it apart starting in the Middle Jurassic period, about 165 million years ago. Pangea split into a northern land mass called

Laurasia, the precursor to the North American and Eurasian continents, and a southern one called Gondwana that comprised the foundations of present-day Africa, Madagascar, Antarctica, Australia, India, and South America. In the Cretaceous period, around 130 million years ago, Gondwana began to divide into its component parts, and Africa separated from South America at the slow rate of about half an inch per year.

As the South Atlantic Ocean widened between Africa and South America, fewer plants were able to disperse from one continent to the other. Since cacti are absent from Africa, with the exception of the widespread, easily dispersed *Rhipsalis* noted above, phytogeographers have concluded that cacti must have evolved in South America after the Atlantic presented a substantial dispersal barrier. Africa does have its own cactus-like plants—known as euphorbias—that have exploited the plethora of suitable cactus habitats on the continent. The similarity of succulent, spine-covered, globular, and columnar forms of many species of African *Euphorbia* (Euphorbiaceae) and species in the Cactaceae is an example of convergent evolution, where two unrelated plant groups have evolved comparable adaptations for surviving in similar but distant climates.

The oceanic barrier to cactus dispersal from South America was effectively in place by the Late Cretaceous, 65 million years ago, when the South Atlantic had grown to 500 miles wide. Following mass extinctions at the close of the Cretaceous period, flowering plants became especially diverse during the Paleogene period. The diversity and distinctiveness of the well-defined cactus family have been used as evidence that the Cactaceae is a relatively old family. Thus, phytogeographers who study plant distribution and the evolution of Cactaceae have placed that family's time of origin at around 65 million years before the present.

The presumed habitat of the first cacti was a hot, humid, seasonally dry scrubland—an environment that was widespread in central and northern South America 65 million years ago when the continent was further south and the Andes had not yet risen. *Pereskia sacharosa,* a spiny, semi-succulent, tree-like cactus with drought-deciduous leaves, is widespread in central South America today and is thought to resemble the earliest cacti more than any other species. Based on the current area of greatest diversity of *Pereskia* and several other cactus genera that share relatively primitive features, as well as evidence from studies of cactus DNA variation, botanists postulate that the cactus family's place of origin was in the area which is now part of the central Andes of western South America.

By 36 million years ago, as the South American plate drifted north—but before it was connected to Central and North America—the large Caribbean islands of Cuba, Hispaniola, and Jamaica, as well as numerous smaller islands, offered new habitats and "stepping stones" that formed a veritable land bridge between South America and Mexico. This island land bridge enabled birds to disperse cactus species north into Mexico, where these cacti would eventually radiate northward, as newly evolved species, into the North American deserts.

Starting about 25 million years ago, the world's climate grew cooler and drier, and this is thought to have instigated a more rapid speciation of the Cactaceae as new suitable habitats emerged. Topographical change also encouraged species diversity. The rise of the Andes in South America, for example, created a rain shadow east of that range by 17 million years ago, and cacti radiated north, south, and east with new species colonizing newly arid or semi-arid habitats.

Recent research suggests that the cactus family may not be as old as previously thought. By performing comparative studies of DNA sequences from relatively primitive cacti, such as *Pereskia* and *Maihuenia,* and genera in the closely related portulaca family (Portulacaceae), molecular geneticists have uncovered evidence that the cactus family arose in the Late Paleogene period, some 30 million years ago. Regardless of whether cacti originated 65 million or 30 million years ago, plant scientists agree that cacti became especially diverse in North America during the spread of deserts there during the Pliocene epoch, from 5 to 2 million years ago.

## Agavaceae

The agave family, Agavaceae, has approximately 300 species in 9 genera that occur from the western U.S. south to Venezuela and Colombia. *Agave* and *Yucca* are the most species-rich genera, accounting for four-fifths of the species in the family. The Agavaceae are most diverse in Mexico, and based on its current center of species diversity, botanists hypothesize that the agave family originated in central or southern Mexico. The oldest known fossils of agave relatives are estimated to be 37.5 million years old. "Agavaceae-like" fossilized pollen grains (microfossils) reported from Mexico have been estimated to be 15 to 25 million years old. The 1988 discovery of a 4-foot long, woody yucca-like megafossil in the rhyolitic lava flows of northwestern Nevada represents the only large fossil Agavaceae known to date. This fossilized stem segment—named and described as *Protoyucca shadishii*—resembled the present-day Joshua tree and occurred here during the warmer Middle Miocene epoch, approximately 14 million years ago.

New genetic research on the Agavaceae and related families, and studies of the rates of evolution within the agave family, suggest the Agavaceae originated less than 40 million years ago and probably about 23 million years ago. *Yucca* is relatively old and is estimated to have originated between 13 and 18 million years ago. In contrast, *Agave* is most likely only 8 to 10 million years old. The low level of genetic differentiation within *Agave* suggests it is relatively young, and because of its large number of species, it must have diversified at a rapid rate.

Climate change contributed to this swift pace of diversification as central Mexico became more arid in the last 30 to 15 million years, with tropical dry forest expanding and the formation of the Sonoran Desert 15 to 8 million years ago. The increasing aridity and changing vegetation during this time allowed for more ecological opportunities for certain plants, and these changes correspond to the diversification of the agave family, most notably in the genus *Agave*.

Top: *Increased aridity has favored the spread of Agavaceae species, such as Harriman yucca. [Cathedral Gorge S.P.]* Bottom: *Banana yuccas develop large fruits, which may have been eaten by Pleistocene megafauna. [Mojave N. Pr.]*

## Packrat Middens and Vegetation History

Our current understanding of recent vegetation history in the desert Southwest—since the last glacial maximum 20,000 years ago—is due largely to the den-building behaviors of a large desert rodent—the woodrat, or packrat. These long-tailed, big-eyed rats are called packrats for their habit of collecting a wide assortment of materials for den construction. There are more than 20 species of packrats, which are found from the tropical forests of Nicaragua to the boreal forests of central Canada. Five packrat species are known in our region, occurring in chaparral and woodland habitats of cismontane California and from the Colorado Desert to the pinyon-juniper woodlands of the Great Basin. Within many habitats, packrats owe their survival to the cacti, agaves, and yuccas that grow nearby.

Succulent cacti, agaves, and yuccas supply packrats with a critical source of water, although these plants do not offer them much nutrition. Packrats do not hibernate and are thought to be under chronic energy stress. Packrat dens, which contain thick, soft nests, help insulate these active rodents from temperature extremes, provide a place for food storage, and offer a haven from coyotes, weasels, owls, and other predators. Packrats construct dens by piling up small rocks, bones, sticks, and many other plant items, and they utilize natural features such as caves, rocky outcrops, and dense vegetation. Some species also place the spiny segments of chollas and prickly-pears in strategic places to deter predators.

Zoologists refer to packrat dens and their surrounding accumulation of debris as middens. Packrats are generally solitary, but many generations will use the same den site, adding new material over time, and excreting abundant urine and feces. As packrat urine dries, it crystallizes and binds together the leaves, seeds, twigs, spines, dried fecal pellets, and other midden debris, forming a hardened mound—a fossilized paleomidden that may persist for thousands of years. The most revealing paleomiddens are those that have been used for centuries and have remained dry under rocky

*Packrats used cholla stems and other plant debris to make a nest in this Mojave yucca. [Lake Mead N.R.A.]*

ledges or in caves. Packrats do not range far from their dens, rarely straying over 100 feet, so the plant parts discarded on middens are very site-specific.

Well-preserved paleomidden macrofossils are readily identifiable and can be radiocarbon dated to give a local picture of ancient plant community composition. These macrofossils offer proof of vegetation changes brought on by an increasingly hotter and drier climate. They show that Joshua trees grew at elevations as low as 900 feet in the Colorado Desert's Picacho Peak area 12,500 years ago. Today the closest Joshua trees are found at higher elevations and 100 miles further north. By examining paleomidden macrofossils, botanists have also concluded that the Newberry Mountains in the Mojave Desert used to be covered with a woodland of junipers and live oaks; the creosote bush scrub and other plants we see here today arrived only 7800 years ago.

## Plant Classification, From Classes to Species

Since the late 19th century, taxonomists have ranked organisms on the basis of their phylogenetic relationships in order to place them in a hierarchical system that has an evolutionary framework. Within this classification system, cacti, agaves, and yuccas—as well as all other flowering plants—belong to the division Angiospermae. Traditionally, the Angiosperm division has been divided into the Dicotyledoneae (dicot) and the Monocotyledoneae (monocot) classes. Based on the new Angiosperm Phylogeny Group (APG) system of classification, angiosperms are no longer broken into two classes; instead they are now alternatively grouped into four basic lineages or clades: the paleoherbs, paleotrees (sometimes referred to as the basal angiosperms or magnoliids), monocots, and eudicots. Monocots and eudicots have evolved independently since the Early Cretaceous period 145 million years ago.

*Left: Brown-spined prickly-pear's bright tepals and numerous stamens are typical of cacti. [Santa Rosa Mtns. N.M.] Right: Harriman yucca, like other Agavaceae species, has flower parts in sets of three. [Cathedral Gorge S.P.]*

Although the cactus and agave families share many physiological and ecological attributes, they fall into different plant lineages. Agaves and yuccas are monocots, while cacti are eudicots. Monocots share several basic characteristics; they produce one cotyleon, or "seed leaf," their leaves usually have parallel venation, and their flower parts are arranged in sets of threes. Examples of other monocots are grasses, orchids, palm trees, and nolinas. Eudicots have two cotyledons, leaves usually with net venation, and floral parts in sets of four, five, or a higher indefinite number. In addition to cacti, other familiar eudicots include roses, penstemons, sagebrush, and cottonwood trees.

Below the level of eudicot or monocot, flowering plants are grouped into orders: the agave family is in the order Asparagales and the cactus family is in the order Caryophyllales. It is interesting to note that fewer than 20 of the world's 400 to 450 plant families produce a pigment called betalain and all are in Caryophyllales. Betalain pigments differ from anthocyanin pigments (a pigment type produced by the rest of the world's plant families) and are responsible for the brilliant red, pink, orange, and yellow colors of many cactus flowers. Most plant families within this order also share certain embryological characteristics, a distinctive pollen grain structure, stem succulence, and CAM photosynthesis (see page 9).

Orders are further divided into families, subfamilies, genera, and species. The most important level—the basic unit of classification—is the species. Each species name is composed of a general (genus) and a specific (species) name, which taken together, are referred to as its scientific name. The scientific names of plants are Latinized and written in italics. They may describe some unique characteristic, commemorate the discoverer or original collector, or associate the species with its habitat or locality. The literal translation of *Yucca brevifolia* (Joshua tree), for example, is "the *Yucca* with short leaves." Carl Wolf named *Cylindropuntia munzii* (Munz cholla) in honor of another well-known California botanist, Philip Munz (1892–1974). George Engelmann connected desert agave with its desert habitat, by calling it *Agave deserti*.

The following table displays the nomenclature for two plants that are featured in this book. It shows how these plants fit within the taxonomic hierarchy used for all organisms. Note that, as in these examples, some species are further divided into subspecies (ssp.) and varieties (var.) depending on their variability. Subspecies is a higher rank than variety, so in general, varieties of a species are more alike than subspecies.

| Cane cholla | Ivory-spined agave |
|---|---|
| Order: Caryophyllales | Order: Asparagales |
| Family: Cactaceae | Family: Agavaceae |
| Subfamily: Opuntioideae | Subfamily: Agavoideae |
| Genus: *Cylindropuntia* | Genus: *Agave* |
| Species: *Cylindropuntia californica* | Species: *Agave utahensis* |
| Variety: *Cylindropuntia californica* var. *parkeri* | Variety: *Agave utahensis* var. *eborispina* |

It should be noted that plant classification at the levels of family, order, and above have seen some dramatic changes since the mid-1990s, leaving botanists either bewildered, eager to adopt this new approach, or undecided with a "wait-and-see" attitude. By comparing DNA sequences from three particular genes from thousands of different species, researchers working together are able to evaluate molecular characters among hundreds of plant families and produce more accurate and sophisticated phylogenetic trees. This field of molecular systematics led to a new plant classification system proposed in 1998 by a group of taxonomists called the Angiosperm Phylogeny Group (APG). This classification system of 462 families has been updated at least once since then (APG II) and will undoubtedly be revised again. The APG system places agaves into Asparagaceae, the very large asparagus family (note the resemblance of the flower stalk), but allows for the alternative recognition of the traditional family, Agavaceae, which is used in this book.

**Adaptations for an Arid Environment**

Anyone who has accidentally knocked off a cholla branch, or been stabbed in the shins by a yucca, can testify that cacti, agaves, and yuccas are plants that command respect. In addition to these defense mechanisms, the Cactaceae and Agavaceae also dis-

*Cacti, such as these teddy-bear cholla, have evolved to survive in an arid environment. [Imperial Co.]*

play an amazing suite of morphological and physiological features—such as succulent plant parts and a water-conserving method of photosynthesis—that enable them to thrive in arid environments.

## Succulence

Water is the source of succulence in the stems and leaves of cacti, agaves, and yuccas. It is stored in the whitish inner tissue called the water-storage parenchyma where it can be accessed in times of drought. The vast amounts of water these succulent plants contain enable them to survive water losses of 70% to 95%, whereas most plants would die after losing 30% of their water volume. The succulent plant parts of cacti, agaves, and yuccas also have features that allow them to retain water. The outer layer—the epidermis—of cactus stems, and agave and yucca leaves, is translucent but covered with a waxy layer called the cuticle that traps plant water and prevents its loss from interior cells. This loss is further retarded by the presence of mucilage, a slimy substance produced in the plants' cells that binds tightly with water, reducing evaporation. The mucilage also confers another benefit: its bad taste probably deters some animals from eating the plant.

Many cacti have nipple-like projections or low bumps called tubercles that are tipped with spiny areoles. Tubercles are formed from the fusion of a leaf petiole with stem tissue. The characteristic ribs on columnar and barrel cacti are actually vertically aligned tubercles that have coalesced to form a ridge. Tubercles and ribs can expand to accommodate water uptake after rainfall or contract in times of drought; their elasticity is an important adaptation that allows cacti to adjust to different water volumes without tearing their all-important cuticle layer. These projections also increase available surface area for uptake of carbon dioxide and exposure to sunlight.

## CAM Photosynthesis

In the process of photosynthesis, plants utilize radiant energy from the sun to turn water and carbon dioxide ($CO_2$) into the sugars and starches they require for maintenance and growth. All non-aquatic plants take up $CO_2$ from the air through the pores

*Top: Spine-tipped tubercles on mountain cactus swell to accommodate water uptake after a rain. [White Pine Co.] Bottom: Pancake prickly-pear (foreground) and other cacti in our region use CAM photosynthesis. [Mojave N. Pr.]*

in their leaves or stems, known as stomata. When these pores are open, $CO_2$ diffuses in from the atmosphere and water vapor escapes. This evaporative water loss (transpiration) poses a problem for plants in arid or saline terrestrial environments, and they have to balance their energy needs with the potential for desiccation.

More than 90% of plant species take up $CO_2$ and photosynthesize when their stomata are open and the sun is shining. This common method of photosynthesis, which fixes carbon in the chloroplasts during the daytime, is called the $C_3$ photosynthetic pathway. All of our region's members of the cactus family, and most members of the agave

*A rapid increase in surface roots helps barrel cactus like these absorb water after a rain. [Mojave N. Pr.]*

family, use an alternative to the $C_3$ photosynthetic pathway known as Crassulacean acid metabolism, or CAM photosynthesis. This special mode of photosynthesis takes its name from the stonecrop family, Crassulaceae. Daily cyclical changes in the acidity levels of leaves in this plant family sparked the curiosity of an early 19th century botanist and eventually led to the realization that there is more than one photosynthetic pathway. CAM plants conserve water by closing their stomata during the day and opening them for $CO_2$ uptake at night, when the relative humidity is greater and water loss from transpiration is less. The $CO_2$ is stored at night in the form of an acid. During daylight hours, photosynthesis proceeds along the standard $C_3$ pathway, but, without a need for an influx of $CO_2$, the plants' stomata can remain closed. CAM plants may take up some $CO_2$ during the day if there is an adequate supply of water. (CAM is also used by plants in highly saline habitats and by epiphytic species challenged by sporadic water availability, such as orchids and bromeliads.)

Among plants of the agave family, succulent-leaved yuccas, such as banana yucca, generally use CAM, and yuccas with less fleshy leaves, such as Joshua tree, do not. Some $C_3$ plants, such as Joshua tree, still manage to reduce water loss by closing their stomata during the hottest and driest period of the year. While this reduces evaporation, it also prevents the influx of $CO_2$ for photosynthesis and thereby stops plant growth, often for months at a time.

### Roots

While succulence and CAM photosynthesis inhibit water loss in cacti, agaves, and yuccas, it is their root systems that are notable for helping with water capture. Many species in the cactus and agave families gather water from a scant rainfall much more quickly and efficiently than other plants. For example, a desert barrel cactus may lose five gallons of water after 40 days of severe drought, but it can absorb the same amount from a moderate rainfall in only a few days. Water absorption feats of this kind are possible, in part, because cacti, agaves, and yuccas begin to grow "rain roots" within hours of the soil getting soaked. These fine, shallow lateral roots take advantage of moisture from rainstorms but die back during dry periods. One study showed that in the two-week period following a heavy rain, a small- to medium-sized desert barrel cactus increased its root area by more than 25%, enlarging its root system to a total of 750 feet.

Most of the roots of cacti, agaves, and yuccas occur 4 to 10 inches below the surface. At this depth they can avoid the top inch or two of soil, which gets lethally hot for roots, but still take advantage of moisture from even a light rainfall. The main roots of agaves and yuccas increase in length and number with age, but like other monocots, their roots remain relatively straight and do not grow wider than about ¼ inch. Cactus roots, too, become longer and more numerous with age, but unlike agaves and yuccas, they also grow thicker. Cactus roots have the added adaptation of producing an insulating layer of bark around their roots that seals them off and prevents water loss. Some cacti, such as sand-cholla, also produce deeper, tuberous roots.

**Spines**
Spines are a salient feature of most plants in this book. In the agave family, spines are found on leaf margins and tips, and they vary in their occurrence. It seems their primary role is to help repel animals that might consume the plants' fleshy leaves and highly palatable flower stalks. In the cactus family, spines are highly variable and perform many functions.

Cactus spines are actually modified leaves. They are produced at a specialized spot on the stem called an areole, from the Latin word for "small area." The presence of areoles is the single most distinctive feature that defines the cactus

*Top: Engelmann prickly-pear pad shows spines and the areoles where they are produced. [Anza-Borrego Desert S.P.] Bottom: New spines of cottontop cactus turn a vivid red in cool, wet winter months. [Ibex Hills, Inyo Co.]*

Evolution, Classification, and Botanical Characteristics 11

family (see illustration on page 29). Areoles are modified short shoots, or branches, and are capable of growing fine wooly hairs, flower buds, leaves, new stems, roots, or spines. Areoles may produce central spines and/or radial spines, or glochids, the deciduous, stiff, barbed, hair-like spines found on chollas and prickly-pears. Sometimes areoles produce no spines at all.

Cactus spines help deter herbivory by large insects, desert tortoises, packrats, rabbits, burros, and other animals. They also help conserve water by shading the stem, reflecting light and heat, and forming a boundary layer around the stem. The spines themselves do not contribute to water loss because, unlike typical leaves, they have no stomata from which to lose water vapor. Modified spines called gland spines, or extrafloral nectaries, secrete nectar that attracts pollinators (see page 19). The spiny stems of some cacti, such as chollas and prickly-pears, even aid vegetative reproduction and distribution. That is because animals easily dislodge the prickly stems, which are knocked to the ground where they may resprout; in addition, some stems become attached to animals that inadvertently serve as dispersal agents.

One of the fascinating things about our regional cacti is that they do not need typical leaves to perform photosynthesis. Instead, cacti photosynethize through their green stems. Some cacti do put forth tiny succulent green leaves on their newest growth, but these leaves wither within a few weeks. Because cactus leaves are no longer essential to the process of photosynthesis, they have become adapted for an impressive array of other services, including spines.

## Flowers

The primary function of cactus, agave, and yucca flowers is to attract pollinators. Whether they are insects, birds, or bats, pollinators enable plants to reproduce sexually by transferring pollen from male to female plant parts within a flower or by depositing pollen from the stamens of one flower onto the receptive stigma of another. This means flowers play a critical role in maintaining a diverse gene pool within a species.

All flowers, when viewed from an anatomical perspective, are actually highly modified leafy branches. In cacti, these branches generally arise from areoles near the stem tip. Flowers in the cactus family are characterized by having many perianth parts, starting from the outermost scale-like leaves and moving inward to sepals, then petals. In cacti, and in many monocots such as *Agave, Yucca,* and *Nolina,* the difference between sepals and petals is so slight no distinction is made between the two, and they are both commonly referred to as tepals.

Set within the bowl or vase-like shape formed by the cactus tepals are dozens to hundreds of stamens, the male reproductive part of the flower. The stamens have pollen-bearing anther sacs attached to the tips of supporting filaments. The center of the flower holds the female reproductive part, or pistil, which consists of an ovary, style, and stigma (see illustration on page 29). The ovary sits at the base of the style and produces ovules. The cactus ovary is located below the other flower parts and so is known as an inferior ovary. But unlike a typical inferior ovary, in which sepals and petals form a tube above the ovary, the inferior ovary of a cactus is formed by being sunken into the stem tissue. The outer tissue of a cactus fruit is essentially stem tissue, often covered with areoles that in some

*Left: The newly opened flowers of this Mojave prickly-pear exhibit yellow tepals. [Death Valley N.P.]*
*Right: The day-old flowers of this Mojave prickly-pear have darkened to orange. [Death Valley N.P.]*

chollas and prickly-pears may produce a new stem, roots, or even new flower buds.

Cactus flowers generally have bright colors or have ultraviolet pigments that attract bees, and their spreading form is adapted to accommodate these busy pollinators. Color is the main attraction, although beavertail and other prickly-pears sometimes emit a watermelon-like fragrance. Some prickly-pears also exhibit a curious trait: their flower color changes with age. Flower tepals of a few of these species darken from yellow to orange through the day, and the filaments of one species, little prickly-pear, mature from orange to red. A number of unrelated species of bees, commonly called cactus bees, are the most important pollinators for the cacti in California and Nevada, with the exception of Mojave mound cactus. The bees feed mostly on the copious pollen, rather than the meager nectar, produced by cactus flowers.

Cholla and prickly-pear flowers have an amazing adaptation that increases the likelihood of pollination: their stamens are stimulated by touch. When a bee lands among the pollen-covered stamens—or if you poke your finger into their midst—the stamens will slowly bend inward, dusting the bee (or your finger tip) with pollen. This helps ensure that a bee is coated with pollen before flying off to the next flower.

In contrast to the numerous perianth parts and abundant stamens of cactus flowers, the flowers of agaves and yuccas are composed strictly of three outer and three inner tepals that surround six stamens. In *Agave,* the inferior ovary sits at the very base of the flower within an upwardly widening tube that extends beyond the ovary's upper rim. The upper part of this tube is formed by the tepals, which are joined near their bases. The lengthy, slender filaments of the stamens arise from within this tube and stretch up into the open, where they display long, teetering anthers. At the base of the tepals is the style, which arises from the ovary tip. In *Agave* the anthers shed their pollen before the stigma is receptive. This strategy—where male flower parts mature before the female—is called protandry, and it guarantees out-crossing of the flower.

*Chaparral yucca blooms only once, but it produces beautiful buds and flowers. [Cleveland N.F., San Diego Co.]*

The ovary of flowers in *Yucca* and *Hesperoyucca,* unlike those of *Agave* and cacti, sits above the thick, broad, white tepals and is referred to as a superior ovary. Stamens in these two genera are short and fleshy, and directly surround the grooved ovary. Yucca flowers are unusual because they are successfully pollinated by a single pollinator. All yucca flowers require yucca moths to effectively transfer pollen to the tip of the stigma, and all yucca moth larvae are dependent on the developing yucca fruits. Yuccas would probably cease to exist if it weren't for the yucca moth (see "Yuccas and Yucca Moths" on page 22).

*Mojave prickly-pear and Engelmann hedgehog (in bloom) with buckhorn cholla. [Providence Mountains S.R.A.]*

CHAPTER TWO

# Ecology and Habitats of Cacti, Agaves, and Yuccas

*The desert floras shame us with their cheerful adaptations to the seasonal limitations. Their whole duty is to flower and fruit, and they do it hardly, or with tropical luxuriance, as the rain admits.*
—Mary Austin, *The Land of Little Rain*, 1903

## A Changing Vegetation

Climatic and geologic changes have profoundly shaped plant life in California and Nevada, and it is fascinating to compare current vegetation types with those of the past. Where chaparral and coastal sage scrub now grow in southern California, a forest of closed-cone pines existed 15 million years ago. Where creosote bush scrub dominates the Mojave Desert, a woodland of evergreen trees covered parts of the land eight million years ago. Cacti, agaves, and yuccas are part of our changing vegetation, and many of them are relatively recent arrivals to this part of North America.

The emergence and spread of cactus and agave family members in our region is tied to climate history. As the Southwest became gradually warmer and drier in the last 5 to 10 million years, these plant families extended north from their origins in South and Central America and began to colonize an increasing array of suitable habitats. During the past 2.4 million years, fluctuations between cold glacial and warm interglacial periods caused different vegetation types to expand and contract, and this "movement" of plants further promoted the dispersal and speciation of cacti, agaves, and yuccas. Over the past 10,000 years, an increasingly hotter and drier climate has been the most significant factor responsible for the extent and composition of today's vegetation types.

Geologic forces have also influenced our region's vegetation patterns. From roughly 5 to 3 million years ago, uplift of California's Sierra Nevada, Transverse, and Peninsular ranges created a significant rain shadow, insuring that vast areas to the east of their crests would become more arid. The biological implications of this long, nearly continuous mountain barrier are so significant that many scientists divide the state into two broad regions: transmontane California, on the eastern—or "other"—side of the mountains, and cismontane

*A late winter rainstorm refreshes the plants in this Joshua tree woodland at Cima Dome. [Mojave N. Pr.]*

California on the western—or "this"—side of the mountains. In Nevada, the primary geologic process that has defined its topography began at least 15 million years ago and continues to the present. As two tectonic plates pull away from each other, the earth's crust is stretching and buckling. This has produced Nevada's distinctive "basin and range" landscape, which is defined by down-dropped valleys flanked by high, narrow ranges, all running parallel to each other. The basins and lower mountain slopes are hotter and drier, and they harbor most of the state's species of cacti, agaves, and yuccas.

Much of transmontane California and Nevada are quite arid, and this is where species in the cactus and agave families are particularly abundant. This territory comprises parts of three distinct North American deserts: Great Basin, Mojave, and Sonoran. In these two states, the Great Basin Desert covers a band of eastern California and much of Nevada and contains approximately 24 species or varieties of cacti, agaves, and yuccas. The Mojave Desert is often described as an ecological transition zone between the higher, cooler Great Basin Desert to the north and the lower, warmer Sonoran Desert to the south. It extends across approximately 35,000 square miles of central-eastern California and southern Nevada, and this part of the desert claims 34 species or varieties from Cactaceae and Agavaceae. The Southwest's vast Sonoran Desert extends into the southeastern corner of California, and the portion within the state is often referred to as the Colorado Desert. Although less than one-tenth the size of the Mojave, the nearly frost-free Colorado Desert has 22 species or varieties of cacti, agaves, and yuccas.

In the more moderate climate of cismontane California, the greatest concentration of cactus and agave family plants occurs in warmer and drier areas. Cismontane California claims 16 species and varieties, and they primarily range from Santa Barbara County southward; 15 of the 16 also extend into Baja California, Mexico. It is notable that there is little overlap with the species of transmontane California: only three species of cismontane California also grow east of the mountains. California's Channel Islands harbor four native cactus species and hybrid prickly-pears, but no yuccas or agaves. Appendix A, "Cactus, Agave, and Yucca Species of California and Nevada" (page 210) lists all the species featured in this book and the major regions where they are found.

**Vegetation Types with Cacti, Agaves, and Yuccas**

Cacti, agaves, and yuccas are found in more than 10 major vegetation types in California and Nevada, ranging from coastal sage scrub to pinyon-juniper woodland. Although they may be locally abundant, these plants rarely dominate large expanses of vegetation. The notable exception is Joshua tree, which sometimes forms relatively dense stands that resemble woodlands. Giant saguaro plays a similar ecological role in areas of the Sonoran Desert outside of California where it grows in greater density.

Vegetation types can cover large areas and are usually defined by their primary growth form,

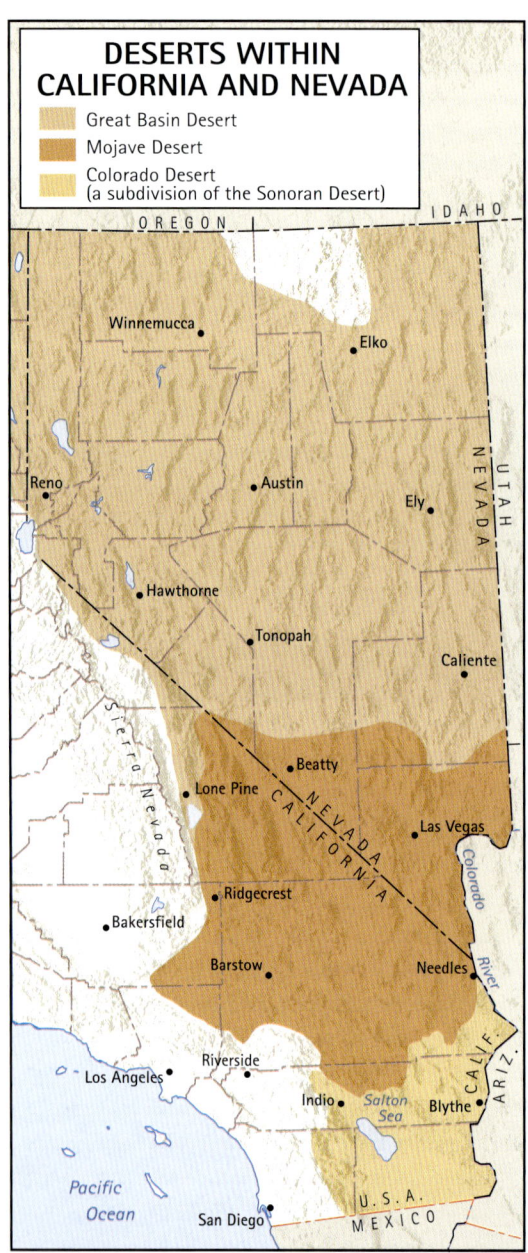

*Buckhorn cholla and Mojave yucca are dominant within this vegetation in Cottonwood Canyon. [Mojave N. Pr.]*

such as woodland, grassland, or scrub. They are often named after a dominant plant species within them, such as sagebrush scrub. Vegetation types are transitional in space as well as in time, with one type grading into another. Ecologists further subdivide vegetation types into smaller units called plant communities, which are groups of species that typically grow together in similar environmental conditions. Some authorities do not make a distinction between broadly defined plant communities and vegetation types. Appendix B, "Major Vegetation Types and Habitats for Cacti, Agaves, and Yuccas" (page 212), summarizes the distribution of cacti, agaves, and yuccas in California and Nevada by vegetation type and habitat.

## Animal Interactions with Cacti, Agaves, and Yuccas

A broad array of wildlife utilizes cacti, agaves, and yuccas as a food source. All parts of these plants are consumed, from fruits, seeds, and flowers to succulent leaves and stems. Their nectar and pollen nourish a host of pollinating insects and bats, and the water stored in succulent plant parts provides a critical supply of moisture. Even though plants in the cactus and agave families are well armored with spines, they also provide shelter and nest- and den-building materials to many animals. Some of the ecological relationships these plants have with animals are mutually beneficial, such as

*Ants feed inside a partially eaten fruit of a coastal prickly-pear. [Torrey Pines S.R.]*

*A hooded oriole and a Scott's oriole (upper right) perch on a Shaw agave. [Baja California]* PHOTO © BILL EVARTS

the interactions between cactus bees and the species they pollinate. Other relationships are parasitic, as when insect larvae feed heavily enough to cause the death of a plant. But perhaps most ecological relationships involving cacti, agaves, and yuccas are commensalistic; the plant or animal benefits at no great cost or advantage to the other.

Scott's oriole is a prime example of a species that takes full advantage of the cacti, agaves, and yuccas that grow throughout much of its spring and summer range in the Southwest. This bird drinks the nectar of desert agave and gleans insects from agaves and yuccas. It also eats the sweet fruits of various prickly-pear species, helping to spread their seeds. Scott's orioles construct woven nests sewn onto Joshua trees, Mojave yuccas, or tall, concealing shrubs, and their preferred nest-building fiber comes from the shredding leaf margins of Mojave yucca.

While the spines of cacti, agaves, and yuccas may deter browsing by some animal species, they guard wildlife that nest within their defensive

*This teddy-bear cholla's spines protect a cactus wren's nest. [Anza-Borrego Desert S.P.]* PHOTO © JOHN EVARTS

sphere. Cactus wrens, for example, are noted for their habit of building large stick nests amongst the protective spines of chollas. Woodpeckers hollow out nests in the stems of saguaros, which later may become the homes of owls, flycatchers, mice, or lizards. Certain packrat species, such as white-throated and desert packrats, fortify their dens with the spiny stem-joints of chollas and prickly-pear cacti to ward off predators.

Loggerhead shrikes have a unique use for cactus spines: they employ them as lethal weapons. These so-called "butcher birds" catch large insects, small birds, and lizards and impale them on a nearby thorn, cactus spine, or Joshua tree leaf, returning later to feed.

Some animals find shelter and food in the cool, dark habitat beneath fallen branches and other succulent plant debris of Cactaceae and Agavaceae. As the debris decays, it attracts fungi, bacteria, mites, fruit flies, termites, and beetles. This prey base draws small predators such as spiders, scorpions, and lizards. Small predators in turn serve as an enticement to larger predators, such as night snakes. The desert night lizard is one species that hunts for prey under Joshua trees and other yuccas. These slim, secretive, olive-gray lizards are actually active during the day, but they have large eyes that allow them to see in the low light conditions under dead yucca limbs.

Cacti, agaves, and yuccas have a mutually beneficial relationship with many of their pollinators. Cacti blooms are so reliable that over 20 species of solitary bees in the Southwest—collectively referred to as cactus bees—specialize in pollinating cactus flowers. Large and fuzzy cactus bees make the best pollinators and, not surprisingly, large, pollen-rich flowers draw the most bees. Researchers have shown that when two species of prickly-pear occur together, the species with wider flowers and more pollen attracts twice as many insect species as its lesser-endowed relative. Agaves reward the bees, moths, hummingbirds, and nectar-feeding bats that visit and pollinate them with healthy amounts of pollen and nectar. Their light-colored flowers attract moths and their long, accessible flower stalks facilitate nighttime visitation by both moths and bats. Edmund Jaeger, desert naturalist and author of *Desert Wild Flowers,* noted that carpenter bees provision the nests they make in Utah agaves with pollen they collect from its flowers.

The areoles of some cacti have modified spines that act as extrafloral nectaries and ooze nectar that acrobat ants and other insects feed on.

*A ground-nesting cactus bee visits a Whipple cholla flower growing in Yucca Valley. [Desert N.W.R.]*

*An acrobat ant seeks nectar from an extrafloral nectary of a Mojave fishhook cactus. [Inyo Mountains]*

*This coastal prickly-pear pad shows evidence of herbivory by rabbits or rodents. [Torrey Pines S.R.]*

This nutritious nectar provides acrobat ants with essential amino acids, carbohydrates, sugars, and—perhaps most importantly—water. Although it is difficult to quantify the reproductive benefit to a cactus of secreting nectar outside of its flower, researchers have demonstrated that greater extrafloral nectar production attracted more ants, which were then able to fend off more cactus bugs—sucking insects that feed on prickly-pears and other cacti. Cacti with extrafloral nectaries may also benefit by growing in soils made more nutrient-rich by nearby ant colonies. Cacti in our region with extrafloral nectaries include buckhorn cholla, teddy-bear cholla, cottontop cactus, desert barrel cactus, brown-spined prickly-pear, Mojave fishhook cactus, and probably others.

The relationship between the cactus longhorn beetle and the cacti it consumes is a parasitic one. This beetle lays its eggs at the base of prickly-pear cacti and Mojave fishhook cactus where its larvae will have a succulent food source readily available. The larvae bore their way through the host plant, weakening it and inviting an invasion of decomposers. The closed carcasses of Mojave fishhook cactus and other species of *Sclerocactus*—held together by their latticework of spines—indicate parasitism by cactus beetle larvae or pyralid moth larvae.

Under some circumstances, animal herbivory can cause measurable impacts on desert plant life. In a U.S. Geological Service study at Joshua Tree National Park during the dry years of 2001 to 2003, scientists found that annual and perennial plants produced little forage, and small mammals turned increasingly to Joshua trees as a source of sustenance. Biologists have long known that antelope ground squirrels, black-tailed jackrabbits, pocket gophers, and other animals eat Joshua tree's bark-like outer tissue, known as periderm. During the drought, these mammals' heavier-than-normal consumption of periderm permanently damaged more than 10% of the park's Joshua trees. There was no recovery for many Joshua trees on which periderm damage was severe, and coupled with the effects of drought, the park may have lost thousands of its namesake species during this time.

Sap beetles are often abundant in cactus flowers, but their relationship to cacti could be considered commensalistic. They congregate in cactus flowers to mate, lay eggs, and feed on nutritious nectar and pollen. Although they are frequently seen covered with pollen, sap beetles do not come in contact with the stigmas of cactus flowers and do not act as pollinators.

**Plant Relationships**

Plant and animal interactions are exciting to observe, whether it involves sighting a Scott's oriole as it gathers yucca fiber to build its nest or watching a cactus bee while it triggers the movement of prickly-pear stamens. Interactions between plants are far subtler, but they are often vital to the survival of an individual or community of plants. Many plants help each other in facilitative interactions. For example, a young diamond cholla that

*A giant saguaro rises above a palo verde—its former nurse plant. [Whipple Mountains, San Bernardino Co.]*

benefits by growing up in the shade of big galleta grass (a desert bunchgrass) in turn helps deter browsers from eating the grass. Plants that shelter growing seedlings are referred to as nurse plants, and the shade they provide can be essential to the survival of young plants, especially in a desert environment. Big galleta grass often acts as a nurse plant to desert agave seedlings. The agaves receive shade from the grass and extra nutrients from its decomposing leaves, but they have to compete with the grass for water. Even though these nursed agaves grow slowly, they stand a better chance of surviving to adulthood than seedlings that grow in the open.

The relationships between plants can change over time, and certain species may out-compete or outlive others to become more prevalent in the vegetation. An interesting model of this is seen in giant saguaros, which are dependent on nurse plants—most notably on palo verde—when they grow in relatively hot and arid sites such as California's Whipple Mountains. Palo verde trees provide the young, vulnerable saguaros with protection from herbivores and extremely high and low temperatures. As saguaros grow, however, they expand their shallow root systems above and beyond that of the nurse palo verdes and may then out-compete them for scant soil moisture. Eventually, the saguaros become large enough to withstand the harsh climate, and the palo verdes slowly die, their demise hastened by the saguaros' expansive root system. But as more saguaros out-compete palo verdes for water, there will be fewer palo verdes to nurse future saguaros, and the balance between the two neighbors may gradually shift again.

# Yuccas and Yucca Moths

Yuccas and yucca moths are entwined in a complex relationship that has been crafted over time by natural selection. This beneficial co-dependency, known as obligate mutualism, provides a fascinating view into the evolutionary ecology of these plants and insects. The crucial role of yucca moths in the pollination of yuccas has been recognized since 1872, and is often cited as one of the classic examples of co-evolution between a plant and an insect. Charles Darwin described the pollination of yuccas by yucca moths as "the most remarkable example of fertilisation ever published."

With the notable exception of Joshua tree, all yuccas depend on a single yucca moth species for pollination. The small white and gray yucca moths in the genera *Tegeticula* and *Parategeticula,* are entirely responsible for the pollination, and hence, seed production, of all yucca species, as well as the yucca relative, *Hesperoyucca whipplei.* Most yucca moths are host specific and rely on the one yucca species they pollinate for larval food and shelter. A few yucca moth species will pollinate and utilize more than one type of yucca.

*A chaparral yucca moth is poised on the style of a chaparral yucca flower. [Point Mugu, Ventura Co.]*

Yucca moth larvae spend much of the year in a state of suspended animation in the soil beneath their host yucca plants and may remain dormant for as long as 17 years. Sufficient winter chilling seems to be crucial to interrupting this deep dormancy, but the moth larvae probably also respond to the same environmental cues that trigger flowering in the host yuccas, such as temperature, precipitation, or day length. As spring progresses and yuccas begin to bloom, the ¼-inch-long larvae pupate. After a few weeks time, yucca moths, measuring nearly ½ inch in length, emerge from their underground silken cocoons. Adult yucca moths are short lived; in less than a week they mate, deposit their eggs into yucca flowers, and pollinate the yuccas before they die.

Yucca moths mate within the safe haven of fragrant, open yucca flowers. After mating, the female gathers pollen from the flowers' anthers using specialized tentacles. She then deftly forms the pollen mass into a sticky ball, which has a mass equivalent to 2% to 10% of her body weight, and tucks it under her head. Next, she flies to another receptive yucca flower and using her ovipositor, she injects one to several thread-like eggs through the flower's ovary wall. The moth then climbs to the stigmatic groove at the end of the flower's ovary, and with a bobbing motion repeated 10 to 20 times, she packs her load of pollen into the groove at the tip of the stigma, pollinating the flower. The moth's eggs develop into larvae in about a week. They spend the next four to five weeks within the protective walls of the ovary, eating some, but not all, of the developing seeds before making their way to the soil beneath the plant.

Yuccas benefit from their relationship with yucca moths because the moths' method of pollination virtually guarantees that ovules in the flower's ovary will be fertilized and will develop into seeds. Yucca moths, in return, receive a reliable food source for their larvae and a safe haven for larval growth. With their pollination by yucca moths assured, yuccas can also channel scarce water resources to fruit production rather than fruit *and* nectar production. All genera in the agave family except *Yucca* produce large amounts of nectar for attracting a wide variety of pollinators, and it is likely that ancestors of modern yuccas did, too. Yuccas now create little, if any, nectar because they have no need to attract pollinators other than yucca moths; bees and other insects that seek nectar from yuccas are incapable of pollinating these specialized flowers. Yuccas require relatively large amounts of water during the flowering and fruiting season, and the fact that yuccas and other Agavaceae produce many more flowers than fruits indicates that fruit production may be limited by water. With yucca moths providing selective pressure for fruit production rather than nectar production, yuccas are free to allocate additional precious water to fruit development, and thus, produce more seeds.

The obligate mutualism of yuccas and yucca moths is stable in an evolutionary sense because both pollinator and host are checked from over-exploiting each other. Yucca moths need to be good enough pollinators to ensure fruit set if their larvae are to survive. For example, if a moth tries to "skimp" on her pollination duty and delivers small amounts of pollen or pollen from the same flower, the yucca flower will drop, or abscise, more readily than a flower that received ample pollen from a separate flower. To select against "greedy" moths that lay too many eggs in one flower, yucca flowers tend to abort if more than five or six loads of eggs are deposited into one ovary. Some female yucca moth species leave a pheromone scent when they oviposit their eggs; the scent serves as a "no vacancy" sign for females that later visit the same flower. A yucca

*These Utah yucca blossoms are dependent on yucca moths for pollination. [Valley of Fire S.P.]*

host species, in turn, is prevented from providing less fruitful rewards, such as fewer seeds, or developing an ovary wall that keeps yucca moths from injecting eggs, by the threat of extinction; in the absence of an alternative host for their yucca moth pollinators, yuccas would inevitably become extinct.

Another facet of this story is the fairly recent evolution of "cheater" yucca moths. These impostors rely on yucca fruits for larval food but lack the specialized pollen-collecting tentacles of true pollinators. Two species of non-pollinators oviposit their eggs into either young fruits *(Tegeticula intermedia)* or fully developed fruits *(Tegeticula corruptrix)* that have already been pollinated by another *Tegeticula* species. The larvae of closely related cheaters and pollinators coexist side by side within the fruits, and there are plenty of seeds to keep both pollinator and cheater species fed. Although several yucca moth larvae may consume up to one-third of the seeds within a fruit, their low abundance and moderate eating habits leave enough seeds for future yucca plants.

*A desert barrel cactus in bloom is surrounded by desert agave. [Anza-Borrego Desert S.P.]*

CHAPTER THREE

# Species Profiles

*Whilst this planet has gone cycling on according to the fixed law of gravity, from so simple a beginning endless forms most beautiful and most wonderful have been, and are being evolved.*
—Charles Darwin, *On The Origin of Species*, 1859

## Introduction to the Profiles

Botanists and horticulturists do not always agree on scientific names, especially for cacti. Most do concur, however, that plant species names sometimes need to change to reflect the most current understanding of a species, its variability, and its evolutionary relationships with other members of its genus and family. The scientific names given in the species profiles that follow are based on three main sources: the *Flora of North America* (FNA); *The Jepson Manual: Vascular Plants of California*, second edition (TJM2); and the *Jepson eFlora*. The contributors to these botanical treatments of the agave and cactus families are regarded as specialists in their field, and by relying on their expertise, this book intends to use names that reflect the most up-to-date nomenclature with the broadest acceptance among botanists. TJM2 includes a few recently revised names for our native cacti, agaves, and yuccas in its updated treatments of the agave family and the cactus family.

The information included under the heading "Identifying Characteristics" is based on the three treatments noted above and other sources listed in the bibliography, as well as field observations of the author. For cacti, descriptions of the spines, such as color, may apply only to new, full-grown spines, as spines tend to age to shades of gray or brown and are often lost altogether from older areoles. The fruit characteristics given for all species, such as color, texture, or succulence, pertain to ripe fruits with mature seeds. Even fruits described as "fleshy" eventually wither, and "dry" fruits are somewhat fleshy for a short time before their seeds are ripe.

Range maps were developed by examining the specimen-based maps made by Lyman Benson in *The Cacti of the United States and Canada*, as well

*Beavertail cactus is one of the most recognizable cacti in the western United States. [Valley of Fire S.P.]*

as the maps in *FNA* and *Sonoran Desert Plants: An Ecological Atlas*. Various papers with specific location information, as well as herbarium collection databases, were also used for location and taxonomic information. These herbaria include Arizona State University, Rancho Santa Ana Botanic Garden, San Diego Natural History Museum, Santa Barbara Botanic Garden, University of Nevada, Reno, University of California, Riverside, and the Wesley E. Niles Herbarium at the University of Nevada, Las Vegas. In addition, the Consortium of California Herbaria website was used to verify some locations.

# Cactaceae

*The Cholla Cactus Garden trail loops through a dense stand of teddy-bear cholla. [Joshua Tree N.P.]*

## Hybridization Among Opuntioids

Prickly-pears and chollas—the opuntioids—are able to reproduce in many ways. They produce new offspring in the usual manner through sexual cross-pollination of individuals within the same species, but they can also reproduce asexually (vegetatively) from detached pads, stem-joints, and fruits. In addition, opuntioids may hybridize with other species. Natural hybrids are the result of successful pollination between similar species, and over time, this process can lead to the evolution of new species and varieties.

Prickly-pear and cholla flowers are adapted to attract generalist pollinators, such as bees, that pollinate a broad variety of species. The pollen they gather can easily be transferred many miles from one species to another. If pollen gathered from one plant species is able to reach and fertilize the ovules of another plant species, then hybrid seeds can form. Botanists are now better able to determine parentage of recognized cactus hybrids than they were in the past because of recent research that details hybrid morphology, provides counts of their chromosomes, and determines pollen fertility. More molecular studies are needed to verify the parentage of certain hybrids, but one thing is clear: prickly-pears and chollas have weak reproductive barriers, and most tend to hybridize with other species in neighboring areas.

The results of hybridization vary widely. A given hybrid may appear intermediate, resembling both parents equally. In other cases, a hybrid may have some characters exactly like those of the seed parent, while others are like those of the pollen parent. This variation occurs because some characters are controlled by several genes and other characters by only one gene. Another factor influencing the appearance of hybrid prickly-pears and chollas is that the parent species may have differing numbers of sets of chromosomes (or ploidy levels). In a cross between such species, the offspring will resemble the parent with the greater number of chromosome sets. In other words, the hybrid progeny express "genomic dosages" in keeping with the different chromosome numbers contributed by each parent. Hybrids (which can and do reproduce vegetatively) may be either sterile, self-pollinating, or have the ability to backcross with one or both parents. With back-crossing it is easy to see how a "hybrid swarm" may result, belying all attempts to pigeonhole individual specimens into one species or another.

Assigning names to cacti has been a challenge ever since Europeans began cultivating them in Britain and Holland in the 17th century. The variability of many cacti species and varieties, the propensity for many of them to hybridize, and the practice of cactus horticulturists to emphasize minor differences, have all led to a long history of what cactus expert Arthur Gibson and his colleagues have called "indiscriminate overnaming" of cacti. The realization that some of the variability is due to hybridization, especially among species with multiple sets of chromosomes (polyploidy), has relegated some cactus "species" to the growing mound of unused synonyms.

Named hybrids are presented later in this chapter. The sidebar "Cholla Hybrids" is on page 55, and "Prickly-pear Hybrids" is on page 128. These hybrids have been known under various varietal and species names for years and are relatively stable in their appearance. The "X" before the specific epithet denotes that the taxon, called a nothospecies, is a cross between two or more species. Most of these hybrids do not have widely accepted common names. Many other hybrids lack assigned scientific names because there are more potential hybridization events between opuntioids than can be discerned and described satisfactorily.

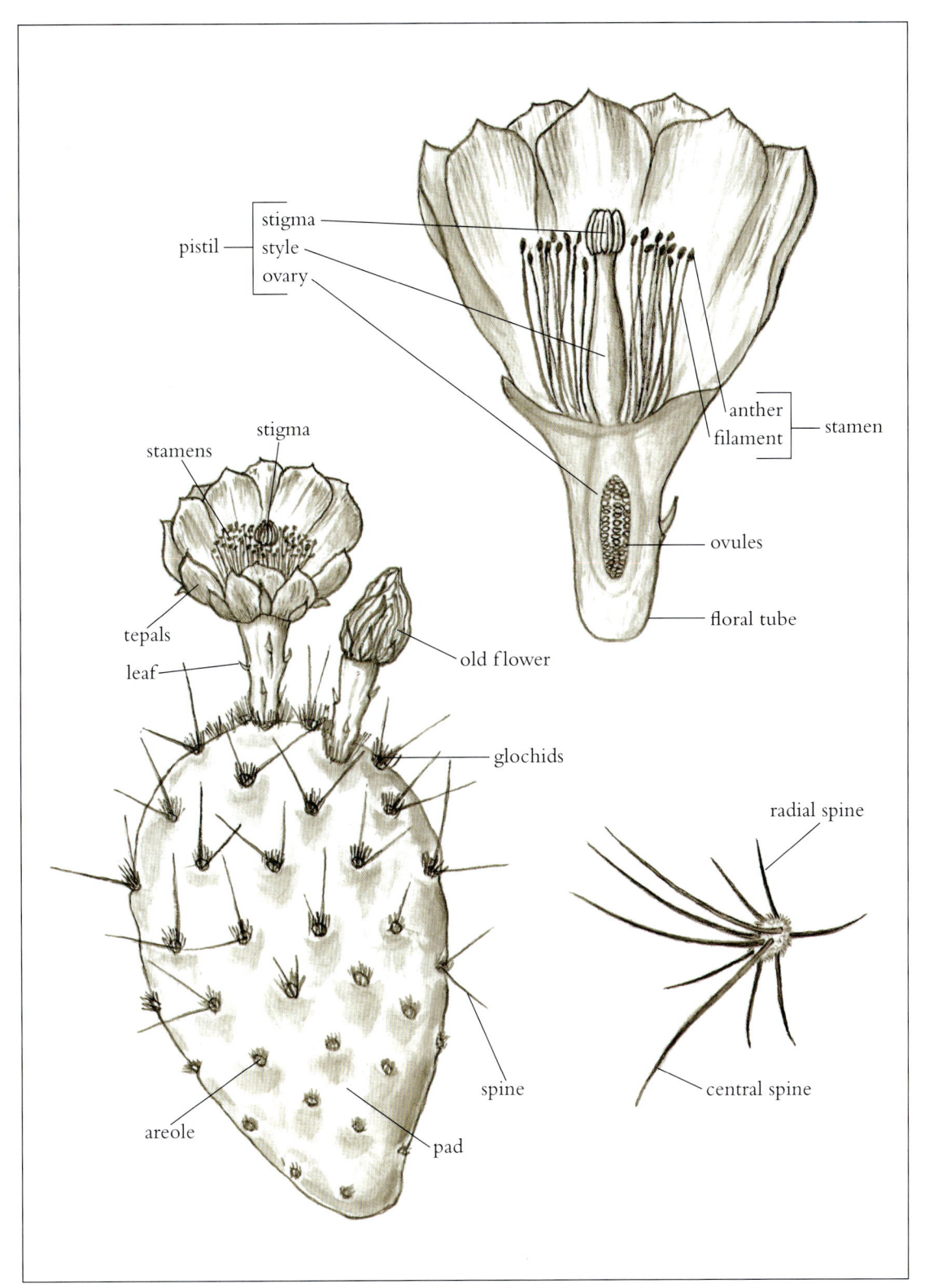

*Prickly-pear pad, dissected flower, and spine detail. Illustration by Susan Bazell.*

Golden cereus • *Bergerocactus emoryi*     ARTWORK BY E.O. MURMAN

# *Bergerocactus*
## GOLDEN CEREUS

*Bergerocactus* is distinguished from other cactus genera in California and Nevada by its growth habit of densely clumped, relatively tall, narrow stems covered with a thick mantle of golden spines. This monotypic (one species) genus was discovered by English naturalist and explorer Thomas Nuttall in 1836 at the site of the first United States/Mexico international boundary marker near Tijuana. Soon after, renowned German-born botanist and St. Louis physician George Engelmann included it in the genus *Cereus* due to the similarity of its seeds and enclosed embryo to those of other *Cereus*. In 1909, Nathaniel Britton and Joseph Rose placed golden cereus in a new genus, *Bergerocactus,* named in honor of the German botanist and cactus specialist Alwin Berger (1871–1931). They believed that golden cereus was different enough from other *Cereus* species to be placed into its own genus. More recent genetic research has supported the dissimilarity of *Bergerocactus* from other related genera and maintained the distinction of this increasingly rare cactus. It is found only in northwestern Baja California, coastal southern San Diego County, and on San Clemente and Santa Catalina islands.

# GOLDEN CEREUS
## *Bergerocactus emoryi*
(ber-ger-oh-KAK-tus EM-or-ee-eye)

**Recent Synonyms**
*Cereus emoryi*

**Other Common Names**
golden-spined cereus, golden club cactus, golden club cereus, velvet cactus, golden snake cactus, button cactus

*A hillside stand of golden cereus begins to bloom. [Cabrillo N.M.]*

*Close-up of a golden cereus flower found at the Otay Mesa revegetation site. [San Diego Co.]*

Golden cereus is perhaps most beautiful when its numerous golden-spined stems are backlit or sidelit; viewed from a distance the stems resemble velvet spires. This spectacular cactus grows in colonies in coastal sage scrub or maritime succulent scrub, typically on steep bluffs or in canyons within a few hundred feet of the ocean. Researchers have found that its growth is more limited by crowding from other shrubs than by light, temperature, or water availability. *Bergerocactus* plants branch near the base, and the ascending stems may live up to 10 years. They may also branch from stems that have fallen to the ground, helping to create impenetrable stands that are typical of this cactus. Bright yellow flowers emerge in the spring from the upper sides and tops of the stems. A few months later, the ripe fruits will ooze out their red pulp and glossy black seeds through an apical pore.

One curious trait of golden cereus is its ability to hybridize with two of its relatives—cardón (*Pachycereus pringlei*) and candelabra cactus (*Myrtillocactus cochal*)—in areas of Baja California where their ranges overlap with golden cereus. The naturally occurring sterile hybrid between golden cereus and cardon, X*Pacherocactus orcuttii*, is found only in small numbers near El Rosario and shows traits intermediate between its two dissimilar-looking parents. The very rare natural hybrid between golden cereus and candelabra cactus, X*Myrtgerocactus lindsayi*, is known only from the Rosario Bay region, south of El Rosario.

*Golden cereus forms thickets in this expanse of coastal sage scrub vegetation in San Diego Co. [Cabrillo N.M.]*

Golden cereus has very specific habitat requirements and occurs only in a few places in coastal Southern California, as well as in northern Baja California. Golden cereus was once found as far north as San Clemente, but due to its preference for ocean-bluff terrain that is highly valued for real estate development, its distribution along California's coast is now mostly confined to protected natural areas from La Jolla southward. Golden cereus grows abundantly on San Clemente and Santa Catalina islands. It can also be seen at Point Loma in Cabrillo National Monument and on slopes above the Tijuana River at Border Field State Park.

## Identifying Characteristics

**Habit:** erect to semi-erect stems branched from the base, usually forming thickets.
**Stems:** green, but obscured by golden spines, long cylindric, with 12 to 18 ribs; 0.75–2 in. (2–5 cm) wide and 1.5–6 ft. (0.5–2 m) tall.
**Spines:** 20 to 45 per areole; radial spines straight, 0.25–1 in. (6–13 mm) long; 1 to 3 central spines up to 2.4 in. (6 cm) long, with longest bent downward; straw-colored becoming dark brown with age.
**Flowers:** 1.5–2.4 in. (3.5–6 cm) across; outer tepals greenish yellow with reddish tips; inner tepals yellow; stigma with about 10 widely spreading lobes, pale yellow; anthers yellow; blooms April to June.
**Fruits:** round, spiny, 1–2.4 in. (2.5–6cm) in diameter; green with reddish tubercles.

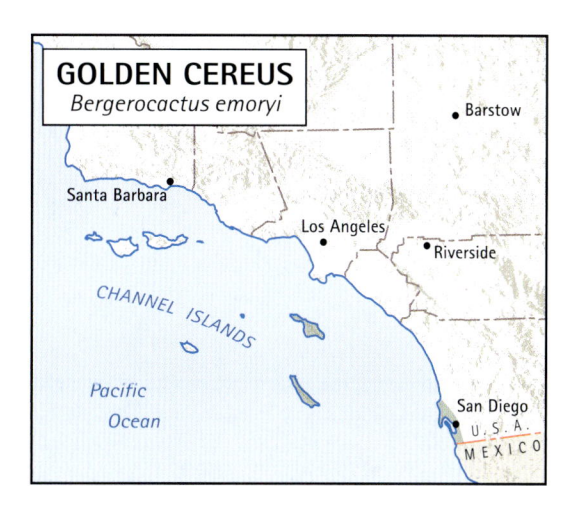

**GOLDEN CEREUS**
*Bergerocactus emoryi*

Species Profiles 33

Giant saguaro • *Carnegiea gigantea*  ARTWORK BY E.O. MURMAN

# *Carnegiea*
## SAGUARO

Giant saguaro—the largest, most stately, and best-known cactus in North America—was originally described and named *Cereus giganteus* by George Engelmann in 1848. In the mid-19th century, when the full diversity of cacti was unknown, most columnar cacti were placed into the genus *Cereus,* which in Latin means "a wax taper," referring to their candle-like shape. This species was given its new (now widely accepted) generic name by Nathaniel Britton and Joseph Rose in 1908 to honor one of America's foremost philanthropists, Andrew Carnegie (1835–1919). In addition to funding public libraries throughout the country, Carnegie was a financial supporter of desert plant research. He sponsored Britton and Rose's 15-year study on the systematics of Cactaceae, which culminated with the publication (between 1919 and 1923) of their classic four-volume work, *The Cactaceae.*

Recent research indicates this monotypic genus is most closely related to *Neobuxbaumia,* a small genus of large columnar cacti from southern Mexico. *Carnegiea* occurs throughout the Sonoran Desert of northern Mexico and southern Arizona and squeezes into California in very few places just west of the Colorado River. Young saguaros can be distinguished from young barrel cacti by their narrower shape and dense covering of straight grayish spines.

# GIANT SAGUARO
*Carnegiea gigantea*
(kar-neh-GEE-uh jy-gan-TEE-uh)

**Recent Synonyms**
*Cereus giganteus*

*A majestic giant saguaro towers above flowering brittlebrush in the Whipple Mountains. [San Bernardino Co.]*

Giant saguaros, symbols of the American Southwest, occasionally appear in the background scenes of old Hollywood Westerns filmed in the California deserts. But the botanically astute viewer will immediately know that the saguaros on the set are fakes. There are probably no more than 100 or so adult specimens of these stately cactus trees in California, and they are most abundant in the Whipple Mountains. This makes giant saguaro one of the rarest of California's cacti.

Saguaro flowers first open in the evening, and each blossom only remains open for about 24 hours. The large white flowers are pollinated by bats, nectar-feeding birds, sphinx moths, and bees. Saguaros don't flower until May or June, but their red, fig-like fruits quickly ripen and drop in June or July, which means that summer rain is crucial for seedling germination and survival.

Tens of millions of seeds are produced for every saguaro that survives long enough to flower and produce its own seeds. Of the few seedlings that do germinate in a favorable site, only about 1% will escape predation by harvester ants, rodents, rabbits, or birds before they develop into spiny tufts no longer palatable to most animals. In addition, environmental conditions do not always favor seedling growth. Botanists studying the Lake Havasu area, for example, have noted that only about 1 year in 10 is suitable for saguaro seedling establishment. To survive, a young saguaro needs to grow up beneath the protective branches of a nurse shrub. Nurse shrubs deter browsing animals, moderate temperature extremes, and provide vital shade. The likelihood that a saguaro will live to the reproductive age of 50 or so—when it will stand 6 to 8 feet tall and weigh nearly 500 pounds—is much better if this long-lived cacti can endure the vulnerable first year or two.

A saguaro may branch after 50 to 100 years, or when it is 6 to 15 feet tall, and it can live as long as 200 years, reaching a height of 40 feet or more. Researchers have noted that saguaros branch less in drier sites, such as at the western extension of their range. In the Whipple Mountains, many saguaros stand 15 to 20 feet tall without branches, and those with branches have relatively few short ones. A population of saguaros without many branches means fewer flowers, fruits and seeds, which in turn will limit the population size.

Giant saguaro is sacred to the Native American tribes of the Sonoran Desert, who have a myriad of uses for its fruits, woody ribs, and saguaro "boots"—woodpecker nest holes surrounded by woody scar-tissue. Ripe fruits, which provide a source of sugar, protein, and vitamin C, can serve as a valuable food source. They can be dried for storage, eaten raw, or cooked to make jam, candies, and syrup. They are also fermented to make a saguaro wine that is associated with rainmaking

*Flowers open on the branch tip of a giant saguaro growing in the Whipple Mountains. [San Bernardino Co.]*

## GIANT SAGUARO
### *Carnegiea gigantea*

celebrations. The saguaro's skeletal ribs have been used for roof beams, fencing, cradle frames, oars, and for reaching and knocking off saguaro fruits. Saguaro boots have been utilized as containers.

Saguaros occur from the central part of Sonora, Mexico, up through the southern third of Arizona and west to the easternmost parts of California, where they are found within a few miles of the Colorado River. Saguaros are most numerous in Arizona and northern Mexico because these areas receive much more summer rainfall than the lower Colorado River Basin. Outside of the eastern Whipple Mountains, saguaros in California are, at best, very few and far between. In 1966, Yale Dawson, author of *Cacti of California,* noted that "a few scattered specimens are found near the Colorado River from the Palo Verde Mountains southward toward Laguna Dam [close to Yuma], near which a fairly large grove occurs." Whether Dawson saw any of these cacti himself, or simply restated earlier observations, is unclear. The saguaro "grove" near Laguna Dam is gone, and roadside saguaros in the area west of Imperial Dam may or may not be of truly native origin. Four widely scattered individuals were verified in the rugged Palo Verde Mountains in 1984. However, the exciting discovery of a large and healthy-looking lone saguaro was made in the Chocolate Mountains in 2011—the only documented saguaro in Imperial County.

## Identifying Characteristics

**Habit:** columnar, unbranched, or with ascending branches above 6 ft. (2 m).
**Stems:** green, unsegmented; 10–30 in. (25–75 cm) wide, up to 50 ft. (15 m) tall; 19 to 26 prominent ribs on adults, 11 to 15 on young plants.
**Spines:** 15 to 30 per areole, straight, rigid and hard, dull white or gray, up to 2 in. (5 cm) long.
**Flowers:** 2–2.5 in. (5–6 cm) across and 3.5–5.5 in. (8.5–14 cm) long; outer tepals strongly reflexed, green with white margins; inner tepals white; stigma yellowish white, with widely spreading lobes; anthers pink to lavender; blooms May to June.
**Fruits:** narrowly pear-shaped, red, scaly; 1–2 in. (2.5–5 cm) wide and 2–3.5 in. (5–9 cm) long; splitting open widely when ripe to expose bright red pulp and black seeds.

Cushion foxtail cactus • *Coryphantha alversonii*   ARTWORK BY SUSAN BAZELL

# *Coryphantha*
## PINCUSHION or BEEHIVE CACTUS

Although pincushion cactus is widespread, it is uncommon and easily overlooked, so finding one in flower is a real treat. Cacti in the genus *Coryphantha* are sometimes confused with cacti in the closely related genus *Mammillaria*. When they are blooming, *Coryphantha* flower clusters take on the appearance of a top hat, in contrast to the ring of flowers characteristic of mammillarias. The genus name *Coryphantha* comes from the Greek words *koryphe,* for head, and *anthos,* for flower. When no flowers or fruits are present, *Coryphantha* can be distinguished from *Mammillaria* in having straight to slightly curved spines that are never hooked. Coryphanthas also have elongate areoles of only one type, while mammillarias have dimorphic flower-producing and spine-producing areoles.

A group of 20 or so *Coryphantha* species, including the 3 from California and Nevada, are often treated in a separate genus, *Escobaria*. These species all have pitted seeds and fringed outer tepals. Edward Anderson's *The Cactus Family* recognizes the genus *Escobaria,* but the more recent *Flora of North America* and *Jepson Manual* do not. *Coryphantha* was first named as a subgenus within *Mammillaria,* but *FNA* treats *Coryphantha* as a separate genus and includes *Escobaria* as a subgenus of *Coryphantha*. It is still unclear whether the subgenus *Escobaria* will emerge from the genus *Coryphantha* as a separate genus to be widely accepted or will continue to cause frustration and disagreement among general botanists and cactus growers.

*Coryphantha* ranges from Cuba through Mexico and north into 15 western U.S. states and southern Canada. Despite their extensive occurrence, the 55 to 75 species of *Coryphantha* are still poorly understood.

# CUSHION FOXTAIL CACTUS
*Coryphantha alversonii*

(kor-if-FAN-tha AL-ver-sun-ee-eye)

**Recent Synonyms**

*Coryphantha vivipara* var. *alversonii*, *Escobaria alversonii*, *Escobaria vivipara* var. *alversonii*

**Other Common Names**

foxtail cactus, foxtail beehive cactus, Alverson pincushion cactus

*Cushion foxtail cactus flowers feature widely spreading pink tepals and white stigma lobes. [Joshua Tree N.P.]*

*Cushion foxtail cactus, shown here in the Hexie Mountains, is a California endemic. [Joshua Tree N.P.]*

Cushion foxtail cactus is an especially attractive, perky little cactus with beautiful pinkish flowers that stand erect from the tops of the narrow barrel-shaped stems. The dark-tipped central spines are straight, relatively stout, and not barbed, which means that cushion foxtail cactus can be cautiously touched. But be warned: the "cushion" in its common name refers to its appearance only and should not be interpreted too literally.

Cushion foxtail cactus was first described in 1894 by American botanist and educator, John M. Coulter (1851–1928), who named this species in honor of its collector, Allen H. Alverson (1845–1916) of San Bernardino, California. Alverson was a jeweler and mineralogist who also traded in cactus and succulents. He collected cushion foxtail cactus in 1892 (when collecting cacti without a permit was legal) near Twentynine Palms, close to Joshua Tree National Park. Coulter's comments about cushion foxtail cactus noted that:

"The covering of stout bushy interlocking spines is like that of var. *deserti* [now *Coryphantha chlorantha*, desert pincushion], but the black and reddish coloration gives a decidedly different appearance. On account of this appearance of a reddish black brush the plant has been popularly called 'foxtail cactus.'"

Unlike other coryphanthas in California and Nevada, cushion foxtail cactus has two layers of hypodermis—the skin layers immediately below the outer epidermis. Hypodermal cells give hard but flexible mechanical support to cacti. Cushion foxtail cactus inhabits drier areas than other coryphanthas, and the extra layer of hypodermis found in this species is probably an adaptation to its relatively dry habitat.

The three species of *Coryphantha* in this book are very similar, but there are several ways to tell them apart. Cushion foxtail cactus differs from desert pincushion cactus in two major ways: it possesses darker spines, as noted by Coulter, and has pinkish flowers with white, widely spreading stigma lobes. Cushion foxtail cactus has shorter tubercles and is generally taller and more robust than both desert pincushion and beehive cactus. In addition, the central and radial spines of cushion foxtail cactus are more numerous than those of beehive cactus.

The range of cushion foxtail cactus does not overlap with either of our other coryphanthas and includes the mountains of the southeastern Mojave and northern Colorado deserts. This California endemic inhabits the transitional zone between these two desert regions and occurs from the Little San Bernardino Mountains southeast to the Big Maria Mountains of Riverside County. Cushion foxtail cactus is not widespread but can be locally common at elevations from 2000 to 5000 feet in plant communities ranging from creosote bush scrub up to Joshua tree woodland. It is locally abundant throughout much of the middle and lower elevations of Joshua Tree National Park and is found on alluvial fans, desert pavement, and other gravelly, rocky areas.

### Identifying Characteristics

**Habit:** erect, roundish to cylindrical; lower stems buried, solitary or in clusters;
**Stems:** green, firm; 1.8–3.5 in. (4.5–9 cm) wide and 2–10.6 in. (5–27 cm) tall; tubercles stiff, to 0.6 in. (1.4 cm) long.
**Spines:** 25 to 51 per areole; radial spines 18 to 33 per areole, white, some with dark tips; central spines 7 to 18 per areole, white with dark reddish black tips or dark with white bases, straight, to 0.9 in. (2–3 cm) long.
**Flowers:** 0.8–1.3 in. (2–3.2 cm) across; outer tepals fringed, dull greenish brown; inner tepals widely spreading, pale rose to violet with paler margins; filaments pink to white, anthers yellow; stigma lobes white; blooms May to June.
**Fruits:** cylindrical, succulent, pale green, floral remnant persistent; 0.6–1 in. (1.6–2.5 cm) long.

*The common name for cushion foxtail cactus is inspired by its reddish black spines. [Joshua Tree N.P.]*

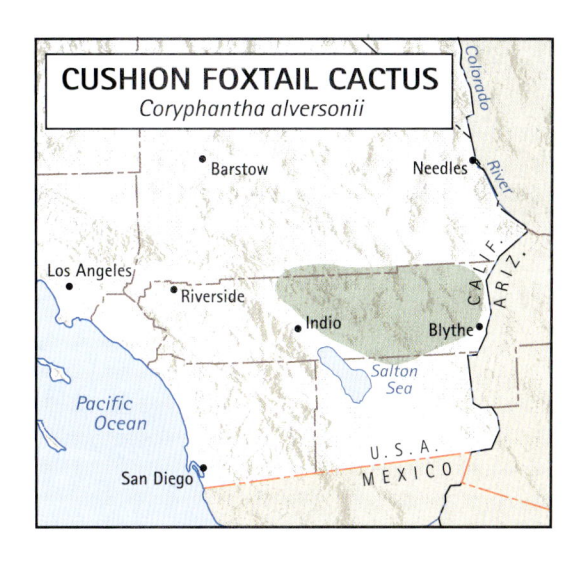

# DESERT PINCUSHION CACTUS
## *Coryphantha chlorantha*
(kor-if-FAN-tha klor-AN-tha)

**Recent Synonyms**
*Coryphantha vivipara* var. *deserti*, *Escobaria vivipara* var. *deserti*, *E. deserti*

**Other Common Names**
yellow-flowered pincushion, pincushion cactus

*Desert pincushion's yellow-orange flowers help distinguish it from beehive cactus. [Mojave N. Pr.]*

*Top: These desert pincushion cacti are growing in their preferred soil substrate—limestone. [Mojave N. Pr.]*
*Bottom: Desert pincushion cactus is an apt name for a plant with multiple interlocking spines. [Mojave N. Pr.]*

Desert pincushion cactus was first collected east of St. George in southern Utah and named *Mammillaria chlorantha* by George Engelmann. Its species name comes from the green flowers (from the Greek words, *chloros* for green and *anthos* for flower) on the dried specimen from which the original description was based. However, most populations have dull orange flowers, and green- or pale pink-flowered plants are rare.

Desert pincushion cactus has been treated as a variety of the variable beehive cactus *(Coryphantha vivipara)* because it shows vegetative similarities to that more widespread species. Its small, compact, dull orange flowers are diagnostic for desert pincushion, but in the absence of flowers, this species can be difficult to distinguish from beehive cactus.

Both species resemble a spiny ball, although the green knobby tubercles of desert pincushion are less visible. Desert pincushion is often perched in cracks of limestone dolomite, while beehive cactus usually protrudes from decomposed granite. Desert pincushion cactus can also be distinguished from beehive cactus by its more numerous (usually 20 to

30) ashy gray, interlocking radial spines.

Based on the ashy appearance of desert pincushion cactus (due to its interlaced spines) and its occurrence on dark dolomite rocks, one might expect this species to have a high heat tolerance. Indeed, experimental research shows that desert pincushion cactus can withstand a temperature of 147°F (64°C). This heat tolerance is similar to that of California fishhook cactus and higher than several chollas and prickly-pears examined in the same experiment. Its dense covering of pale radial spines helps desert pincushion cactus reflect excessive heat.

Desert pincushion cactus is virtually restricted to limestone-derived soils and rocks and can often be found growing on dolomite outcrops with Utah agave. This species occurs from about 1600 to at least 5600 feet in elevation and grows in pinyon-juniper woodland, Joshua tree woodland, and other plant communities of eastern Mojave Desert mountains. It ranges as far northwest as Death Valley National Park's Funeral Mountains and south through the Kingston, Clark, and Ivanpah mountains of California's eastern Mojave. In Nevada it is distributed from the Spotted Range south to the Spring Mountains; it is also found in southwestern Utah and northwestern Arizona.

*A dense covering of spines helps desert pincushion cactus reflect heat. [Clark Mountains, Mojave N. Pr.]*

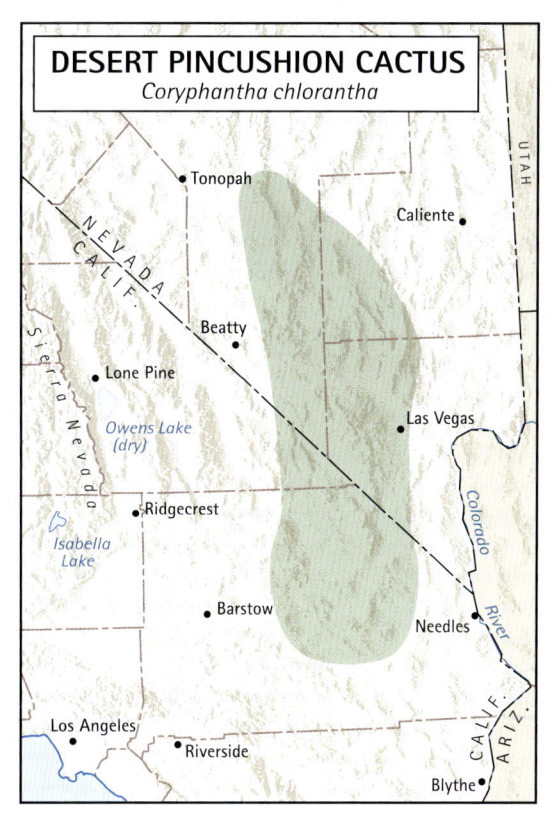

## Identifying Characteristics

**Habit:** erect, globular to short cylindrical, solitary or occasionally clustered.
**Stems:** pale green but obscured by spines, firm; 2.8–3.7 in. (7–9.5 cm) wide and 2.8–6 in. (7–15 cm) tall; tubercles to 0.7 in. (1.5–1.8 cm) long.
**Spines:** 18 to 41 per areole; radial spines 16 to 33 per areole, slender, white-gray, most with dark tips; central spines 2 to 18 per areole, white with dark tips, straight, to 0.8 in. (2 cm) long.
**Flowers:** About 1 in. (2–3 cm) across; outer tepals fringed; tepals pale yellow-orange with darker midstripes; filaments pink to white; anthers yellow; stigma lobes white to greenish white; blooms April to June.
**Fruits:** ovoid, succulent, green to brownish red, floral remnant strongly persistent; 0.5–1.2 in. (1.2–3.1 cm) long.

# BEEHIVE CACTUS
*Coryphantha vivipara* **var.** *rosea*
(kor-if-FAN-tha vy-VIP-ah-ra ro-ZEE-ah)

**Recent Synonyms**

*Coryphantha vivipara* var. *arizonica, C. vivipara* var. *bisbeeana, C. vivipara* var. *radiosa, Escobaria vivipara* var. *rosea, Mammillaria vivipara*

**Other Common Names**

foxtail cactus, viviparous foxtail cactus, desert beehive cactus, rose beehive cactus, pincushion cactus, spinystar

*A cluster of beehive cacti blooms in the eastern foothills of the Snake Range. [White Pine Co.]*

Beehive cactus was first collected by Thomas Nuttall "near the Mandan towns on the Missouri" (North Dakota) in 1811. Nuttall described and named this species for its trait of producing vegetative buds that fall to the ground and root near the mother plant. Vivipary is an unusual characteristic among flowering plants, but it also occurs in coastal cholla and teddy-bear cholla, to name a few.

As expected for a cactus that grows from the Joshua tree woodlands in the Mojave Desert to the badlands of North Dakota, beehive cactus has to withstand both extremely hot and subzero temperatures. Throughout its range, beehive cactus can tolerate summertime ground-surface temperatures over 140°F (64°C) and survive a freezing temperature of -8°F (-22°C) if it has time to acclimate to cold weather.

The range of beehive cactus rivals that of little prickly-pear, stretching from Sonora, Mexico to Saskatchewan, Canada—more than 20° in latitude—making it our region's most cosmopolitan cactus. It is also the most widespread and variable species of *Coryphantha,* with numerous common and varietal names assigned to it by botanists and horticulturists. George Engelmann wrote of beehive cactus: "The extreme forms are certainly very unlike one another, but the transitions are so gradual that I can not draw strict limits between them." Lyman Benson recognized seven varieties in *The Cacti of the United States and Canada* (1982), two of which are now treated as separate species and the others treated as synonyms of *Coryphantha vivipara*. But he did acknowledge that further study was needed to delineate these variable cacti.

Beehive cactus and desert pincushion cactus are very similar vegetatively, but beehive cactus has

*The upper stem of a young beehive cactus rises above the surface of this granitic soil. [Mojave N. Pr.]*

*Beehive cactus, seen here in Nevada's Quinn Canyon Range, can withstand extreme heat and cold. [Nye Co.]*

eastward through all but the lowest elevations of southern and central Nevada. It occurs in sagebrush scrub, Joshua tree woodland, and pinyon-juniper woodland, either in the open or under the cover of protective shrubs.

### Identifying Characteristics

**Habit:** erect, globular to short cylindrical; lower stems buried, solitary, or occasionally clustered.
**Stems:** green, firm; 1.2–4.3 in. (3–11 cm) wide and 2.8–7 in. (7–18 cm) tall; tubercles prominent, to 1 in. (2.5 cm) long.
**Spines:** 22 to 30 per areole; radial spines 12 to 18 per areole, white to pale brown; central spines 10–12 per areole, white with dark tips, straight, to 1 in. (2.5 cm) long.
**Flowers:** 1.2–2 in. (3–5 cm) across; outer tepals fringed, midrib greenish with pink-brown margins; inner tepals pink (pale rose to magenta), darkest at tips; filaments pink to white; anthers yellow; stigma lobes white to pale yellow; blooms April to June.
**Fruits:** ovoid, juicy, green to brownish red, floral remnant persistent; 0.5–1.1 in. (1.2–2.8 cm) long.

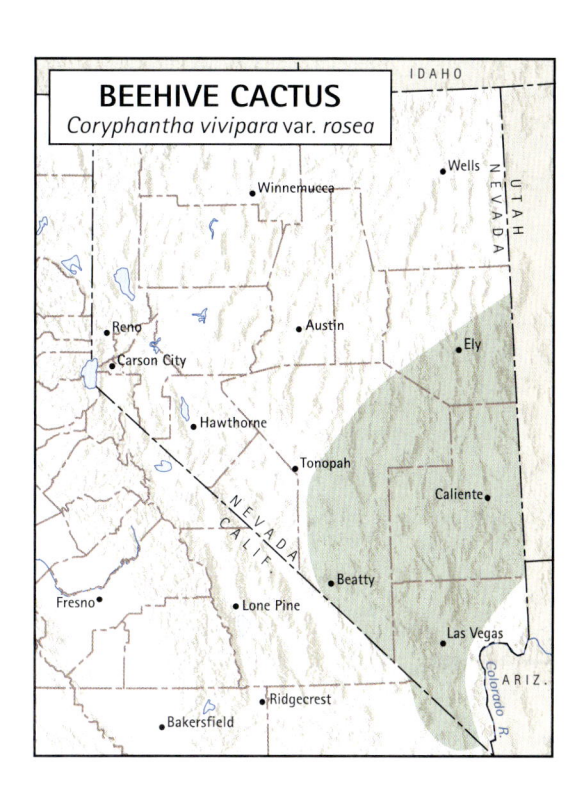

fewer radial spines than desert pincushion cactus. It is more commonly found on granitic alluvium in California, while desert pincushion cactus is nearly always found on limestone. However, in the Great Basin of Nevada, beehive cactus is often found in limestone soils, alongside the similar-looking mountain cactus. Beehive cactus has pink flowers in contrast to the dull orange or yellow flowers of desert pincushion cactus, and it occurs at higher elevations (3500 to 8000 feet) and farther north than cushion foxtail cactus. In the Mojave National Preserve, the well-camouflaged beehive cactus often appears like a knobby, spine-covered ball half submerged in the coarse, granitic sand. During the late spring, however, its gorgeous pink flowers stand out in contrast to its pale brown substrate, signaling to any bees in the vicinity.

Within our region, beehive cactus can be found in California's eastern Mojave Desert and

**BEEHIVE CACTUS**
*Coryphantha vivipara* var. *rosea*

Buckhorn cholla • *Cylindropuntia acanthocarpa* var. *acanthocarpa*  ARTWORK BY E.O. MURMAN

# *Cylindropuntia*
## CHOLLA

Many desert visitors are familiar with *Cylindropuntia*—the chollas—and they tend to stay a respectable distance from these cacti. Chollas have a well-deserved reputation for their formidable armament and the tendency of their stem-joints to easily detach and "jump" onto the nearest passing foot.

When the name *Cylindropuntia* was first published by George Engelmann in 1856, it was described as a subgenus of *Opuntia*. Members of this subgenus were differentiated from other *Opuntia* by their characteristic cylindrical-shaped stem-joints. Chollas continued to be treated as a subgenus by most botanists until around 2001 when seed and pollen morphology and genetic studies showed that it was clearly distinct from *Opuntia* and its other relatives, such as *Grusonia*. (This genus is therefore absent from older floras and plant lists in California and Nevada.) While *Cylindropuntia* species can be distinguished from *Opuntia* species by their cylindrical stem-joints, they are differentiated from both *Grusonia* and *Opuntia* by the presence of papery sheaths that entirely cover their new spines.

Most of the roughly 36 species of *Cylindropuntia* are found in Mexico, and more than half occur in Baja California. Chollas are also found on Hispaniola and throughout the southwestern U.S. There are 14 species in California and Nevada. Many diagnostic characters are used to separate cholla species, but the most important ones include tubercle size and shape, tepal and filament color, and fruit type. Like their close kin the prickly-pears, chollas tend to hybridize, and a few named hybrids are found in our region (see "Cholla Hybrids" on page 55). An abbreviated summary of identifying characteristics of cholla species profiled in this book is found in Appendix D "Cholla Species Comparison" on page 220.

# BUCKHORN CHOLLA
*Cylindropuntia acanthocarpa* var. *acanthocarpa*
(sil-in-droh-PUN-tee-ya ah-kanth-oh-CAR-pa)

**Recent Synonyms**
*Opuntia acanthocarpa* var. *coloradensis*

**Other Common Names**
Colorado buckhorn cholla, staghorn cholla

*Colorful blossoms decorate this buckhorn cholla growing in the Newberry Mountains. [Lake Mead N.R.A.]*

Buckhorn cholla is what many people think of as the "generic" cholla of the deserts of southern Nevada and southeastern California. However, the colorful flowers of buckhorn cholla are hardly generic. Purplish red filaments topped with bright yellow pollen-bearing anthers and beautiful yellowish orange tepals—the outer ones often suffused with red—surround the pale yellow style and stigma. No other cactus flower in our region has this combination of colors, though Wolf cholla comes closest with its red filaments and red- to yellow-colored tepals.

The flower buds of buckhorn cholla were once an important food source for Native Americans throughout the southwestern U.S. and northern Mexico. The buds were harvested, cleaned of glochids, and steam roasted overnight in pits lined with heated stones and covered with succulent leaves. Steamed buds served as a good source of calcium and iron and could be dried and eaten year-round.

Buckhorn cholla is nearly as widespread as silver cholla. Where both species overlap, buckhorn cholla is usually found in greater abundance. It stands taller than silver cholla, and while in flower, buckhorn cholla is readily discerned from silver cholla by its orange tepals and red filaments. When not in bloom, these two common chollas can be distinguished by the length of their joints, the shape of their tubercles, and their growth habits. Buckhorn cholla has longer stem-joints with more open branching and tubercles that are two to four times longer than broad. Chollas that have reddish filaments and short tubercles are sometimes found where both species occur, such as the New York Mountains and other ranges of the southeastern Mojave Desert. These are known as the hybrid *Cylindropuntia Xdeserta*. Buckhorn cholla can be discerned from Wolf cholla, the only other cholla with red filaments, by buckhorn's much larger range of occurrence, its more elongate tubercles, narrower stem-joints, and more ascending growth habit.

Since it is so variable, most botanists recognize three distinct varieties of buckhorn cholla that differ in their tubercle length, size and growth habit, spine and stem color, and range. Variety *acanthocarpa* is the most common and widespread, and it is the only variety known from California and Nevada. This variety is found in the Colorado and eastern Mojave deserts of southeastern California, southern Nevada, and east into southwestern Utah, western Arizona, and Sonora, Mexico. Buckhorn cholla grows in gravelly and rocky soils and is a common inhabitant in many desert plant communities from around 1000 to 4200 feet in elevation. Its broad distribution puts buckhorn cholla in close contact with many other species of *Cylindropuntia*, so it is not surprising to find that buckhorn cholla

*Buckhorn cholla is a common but beautiful cholla widespread in the Southwest. [Red Rock Canyon N.C.A.]*

is known to hybridize with no fewer than eight other species (see "Cholla Hybrids" on page 55).

## Identifying Characteristics

**Habit:** shrub or occasionally tree-like, erect, openly branched; 3–10 ft. (0.9–3 m) tall.
**Stems:** pale green, joints 0.8–1.25 in. (2–3 cm) wide and 4–12 in. (10–30 cm) long; tubercles prominent, elongate, 0.8–1.5 in. (2–4 cm) long and approximately 0.4 in. (1 cm) wide.
**Spines:** 12 to 30 per areole, straight, 0.5–1.5 in. (1.2–3.8 cm) long.
**Flowers:** outer tepals suffused with red, 0.8–1.4 in. (2–3.5 cm) long; inner tepals yellow-orange; stigma lobes pale yellow, white, or pale green; filaments purplish red to dark red; blooms April to June.
**Fruits:** tan, dry, tuberculate, densely spiny, 0.6–1.4 in. (1.5–3.5 cm) long.

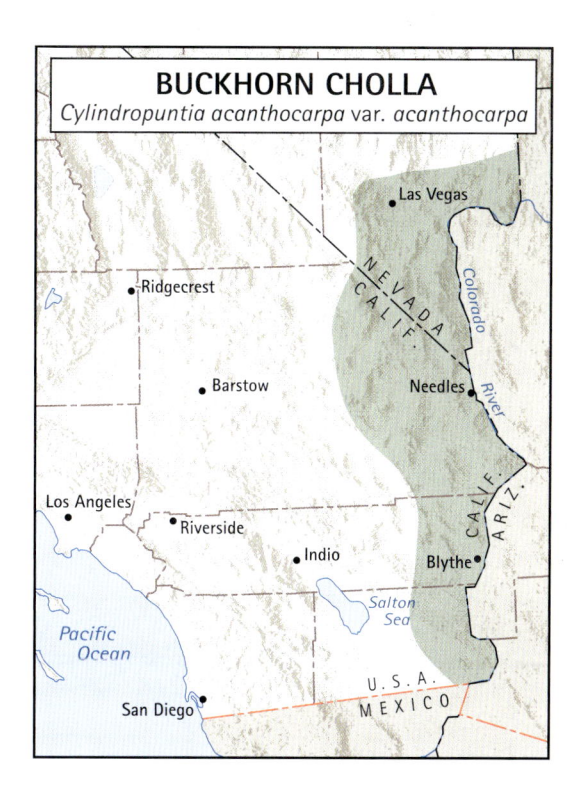

**BUCKHORN CHOLLA**
*Cylindropuntia acanthocarpa* var. *acanthocarpa*

# TEDDY-BEAR CHOLLA
*Cylindropuntia bigelovii*
(sil-in-droh-PUN-tee-ya BIG-eh-lov-ee-eye)

**Recent Synonyms**
*Opuntia bigelovii*

**Other Common Names**
Bigelow cholla, jumping cholla, golden-spined jumping cholla

*Teddy-bear cholla's easily detached stem-joints encourage vegetative reproduction. [Anza-Borrego Desert S.P.]*

Most people recognize the gregarious teddy-bear cholla not as a soft and fuzzy friend but as a "jumping cholla" that hitches rides on the nearest vector, which may be a boot or a bare ankle. (A wide-toothed comb or stick helps dislodge a stem-joint from skin or clothing.) Teddy-bear cholla seeds are usually infertile, but fallen stem-joints and fruits readily root and grow into new plants; as a result, this species relies almost exclusively on its easily detached stem parts for vegetative reproduction. Teddy-bear cholla thus tends to form dense colonies of individuals, with young plants surrounding their taller parent plants and spiny stem-joints littering the desert floor.

A thick covering of long, barbed spines benefits this well-known cholla in several other ways, but at some cost to its productivity. The most obvious benefit is protection from potential "cholla-vores," such as rabbits and rodents. (Pack-rats commonly use detached stem-joints in their nests to deter predators.) However, teddy-bear cholla spines reduce photosynthesis by acting as a natural shade-cloth, shading the stem surface by 30% to 40%. Although this spiny covering helps reduce heat and water loss, experiments by plant physiologist Park Nobel have shown that teddy-bear cholla can produce 50% more stem volume with its spines trimmed off. This trade-off is one example of the evolutionary compromises that seem so common among cacti and other desert plants.

The scientific name for teddy-bear, or Bigelow cholla, was bestowed in 1856 by George Englemann in honor of John M. Bigelow (1804–1878). As part of the Pacific Railroad Survey of 1853–1854, Bigelow was responsible for collecting plants and reporting on the "Botany of the Expedition." Numerous plants of the desert Southwest are named for him, including *Nolina bigelovii*.

Teddy-bear cholla puts its resources into its propagule-forming upper segments, and the lower portions of the plant die back and take on a burnt look. This makes teddy-bear cholla easy to recognize, even from a distance, with its dark brown or black lower trunk topped with a stout, spiny, greenish yellow cluster of stems. When backlit by a low sun, this cholla becomes rimmed with warm light.

Teddy-bear cholla is most often found on southern or western exposures on rocky hillsides and bajadas at elevations from 1000 to 3000 feet. It is one of the most widespread North American chollas and occurs throughout the Sonoran Desert of western Arizona, northern Mexico, and southeastern California and extends north through the southern Mojave Desert to the tip of Nevada.

*Teddy-bear cholla with blooming desert senna in the U.C. Sacramento Mountains Reserve. [San Bernardino Co.]*

## Identifying Characteristics

**Habit:** tree-like or shrubby, usually with a single trunk and short lateral branches; lower branches and trunk becoming dark brown; 1–5 ft. (0.3–1.5 m) tall.

**Stems:** green to grayish green, usually somewhat whorled; joints 1.6–2.2 in. (4–5.5 cm) wide and 1.6–7 in. (4–18 cm) long; tubercles prominent, broadly oval, 0.15–0.3 in. (0.4–0.8 cm) long.

**Spines:** 8 to 15 per areole, straight, yellowish, spreading, interlaced, 0.4–1 in. (1–2.5 cm) long.

**Flowers:** tepals pale green to yellowish green with red tips, 0.6–1 in. (1.5–2.5 cm) long; style and stigma lobes greenish; filaments green; blooms March to June, occasionally in September.

**Fruits:** usually sterile, fleshy to leathery, yellow, egg-shaped, becoming spineless, tubercles prominent, 0.6–1.6 in. (1.5–4 cm) long.

**TEDDY-BEAR CHOLLA**
*Cylindropuntia bigelovii*

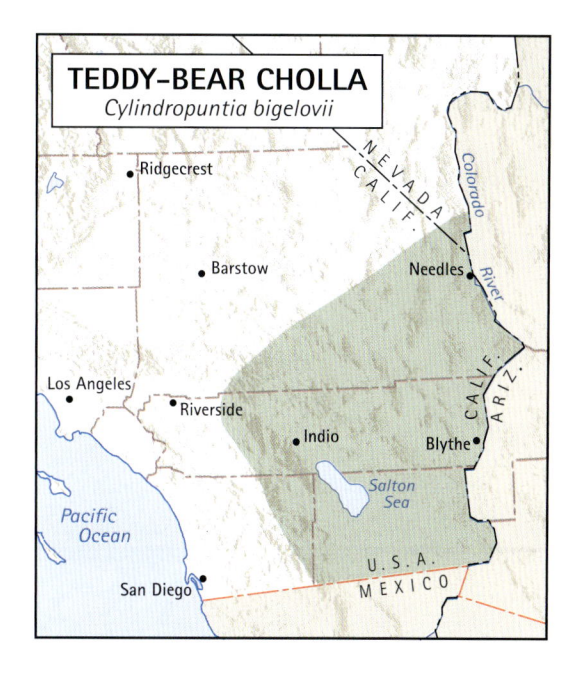

Species Profiles 51

## SNAKE CHOLLA
*Cylindropuntia californica* var. *californica*
(sil-in-droh-PUN-tee-ya kal-i-FOR-ni-kah)
**Recent Synonyms**
*Opuntia serpentina, O. parryi, O. parryi* var. *serpentina*

## CANE CHOLLA
*Cylindropuntia californica* var. *parkeri*
(PAR-ker-eye)
**Recent Synonyms**
*Opuntia parryi, O. californica* var. *parkeri*
**Other Common Names**
valley cholla

*Cane cholla is not a desert species and is found even in oak woodlands. [Cleveland N.F.]*

*Snake cholla, cultivated here at a native plant nursery, is becoming increasingly rare. [San Diego Co.]*

**Snake cholla** is usually a sprawling, low-growing cholla that occurs in the coastal sage scrub understory in a few locations from the San Diego area south into northern Baja California. In contrast, cane cholla (*Cylindropuntia californica* var. *parkeri*) is a tall and lanky cactus that is found throughout cismontane southern California in chaparral and oak woodland habitats. Though lumped together at various times, these two chollas are now considered to be two distinct varieties of *Cylindropuntia californica* that occur in southern California. Two other varieties are found only in Baja California.

Like many cacti that were first collected and described over 150 years ago, snake cholla has a long and confusing history of scientific name changes, beginning in 1840 and ending (for the time being) in 2001. Snake cholla, which was first collected "near the seacoast about San Diego" in 1838 by Thomas Nuttall, was given the provisional name *Cereus californicus* by renowned American botanists John Torrey and Asa Gray. It was then more completely described and (more aptly) renamed *Opuntia serpentina* by George Engelmann in 1852. In 1899, taxonomists returned snake cholla closer to it original scientific name by giving it the Latin name *Opuntia californica*. Since then, the scientific names assigned to snake cholla changed depending on its currently accepted status as a distinct species, a variety, or as merely a variant growth form of cane cholla. The prior Latin name, *Opuntia californica*, was resurrected in 1996 by cactologist Donald Pinkava to be consistent with the botanical rules of nomenclature. Because snake cholla's most recent scientific name, *Cylindropuntia californica* var. *californica*, is based on a more complete understanding of

*A cane cholla grows in valley grassland vegetation in Cajon Canyon. [San Bernardino Co.]*

its relationship to other chollas, its current taxonomic identity should stick, at least for a while.

This cholla's unique growth habit of snaking its way along the ground and through shrubs helps to distinguish it from other chollas and explains the origin of its common name. In addition to this sprawling growth habit, snake cholla differs from cane cholla in having tubercles that are shorter and more rounded, areoles that grow closer together, and brown radiating spines that are all of equal length. Another similar species, coastal cholla, can also assume a low-growing to sprawling growth habit, but its stem-joints are generally much thicker, more easily detached, and its tubercles are larger than those of snake cholla.

Snake cholla grows in sandy soils in openings or beneath shrubs in coastal sage scrub plant communities within 10 miles of the ocean. It has become increasingly rare and now occurs in scattered small populations on xeric sites from Florida Canyon in Balboa Park, San Diego, south to Otay Mesa at elevations below 300 feet.

**Cane cholla** has long gone by the scientific name of *Opuntia parryi,* bestowed by George Engelmann in 1852. Charles C. Parry (1823–1890), a physician, geologist, and botanist, first collected specimens of this cholla in 1851 in the San Felipe Valley northeast of San Diego while on the United States and Mexican Boundary Survey. In *The Native Cacti of California* (1969), Lyman Benson treated cane cholla and snake cholla as varieties of *Opuntia parryi*. They can be difficult to distinguish as herbarium specimens but differ markedly in growth habit, range, tubercle size, and spination.

The most noticeable trait of cane cholla is its growth form of long narrow stems with relatively few spines. The stem-joints grow up to a foot long, but appear much taller because they grow in a straight angle, one upon another. Plants are usually 4 to 6 feet tall, but one individual observed in Oak Grove (San Diego County) grew at least 14 feet high using the support of a red shank tree. The yellowish flowers are crowded near the stem tips, similar to Gander cholla, but cane cholla's lack of

*Cane cholla's stem-joints grow in straight angles, enhancing its upright habit. [Cleveland N.F]*

**SNAKE CHOLLA, CANE CHOLLA**
*Cylindropuntia californica*
var. *californica* (snake cholla)
var. *parkeri* (cane cholla)

overlapping spines on longer tubercles can usually be used to distinguish these two cacti.

Cane cholla is one of only three chollas in California (the others being snake cholla and coastal cholla) that does not inhabit true desert environments. It grows to the western edge of California's Colorado and Mojave deserts and is typically found in openings in inland chaparral, valley grassland, and oak woodland plant communities at elevations from 2000 to 5000 feet. Cane cholla occurs from northern Baja California north through the Peninsular and western Transverse ranges as far north as Cuyama Valley in eastern Santa Barbara County.

## Identifying Characteristics

**Habit:** shrub, sprawling, prostrate to semi-erect in var. *californica*, or erect in var. *parkeri*, openly branched; 1–4 ft. (0.3–1.2 m) long in var. *californica*; 1–10 ft. (0.3–3 m) tall in var. *parkeri*.
**Stems:** dark green, joints 0.6–1 in. (1.5–2.5 cm) wide and 2.4–12 in. (6–30 cm) long; tubercles prominent, sometimes forming ribs, 0.3–0.6 in. (0.7–1.5 cm) long and less than 3 times longer than wide in var. *californica*; 0.6–1.2 in. (1.5–3 cm) long and usually 3 to 5 times longer than wide in var. *parkeri*.
**Spines:** 7 to 20 per areole or absent; brown in var. *californica*; white to pale yellow in var. *parkeri*; spines of similar length in var. *californica*; 1 to 3 central spines much longer in var. *parkeri*, 0.4–1.2 in. (1–3 cm) long.
**Flowers:** tepals yellow, greenish yellow or orange; outer tepals tipped reddish brown, 0.6–1.2 in. (1.5–3 cm) long; style white to yellow or pink; stigma lobes white to yellow; filaments greenish yellow; blooms April to June in var. *californica*, April to July in var. *parkeri*.
**Fruits:** green to yellow, drying to tan, dry, spines few or absent, 0.6–1.3 in. (1.5–3.2 cm) long for both varieties.

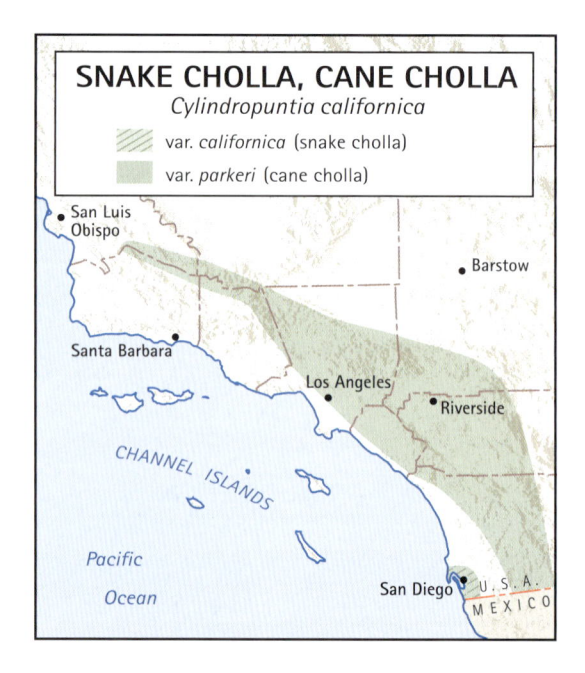

*Mason Valley cholla was previously considered a hybrid (see page 60). [Anza-Borrego Desert S.P.]*

## Cholla Hybrids

Hybridization between cholla species is a common occurrence. In fact, every cholla species is suspected of hybridizing with at least one other, and a few, such as buckhorn cholla, have crossed with as many as eight other cholla species. Some of these hybrids have been formally named and described, but most have not. Reputed cholla hybrids from California and Nevada include the following:

*Cylindropuntia acanthocarpa* var. *acanthocarpa* X *Cylindropuntia echinocarpa:* known as *Cylindropuntia* X *deserta,* this hybrid of two highly variable species is reported from the Iron Range in the eastern Mojave Desert and is likely in many other areas of southeastern California and southern Nevada.

*Cylindropuntia acanthocarpa* X *Cylindropuntia multigeniculata:* known from the Blue Diamond Hill and probably elsewhere in southern Nevada.

*Cylindropuntia echinocarpa* X *Cylindropuntia munzii:* known only from the range of Munz cholla, south of the Little Chuckwalla Mountains, California.

*Cylindropuntia echinocarpa* X *Cylindropuntia ramosissima:* documented from the Whipple Mountains and probably found in other parts of southeastern California.

*Cylindropuntia echinocarpa* X *Cylindropuntia whipplei:* known from the Sheep Range within Nevada's Desert National Wildlife Refuge and probably elsewhere in southeastern Nevada.

*Cylindropuntia californica* var. *parkeri* X *Cylindropuntia ganderi:* known from the upper San Felipe Valley area west of Anza-Borrrego Desert State Park; near Aguanga, on the Riverside-San Diego County line; and probably elsewhere in the eastern Peninsular Ranges of California.

*Cylindropuntia ganderi* X *Cylindropuntia wolfii:* known from near Ocotillo, at the southern edge of the California range of Wolf cholla, just south of Anza-Borrego Desert State Park.

# CHUCKWALLA CHOLLA
## *Cylindropuntia chuckwallensis*
(sil-in-droh-PUN-tee-ya chuck-wall-EN-sis)

*Chuckwalla cholla produces flowers with reddish styles but variable tepal colors [Joshua Tree N.P.]*

*One-third of Chuckwalla cholla flowers are dark red [Chuckwalla Mountains Wilderness]*

Chuckwalla cholla is California's newest cactus species, and was first described in 2014. This enigmatic cholla had been hiding in plain sight for nearly a century. Although collected by Willis Linn Jepson, Philip Munz, Frank Peirson, and others in the 1920s, they all identified it as silver cholla. Peirson, however, did note the "peculiar dull reddish purple" of the flowers, a key feature that separates Chuckwalla from silver cholla.

In the absence of flowers, Chuckwalla cholla could be mistaken for an especially spiny, gnarly-looking silver cholla. These species, which may co-occur, have similar sized branches, and their spine lengths and spine numbers are a close match. Chuckwalla cholla has much more crowded branching that is organized in whorls, giving it a low, broad, compact and spinier appearance. With its whorled branching growth habit, Chuckwalla cholla most closely resembles Blue Diamond cholla from southern Nevada and adjacent Arizona. Even if these two species did have overlapping ranges, they would not be easily confused with one another. Chuckwalla cholla is larger in every measurable character, and it does not have green flowers like Blue Diamond cholla.

Botanists Marc Baker and Michelle Cloud-Hughes, who described Chuckwalla cholla as a new species, made a detailed comparative study of Chuckwalla cholla and three other cholla species, and discussed its likely taxonomic relationships. Although Chuckwalla cholla does not have any specific characters that distinguish it from other chollas, it does exhibit a unique suite of characters that set it apart. Like Wolf cholla, Chuckwalla cholla is hexaploid, meaning it has six sets of chromosomes. Because its morphology most resembles Blue Diamond cholla and its flower color is most similar to buckhorn cholla, the researchers hypothesize that Chuckwalla cholla may have evolved from ancient hybridization between Blue Diamond cholla and buckhorn cholla or similar precursors to those species.

The researchers noted that, similar to Wolf cholla, Chuckwalla cholla is also gynodioecious, producing either perfect flowers (bisexual with fertile stamens and pistils), or only female, pistillate flowers that have pollen-sterile stamens. Because polyploid plant species tend to have higher rates of self-fertilization, or inbreeding, than their more

*The white spines and densely whorled branches help distinguish Chuckwalla cholla from other chollas [Joshua Tree N.P.]*

common diploid relatives, there may be selective pressure in polyploid plants to evolve flowers that promote outcrossing—such as the partially dioecious flowers of Wolf and Chuckwalla cholla. The flowers of Chuckwalla cholla are also noteworthy for their color variability. In populations studied by botanists, roughly half of the flower tepals are orange, one-third are dark red-purple, and one-eighth are yellow.

Chuckwalla cholla was named for its occurrence in the Chuckwalla Mountains of the Colorado Desert. It grows at elevations of 1300 to 5250 feet in a variety of soil types and habitats, from desert washes to rocky slopes. Chuckwalla cholla is restricted to Riverside and Imperial counties, and ranges from the northern Chocolate Mountains through the Chuckwalla Mountains and then extends northwest into the Eagle and Cottonwood mountains of Joshua Tree National Park.

## Identifying Characteristics

**Habit:** shrub generally wider than tall with several trunks, densely branched, mostly in whorls; 1.5–4.0 ft. (0.5–1.2 m) tall, and up to 6.5 ft. (2 m) wide.
**Stems:** green, joints 0.7–1.1 in. (1.7–2.9 cm) wide and 1.2–4.0 in. (3–10 cm) long; tubercles oval, 0.3–0.6 in. (0.7–1.6 cm) long.
**Spines:** 10 to 21 per areole; straight, translucent white, mostly obscuring stems; 0.7–1.6 in. (2–4 cm) long.
**Flowers:** tepals yellow-orange to pink-purple; 1.2–2 in. (3–5 cm) long; style and stigma lobes pink to purple; filaments pink to purple, occasionally pale green; blooms March to April.
**Fruits:** gray-tan, dry, densely spiny, bur-like; 0.5–0.9 in. (1.3–2.3 cm) long.

# SILVER CHOLLA
*Cylindropuntia echinocarpa*
(sil-in-droh-PUN-tee-ya ek-in-oh-CAR-pa)
**Recent Synonyms**
*Opuntia echinocarpa, O. wigginsii*
**Other Common Names**
golden cholla

*Some of the spines on this silver cholla still have straw-colored tips. [Lake Mead N.R.A.]*

*Flower buds and spiny fruits of a silver cholla growing in the Newberry Mountains. [Lake Mead N.R.A.]*

Judging by the two common names for this cholla, one might wonder how one person's silver could be another's gold. The explanation lies in the coloration of the sheaths that cover the newest spines. Cholla spines, in contrast to the spines of prickly-pears and club-chollas, produce an epidermal sheath that covers the entire spine and eventually falls off. The tips of these baggy, paper-like sheaths are straw-colored, giving the outermost spiny stems of this cholla a golden hue. But once the sheath color fades or the sheaths fall off, the numerous, relatively long, white to gray spines impart a more silvery appearance.

Silver cholla is extremely variable, and it comes in sizes ranging from bushy 2-foot-tall mature plants in the northern and eastern Mojave Desert to intricately branched "trees" 5 to 6 feet tall in the southern and central parts of its range. Even though its size and general appearance can vary greatly, characteristics of the stem, flower, and tubercle are fairly consistent across its range. Short stem-joints 1 to 3 inches long, yellowish green flowers with green filaments, and prominent tubercles no more than twice as long as they are wide, are good distinguishing features of silver cholla. The small tubercles account for the crowding of the spines, which completely obscure the pale green stem surface, adding to its silver appearance.

No other cholla in our region occurs as far north or in such an expansive range as silver cholla. It is found from the southern reaches of the Great Basin in central Nevada and Mono County, California through the entire Mojave and south to the Sonoran Desert of California, Arizona, and Mexico. Silver cholla grows alongside many other cacti and thrives in some of the driest habitats of any cactus in our region. It is often the only other perennial plant to survive over vast expanses of Mojave Desert territory dominated by creosote bush and burrobush. With the exception of at least

*Silver cholla thrives in extremely arid regions and has a very expansive range. [Valley of Fire S.P.]*

one small population of diamond cholla found in Death Valley National Park, silver cholla is the only cholla found in California's northern Mojave region. It occurs at elevations from approximately 200 to nearly 6000 feet on valley floors, bajadas, or rocky slopes and in vegetation types ranging from creosote bush scrub to Joshua tree woodland and pinyon-juniper woodland.

## Identifying Characteristics

**Habit:** shrub to tree-like, erect, densely branched from the base; 1.5–6.5 ft. (0.5–2 m) tall.
**Stems:** green to grayish green, joints 0.4–1.2 in. (1–3 cm) wide and 1.2–4.7 in. (3–12 cm) long; tubercles prominent, oval, 0.2–0.5 in. (0.4–1.3 cm) long.
**Spines:** 6 to 22 per areole; straight, whitish, interlaced and obscuring stems; 0.8–1.8 in. (2–4.5 cm) long.
**Flowers:** inner tepals pale green to yellow-green; outer tepals sometimes suffused with maroon, 0.8–1 in. (2–2.3 cm) long; style and stigma lobes whitish; filaments green to yellow-green; blooms March to June.
**Fruits:** gray-tan, dry, roundish, densely spiny, bur-like; 0.5–0.9 in. (1.3–2.3 cm) long.

**SILVER CHOLLA**
*Cylindropuntia echinocarpa*

# MASON VALLEY CHOLLA
*Cylindropuntia fosbergii*
(sil-in-droh-PUN-tee-ya fos-BERG-ee-eye)

## Recent Synonyms
*Opuntia fosbergii, Opuntia bigelovii* var. *hoffmannii*

*The pale green flowers of Mason Valley cholla produce fruits with sterile seeds [Anza-Borrego Desert S.P.]*

Mason Valley cholla is one of the few chollas that is easily recognizable from a distance because of its large size and pinkish hue. It grows in valley bottoms and alluvial fans alongside teddy-bear cholla, Gander cholla, ocotillo, and desert agave and stands taller than any other cactus in its territory. This territory, however, is quite small, stretching only about 18 miles (30 km) along California Highway S-2 between Mason Valley in the northwest and Carrizo Valley in the southeast. The entirety of Mason Valley cholla's range lies within or adjacent to the southern portion of Anza-Borrego Desert State Park, making this species one of California's most limited endemics.

Its stout trunk with terminal branches, which are easily detached and litter the ground around it, account for its other common name—pink teddy-bear cholla. Both Mason Valley and teddy-bear cholla are triploid (with three sets of chromosomes) and produce sterile seeds, making their reproduction entirely vegetative. Their colonial nature attests to this "jumping cholla" mode of reproduction. In fact, Mason Valley cholla was long considered to be a natural hybrid between teddy-bear cholla, the species it most closely resembles, and a second parent, most likely its other cholla neighbor, Gander cholla. Lyman Benson, the eminent cactus expert who wrote *The Cacti of the United States and Canada* (1982), treated Mason Valley cholla as a variety of teddy-bear cholla.

The earliest name for Mason Valley cholla is *Opuntia fosbergii*, described and named by Carl Wolf (see page 74) in honor of Francis Raymond Fosberg (1908-1993). Fosberg was a botanist and plant conservationist with the U.S. Geological Survey and the Smithsonian Institution, and a collector of the California flora.

A comparative genetic study of Mason Valley cholla and its four possible hybrid relatives, made by Michael Mayer of University of San Diego and his colleagues in 2011, showed that while Mason Valley and teddy-bear cholla are each other's closest relatives, Mason Valley cholla is most likely not of recent hybrid origin with teddy-bear cholla as one parent species, nor is it a variety of teddy-bear cholla. In addition, Mason Valley cholla is not closely related to the other chollas studied (Gander, Wolf, cane, and silver cholla).

Mason Valley and teddy-bear cholla are best thought of as sister species, meaning they are derived from a common ancestor not shared by any other living cholla species. The authors of the study noted above speculate that Mason Valley cholla may have evolved from isolated populations of widespread ancestral teddy-bear cholla and

*The tall stature and beige to pink color of Mason Valley cholla distinguish it. [Anza-Borrego Desert S.P.]*

eventually had its range restricted and its genetic variability diminished. Although it is now known that Mason Valley cholla is distinct genetically, its evolutionary past remains unclear.

## Identifying Characteristics
**Habit:** tree-like or shrubby, usually with a single trunk and ascending lateral branches; lower branches and trunk becoming dark brown; 3–8 ft. (1–2.5 m) tall.
**Stems:** green to pinkish-brown, usually somewhat whorled; joints 1.6–2.5 in. (4–6 cm) wide and 1.6–7 in. (4–18 cm) long, easily detached; tubercles prominent, broadly oval, 0.4–0.8 in. (1–2 cm) long.
**Spines:** 7 to 10 per areole, straight, pale red-brown with yellow sheath, 0.6–1 in. (1.5–2.5 cm) long.
**Flowers:** tepals pale reddish-brown to yellowish-green, 0.6–1 in. (1.5–2.5 cm) long; style and stigma lobes greenish; filaments green; blooms from March to May.
**Fruits:** dry to leathery, yellow, egg-shaped, 0 to few spines, tubercles prominent, seeds sterile.

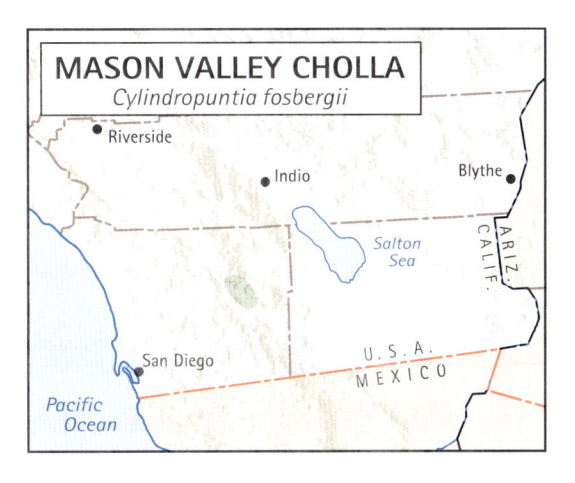

**MASON VALLEY CHOLLA**
*Cylindropuntia fosbergii*

# GANDER CHOLLA
*Cylindropuntia ganderi*
(sil-in-droh-PUN-tee-ya GAN-der-eye)

**Recent Synonyms**
*Opuntia acanthocarpa* var. *ganderi*, *O. ganderi*

*Recent research has established Gander cholla as a distinct species. [Anza-Borrego Desert S.P.]*

If a cholla can ever be considered elegant, then Gander cholla would certainly qualify. Its multiple, ascending, pale green stems are covered with whitish spines and bear bright yellow-green flowers crowded near the stem tips. The red-brown buds first open as bright green cup-shaped flowers, but with warm sunlight some flowers eventually open much wider to resemble dazzling yellowish green saucers that expose the green filaments, yellow anthers, and cream-colored style and stigma.

Gander cholla is a common cactus of California's Colorado Desert, despite its absence from many recent field guides and floras. Its place in the California flora has been poorly known and unappreciated because of its treatment as either a fifth variety of the widespread buckhorn cholla, or as a hybrid between cane cholla and silver cholla. However, recent research by cholla expert Jon Rebman shows that Gander cholla is not closely related to buckhorn cholla, is not a hybrid, and should be acknowledged as a distinct species.

Gander cholla can be difficult to distinguish from cane cholla due to these two species' somewhat similar growth habits and because they both have dry spiny fruits and greenish yellow flowers. Gander cholla, however, typically has shorter, paler green, more upward-curving stems, spinier fruits, and shorter tubercles that bear more spines. Chollas that appear intermediate—and are probably hybrids between these two species—are found in eastern San Diego County near San Felipe Valley and north of the community of Oak Grove. The

*Gander cholla resembles cane cholla with its upright stems and greenish yellow flowers. [Anza-Borrego Desert S.P.]*

*Gander chollas with backlit spines surround blooming beavertail cacti. [Anza-Borrego Desert S.P.]*

branching pattern and growth habit of Gander cholla readily separate it from silver cholla, and greenish filaments distinguish Gander from Wolf cholla. Gander cholla is suspected of hybridizing with Wolf cholla at the southern part of its range.

Gander cholla occupies a unique range from 300 feet elevation on the floor of the Colorado Desert westward into chaparral vegetation at 3000 feet in the Santa Rosa Mountains. It is locally abundant in the valleys and foothills in the southern part of Anza-Borrego Desert State Park, where it is commonly found with desert agave, Englemann hedgehog, desert barrel cactus, ocotillo, and other plants of Sonoran creosote bush scrub. It also grows in northern Baja California.

## Identifying Characteristics

**Habit:** shrub, diffusely branched, ascending; 1.5–5 ft. (0.5–1.5 m) tall.
**Stems:** pale green, joints 1–1.6 in. (2.5–4 cm) wide and 4–10 in. (10–26 cm) long; tubercles prominent, elliptic, 0.5–1 in. (1.3–2.6 cm) long.
**Spines:** 11 to 28 per areole, white to pale yellow, mostly straight, 0.8–1.4 in. (2–3.5 cm) long.
**Flowers:** tepals greenish yellow; outer tepals tipped reddish brown, 0.8–1.2 in. (2–3 cm) long; style and stigma lobes white to yellow; filaments green; blooms March to May.
**Fruits:** yellow-tan, dry, bur-like, densely spiny, 0.6–1.4 in. (1.5–3.5 cm) long.

**GANDER CHOLLA**
*Cylindropuntia ganderi*

# BLUE DIAMOND CHOLLA
## *Cylindropuntia multigeniculata*
(sil-in-droh-PUN-tee-ya mul-tee-jeh-nik-yoo-LAH-ta)

**Recent Synonyms**
*Opuntia whipplei* var. *multigeniculata*,
*Cylindropuntia Xmultigeniculata*

*Blue Diamond cholla is distinguished by its short, highly spiny, whorled stems. [Desert N.W.R.]*

*The leathery yellow fruits of Blue Diamond cholla have few glochids. [Desert N.W.R.]*

Blue Diamond cholla was first collected and described in 1943 by prolific plant collector and botanist, Ira Clokey (1878–1950). For the next 60 years it was thought to be endemic to the Blue Diamond Hill, just west of Las Vegas. In 2002 and 2003 more populations were discovered to the south, northwest, and north of Las Vegas and east near Kingman, Arizona. Although this cholla was described originally as *Opuntia multigeniculata*, it has been treated by many botanists as either a variety of Whipple cholla or as a hybrid between Whipple and silver cholla. In 2005, cactus expert Marc Baker determined that Blue Diamond cholla was distinct enough to be treated as a species, including a spiny-fruited form found in the northeastern part of its known range.

The Latin species name for Blue Diamond cholla, *multigeniculata,* translates to "with many sharp bends" and is an apt description for this cactus. Although it is similar to both silver and Whipple cholla, Blue Diamond cholla can most readily be distinguished by its abundance of very small, highly spiny, persistent branches that line its main stems from base to tip. The uppermost branches of Blue Diamond cholla are distinctively whorled and produce greenish yellow flowers on the previous season's growth.

Both silver and Whipple cholla can also be small and densely branched, and they yield greenish yellow flowers, but there are good field characters that distinguish these three chollas. The yellow fruits of Blue Diamond cholla have few glochids, and even within those populations that have more spiny fruits, their fruits are not nearly as spiny as the bur-like fruits of silver cholla. The stem-joints of Blue Diamond cholla are only 1 to 2 inches long, and they are narrower than the longer stem-joints of both silver and Whipple cholla. Silver cholla is usually more openly branched and has a lower trunk devoid of lateral branches. Whipple cholla also has fewer spines (three to eight per areole) and its spines are thicker and shorter than those of Blue Diamond cholla.

*Blue Diamond cholla is a feature of the Mojave creosote bush scrub vegetation at Gass Peak. [Desert N.W.R.]*

Blue Diamond cholla is found in relatively dense, healthy populations that are widely scattered in the northeastern Mojave Desert. In Nevada, Blue Diamond cholla is known from the Blue Diamond Hill, the McCullough Range, the vicinity of La Madre Mountain north of the Red Rock Canyon area, and Gass Peak in the Las Vegas Range; the spiny-fruited form is located in the vicinity of Bonelli Peak and in the Gold Butte area of eastern Clark County. Blue Diamond cholla grows most commonly in open Joshua tree woodland and is associated with blackbrush, creosote, burrobush, and many other desert plants. It can be found in washes or on open, steep, rocky slopes at elevations from 2800 to 5800 feet and prefers soils derived from sedimentary, basaltic, or granitic substrates.

**Flowers:** tepals pale green-yellow; 0.6–0.8 in. (1.5–2 cm) long; style and stigma lobes cream to pale yellow; filaments whitish to yellow-green; blooms April to early June.
**Fruits:** leathery, yellow, round; tubercles prominent, spineless with few or no glochids; 0.8 in. (2 cm) long.

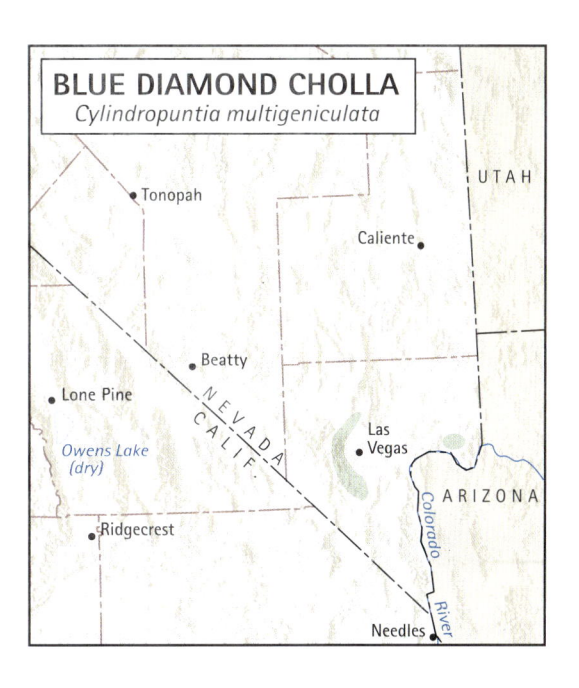

## Identifying Characteristics

**Habit:** low shrub, compact; up to 5 ft. across (1.5 m) and 20 in. tall (0.5 m), with 1 to several trunks and lateral, dense branches.
**Stems:** green to grayish green, whorled; joints 0.6–0.8 in. (1.5–2 cm) in diameter and 0.8–2.8 in. (2–7 cm) long; tubercles prominent, crowded, oval; 0.2 in. (0.4–0.6 cm) long and half as wide.
**Spines:** 12 to 14 per areole, white, spreading, interlaced, nearly concealing stem; 0.3–0.8 in. (0.8–2 cm) long.

# MUNZ CHOLLA
## *Cylindropuntia munzii*
(sil-in-droh-PUN-tee-ya MUNZ-ee-eye)
**Recent Synonyms**
*Opuntia munzii, O. Xmunzii*
**Other Common Names**
golden cholla

*The uppermost branches of Munz cholla have a drooping habit and detach easily. [Imperial Co.]*

*In California, Munz cholla is found in the Colorado Desert and has a very limited distribution. [Imperial Co.]*

Munz cholla is a giant among California chollas. It commonly reaches a height of 6 feet and occasionally grows to 10 feet tall. Despite its tree-like stature, this is not a cholla under which to spread a picnic blanket. The branch tips hang down menacingly and are easily detached. Munz cholla's large surface area, coupled with its relatively shallow root system (typical of cacti), may explain why it has a propensity to blow over in high winds. Not everything about this cholla is big: its reddish brown flowers are rather small and inconspicuous.

Desert naturalist Edmund Jaeger (1887–1983) first brought this distinctive cholla to the attention of southern California botanists in 1922. Carl B. Wolf described and named this species in 1938 for California botanist Philip Munz (1892–1974), Wolf's successor at Rancho Santa Ana Botanic Garden and its director from 1946 to 1960.

Munz cholla has been treated in the past as a natural hybrid between either buckhorn cholla and teddy-bear cholla, or silver cholla and teddy-bear cholla (see "Cholla Hybrids" on page 55). However, Munz cholla differs from buckhorn cholla in having shorter stem-joints with shorter tubercles, a tree-like growth habit, and very different flower characteristics. Munz cholla is distinguished from silver cholla by its larger tubercles, longer stem-joints with fewer spines, and a fruit with deciduous spines. In fact, the fruits of Munz cholla are somewhat unusual because they sport a formidable cover of long glochids, but no fixed spines. In contrast, two of the purported parents of a hybrid Munz cholla—silver and buckhorn—both have extremely spiny fruits. Munz cholla contrasts with its third purported parent, teddy-bear cholla, in

*Munz cholla, seen here with the Chuckwalla Mountains behind it, exhibits a tree-like stature. [Imperial Co.]*

having longer tubercles with fewer spines and a much more spreading and larger growth form. These two species also have numerous dissimilar flower characteristics.

Although locally common in northeastern Baja California, Munz cholla's distribution north of the border is quite limited. It primarily occurs on the southern flanks of the Chuckwalla Mountains in Riverside County and is also known from a few populations within the Chocolate Mountain Aerial Gunnery Range of Imperial County. Munz cholla grows in sandy to gravelly soils in Sonoran creosote bush scrub at elevations of 1300 to 2300 feet. It often occurs on lower bajadas and flats, with ocotillos and ironwood, as well as teddy-bear cholla and Engelmann hedgehog cactus.

## Identifying Characteristics

**Habit:** tree-like, branches spreading with uppermost ones drooping; 5–10 ft. (1.5–3 m) tall.
**Stems:** grayish green, joints 0.8–1.4 in. (2–3.5 cm) wide and 1.6–6.3 in. (4–16 cm) long, but older main stems larger; tubercles prominent, narrowly oval, 0.5–0.8 in. (1.2–2 cm) long and approximately 0.25 in. (4–7 mm) wide.
**Spines:** 7 to 15 per areole, straight, yellowish, of equal length, 0.5–1.2 in. (1.2–3 cm) long.
**Flowers:** tepals reddish brown, sometimes suffused with green or maroon; inner tepals longer, 0.5–0.8 in. (1.4–2 cm) long; style and stigma lobes whitish; filaments green; blooms April to May.
**Fruits:** yellow, but slowly drying to tan, roundish, spineless but with long glochids, 0.7–0.9 in. (1.7–2.4 cm) long.

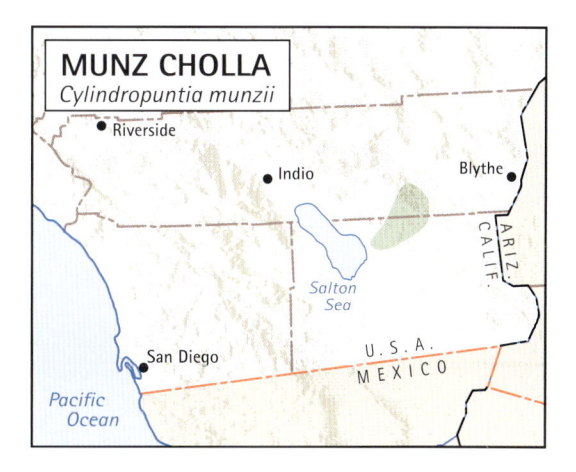

**MUNZ CHOLLA**
*Cylindropuntia munzii*

# COASTAL CHOLLA
## *Cylindropuntia prolifera*
(sil-in-droh-PUN-tee-ya pro-LIF-er-a)

**Recent Synonyms**
*Opuntia prolifera*

**Other Common Names**
jumping cholla

*A few of the stamens of this coastal cholla flower are aberrant and possess a "mini-style." [Cabrillo N.M.]*

Coastal cholla shares this asexual reproductive attribute with a close relative, teddy-bear cholla. Both species rarely produce viable seeds, and both also have three sets of chromosomes. This inability to produce adequate seeds through normal fertilization can be traced to the origin of coastal cholla. Genetic research with DNA markers has shown that *Cylindropuntia prolifera* almost certainly originated as a hybrid between *Cylindropuntia alcahes* and *Cylindropuntia cholla*, both from Baja California. It is noteworthy that the genetically variable coastal cholla ranges farther north and into a different vegetation and climate zone than either of its parents.

The beautiful flowers of coastal cholla feature pink to purple tepals surrounding greenish yellow filaments. But there is a curious aspect to some of the flowers: they have style-like appendages connected to the anthers. A short pink "mini-style" grows from between the two anther sacks of the stamen and has a whitish "mini-stigma" attached to its end. These mutations usually occur on the outermost anthers and are thought to be the result

*The fruits of coastal cholla, like these pictured here, rarely produce viable seeds. [Cabrillo N.M.]*

Coastal cholla derives its scientific name, *prolifera*, from its proliferating fruits. These fruits, however, very rarely contain viable seeds, and this species reproduces almost entirely from the rooting and growth of its easily detached fruits and stem segments. As a consequence of this vegetative reproduction, coastal cholla tends to form very dense thickets. Despite its clonal nature, coastal cholla is quite variable in its growth form depending on its specific habitat and local environmental conditions.

*This blooming coastal cholla grows in coastal sage scrub vegetation near Chula Vista. [San Diego Co.]*

to its maritime proclivity, coastal cholla is common on all northern and southern Channel Islands and is the only cholla found on both the islands and immediate coast.

### Identifying Characteristics

**Habit:** shrubby or tree-like, erect, densely branched above, often whorled; 3–8 ft. (1–2.5 m) tall.

**Stems:** dark green to grayish green, easily detached; joints 1.4–2 in. (3.5–5 cm) wide and 1.5–6 in. (4–15 cm) long; tubercles prominent, broadly oval, 0.5–1 in. (1.2–2.4 cm) long.

**Spines:** 6 to 12 per areole, straight, spreading, pale red-brown to dark brown, 0.4–0.8 in. (1–2 cm) long.

**Flowers:** tepals pink to reddish purple, 0.8 in. (2 cm) long; stigma lobes yellow-white; filaments yellow-green, occasionally few with pink style-like appendages; blooms April to July, occasionally September to October.

**Fruits:** fleshy, spineless, round, green, usually forming chains, 0.8–1.4 in. (2.1–3.5 cm) long.

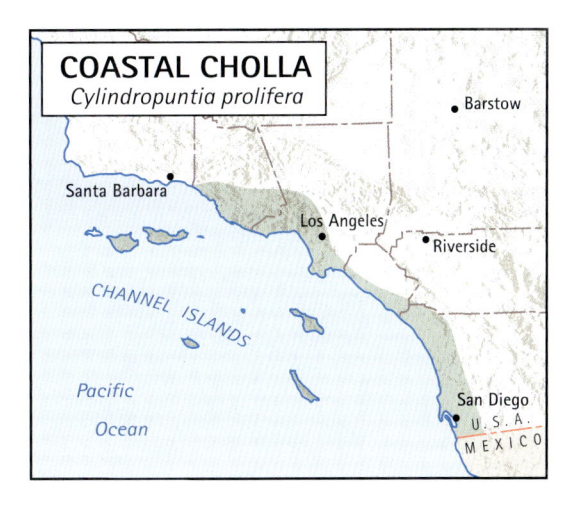

of a hormone imbalance during the flower bud's development, which in turn is probably related to its hybrid origin and triple set of chromosomes. Similar mutations are known from a handful of other plant families but have not been documented in other cacti.

Like Shaw agave and golden cereus, coastal cholla occurs in both Sonoran Desert scrub in Baja California and coastal sage scrub of southern California. Coastal cholla is found on hills and bluffs within a few miles of the coast, ranging as far north as the Ventura River drainage and extending south into central Baja California's west coast. True

# DIAMOND CHOLLA
*Cylindropuntia ramosissima*
(sil-in-droh-PUN-tee-ya ram-oh-SIS-si-ma)

**Recent Synonyms**
*Opuntia ramosissima*

**Other Common Names**
pencil cholla, pencil cactus, holy cross cholla

*Diamond cholla features multi-branched stems and long spines. [Joshua Tree N.P.]*

*Blossoms add a bright accent to the stems of this diamond cholla in the Ivanpah Valley. [San Bernardino Co.]*

Diamond cholla's multi-branched slender stem-joints and impressively long spines make it stand out among our region's cholla species. The main spines stick out perpendicular to the stem-joints, and they may be restricted to the plant's uppermost growth or are absent altogether. The spine length can exceed the stem diameter by three or four times. New spines are covered with a beautiful, yellow-tipped, papery sheath. Diamond cholla produces flowers in a broad range of colors, often in some shade of orange. Few people observe them, however, because they tend to flower during mid-summer, when desert temperatures are formidable. Also, they do not bloom dependably every year, unlike more succulent cacti that do bloom regularly.

Diamond cholla displays several specialized traits that exemplify its advanced evolutionary state compared to other chollas. It has highly branched stems, diamond-shaped tubercles that seem etched onto the stems, and dry, bur-like fruit. According to cholla expert Jon Rebman, the more primitive chollas occur nearer the center of cholla species diversity—in the southern parts of the *Cylindropuntia* range in Mexico and the Caribbean. These more primitive chollas generally have simple branching, fleshy fruits, and mostly bumpy tubercles. More advanced species, such as diamond cholla, have more complex branching patterns and dry fruits, and they tend to occur farther north from the theorized subtropical origin of chollas.

The distribution and elevational range of diamond cholla indicate that it can tolerate some of the driest, hottest, and coldest desert habitats of any cholla species. Its frost tolerance of 25°F (−4°C) enables diamond cholla to extend its range into the northern Mojave Desert where it thrives at elevations up to 4000 feet. Diamond cholla grows in the Greenwater Valley of Death Valley National Park and is the only cholla, besides silver cholla, found in the park. In southern Nevada, diamond cholla occurs as far north as southern Esmeralda County west of Lida and east to the Mormon Mountains. Diamond cholla is found to the south throughout much of the Sonoran Desert of northern Mexico and western Arizona and in southeastern California

*A blooming bladderpod grows among the stems of this diamond cholla in the Pinto Valley. [Joshua Tree N.P.]*

## DIAMOND CHOLLA
*Cylindropuntia ramosissima*

from the Colorado River Basin to the eastern slopes of the Peninsular Ranges. Diamond cholla prefers relatively fine sandy and gravelly soils of washes and flats and grows in an array of vegetation types from Sonoran creosote bush scrub to Joshua tree woodland.

### Identifying Characteristics

**Habit:** shrub, highly branched, 1.6–6.6 ft. (0.5–2 m) tall.
**Stems:** green or grayish green; joints less than 0.5 in. (0.5–1 cm) wide and 0.8–4 in. (2–10 cm) long; tubercles flat, diamond-shaped, less than 0.3 in. (4–8 mm) long.
**Spines:** 0 to 5 per areole (usually 1 or 0), straight, brownish; main spine 1–2.4 in. (2.5–6 cm) long; basal spines, if present, less than 0.4 in. (1 cm) long.
**Flowers:** tepals greenish yellow, orange or red-brown, 0.25–0.5 in. (0.6–1.3 cm) long; style and stigma lobes whitish; filaments pale green; blooms April to August.
**Fruits:** tan, dry, spiny and bur-like, oval, 0.6–1.2 in. (1.5–3 cm).

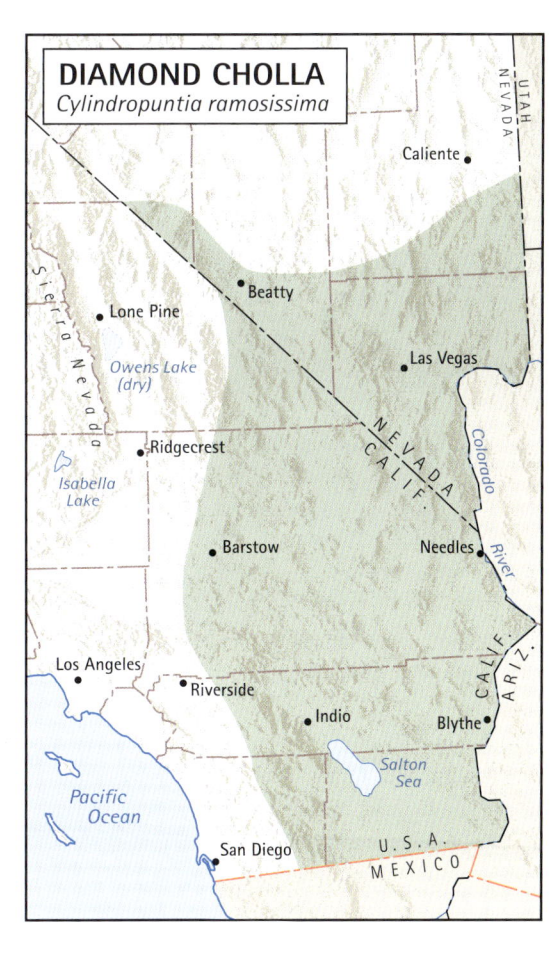

# WHIPPLE CHOLLA
## *Cylindropuntia whipplei*
(sil-in-droh-PUN-tee-ya WHIP-pull-eye)

**Recent Synonyms**
*Opuntia whipplei, Opuntia whipplei* var. *enodis*

**Other Common Names**
Clokey cholla, plateau cholla

*The fleshy greenish yellow fruits of Whipple cholla have prominent tubercles. [Desert N.W.R.]*

*Flowers top the ascending stems of this Whipple cholla in Yucca Valley. [Desert N.W.R.]*

In its most common growth form, Whipple cholla displays erect stems encircled by ranks of short, whorled, upward-angled branches of equal lengths. In this form, it can take on a primeval appearance that resembles the branching of a giant horsetail plant. Whipple cholla can also develop a mat-like form; this happens when its main stems are prostrate, rather than erect, and send out upright branches. Regardless of form, this cholla produces plump, spineless fruits, which resemble a yellow raspberry attached to the stem with its wide end uppermost.

Whipple cholla is named for Lieutenant Amiel W. Whipple (1817–1863), the engineer and surveyor who led the Pacific Railroad Survey from Fort Smith, Arkansas to Los Angeles in 1853–1854. The expedition's surgeon and botanist, John M. Bigelow (1804–1878), collected this cholla during their journey, and with George Engelmann, named and described Whipple cholla in 1857. Lieutenant Whipple is also commemorated in the scientific name for chaparral yucca.

Whipple cholla's spines and fruits help set it apart from its two most similar cholla neighbors in Nevada, which are Blue Diamond and silver cholla. The spines of Whipple cholla are not especially numerous, though they are noticeably distinct. The stout central spines number four (or occasionally five or six) and spread-out like a cross within the smaller, deflexed radial spines. Blue Diamond and silver cholla both possess more spines per areole, and their spine lengths are variable rather than of two distinct lengths as in Whipple cholla. In addition, the longer whorled branches of Whipple cholla are ascending, in contrast to the short, perpendicularly whorled branches of Blue Diamond cholla. Silver cholla, whose range overlaps with Whipple cholla in the lower elevations of the Sheep Range, can resemble Whipple cholla with its erect stems and somewhat whorled branches, but its bur-like fruits are much spinier than those of Whipple cholla.

Whipple cholla is considered by some botanists to be one of the parents—with co-parent silver cholla—of Blue Diamond cholla. Cactus expert Marc Baker, who has studied Blue Diamond cholla, believes Whipple cholla may be closely related to Blue Diamond cholla and may hybridize with it, but is not the parent of Blue Diamond cholla.

The southwestern edge of Whipple cholla's distribution is in the Sheep and Las Vegas ranges of Nevada's Desert National Wildlife Refuge. From here, Whipple cholla extends northeast to near Pioche in Lincoln County; it continues east into southern Utah and across the northern third of Arizona to the Four Corners region. This species grows in Joshua tree woodland up into pinyon-juniper woodland on mountain slopes, washes, and ridges from 5000 to 7400 feet and inhabits slightly higher elevations than most of our other chollas.

## Identifying Characteristics

**Habit:** Mat-forming to erect and shrubby; 1–4.3 ft. (0.3–1.3 m) tall, with few to many branches.
**Stems:** green, branches in whorls, slender; joints 0.2–0.9 in. (0.5–2.2 cm) wide and 1.2–6 in. (3–15 cm) long; tubercles very prominent, short, 0.3 in. (0.5–1 cm) long.
**Spines:** 3 to 8 per areole; white to pale red-brown, interlaced; radial spines slender, with flattened bases, 0.2 in. (0.5–0.8 cm) long; central spines usually 4, stout, spreading into a cross, 0.8–1.8 in. (2–4.5 cm) long.
**Flowers:** tepals yellow to greenish yellow; 0.6–1.2 in. (1.5–3 cm) long; style white to yellowish; stigma lobes whitish to pale green; filaments yellow to yellow-green; blooms May to June.
**Fruits:** fleshy, greenish yellow, broadly cylindrical with prominent tubercles, no permanent spines and few or no glochids; 0.7–1.4 in. (1.8–3.5 cm) long.

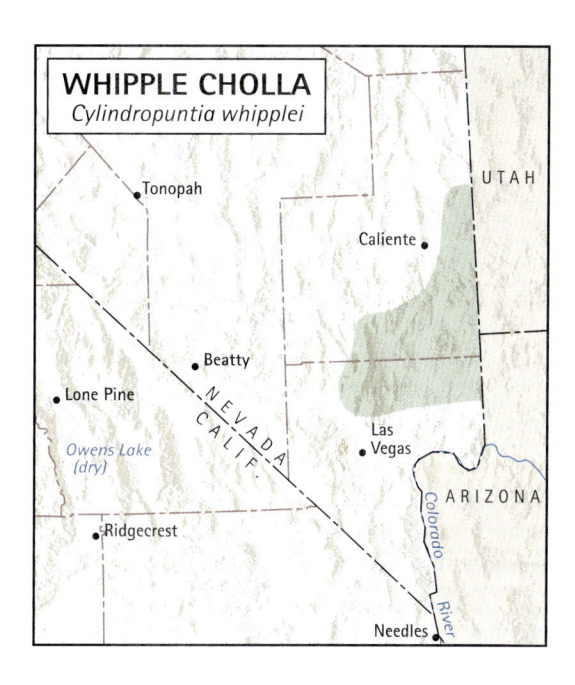

*Unlike Blue Diamond or silver cholla, Whipple cholla displays spines of two distinct lengths. [Desert N.W.R.]*

# WOLF CHOLLA
## *Cylindropuntia wolfii*
(sil-in-droh-PUN-tee-ya WOLF-ee-eye)
### Recent Synonyms
*Opuntia echinocarpa* var. *wolfii*, *O. wolfii*

*Maroon is one of the many different tepal colors found in Wolf cholla. [Anza-Borrego Desert S.P.]*

*This Wolf cholla in lower Mortero Wash displays coppery orange tepals. [Anza-Borrego Desert S.P.]*

Wolf cholla is one of the first chollas to bloom in California. It starts flowering in March, ahead of its two close relatives, silver and teddy-bear cholla. Its flowers' yellow, red, or copper-colored tepals and red filaments make this cholla unique and especially attractive. On rare occasions, one may notice Wolf cholla flowers with filaments tipped by white abortive anthers that have no yellow pollen. That is because Wolf cholla is gynodioecious, meaning that some of its flowers have male and female parts and others are functionally female since they produce no pollen. Wolf cholla is also unusual among chollas because it has six sets of chromosomes.

Although Wolf cholla appears robust and fierce enough to be named after a large canine, it was actually named in honor of Rancho Santa Ana Botanic Garden botanist, Carl B. Wolf (1905–1973). Lyman Benson originally described Wolf cholla as a variety of the widespread and highly variable silver cholla. However, Benson recognized that "The shrub is as big as var. *echinocarpa,* but so much more dense as to seem a different species." Recent research on genetic relationships, species distributions, and the variability and importance of different cholla characters has advanced our understanding of their taxonomy. Like Gander cholla, which had previously been considered a variety of buckhorn cholla, Wolf cholla is now recognized as a species distinct from silver cholla. Wolf cholla differs from silver cholla in having simpler branching, stout stems that are more erect, longer tubercles, and different-colored styles, filaments, and tepals.

Wolf cholla is found only in a relatively small area of southeastern San Diego County, western Imperial County, and in one population

*Wolf chollas grow on a rocky slope, surrounded by brittlebrush and phacelia. [Anza-Borrego Desert S.P.]*

in adjacent Baja California. It occurs between approximately 1000 and 4000 feet elevation and grows in gravelly washes and bajadas or on rocky slopes among granite boulders. Wolf cholla is locally abundant in the Jacumba Mountains at the southern edge of Anza-Borrego Desert State Park, in locations such as Mortero Canyon and in the Mountain Springs area along Interstate 8.

## Identifying Characteristics

**Habit:** shrub, erect, densely branched from the base; 1.5–5 ft. (0.5–1.5 m) tall.
**Stems:** pale green, stout; joints 1–1.6 in. (2.5–4 cm) wide and 2.4–15.7 in. (6–40 cm) long; tubercles prominent, 0.4–1 in. (1–2.5 cm) long and approximately half as wide.
**Spines:** 12 to 30 per areole, straight, 0.4–1.2 in. (1–3 cm) long.
**Flowers:** inner tepals yellow-green, suffused with red or purple-brown, 0.8–1.4 in. (2–3.5 cm) long; style red-pink; stigma lobes pink-white; filaments dark red to bronze; blooms March to May.
**Fruits:** gray-tan, dry, densely tuberculate, spiny, 1–1.2 in. (2.5–3 cm) long.

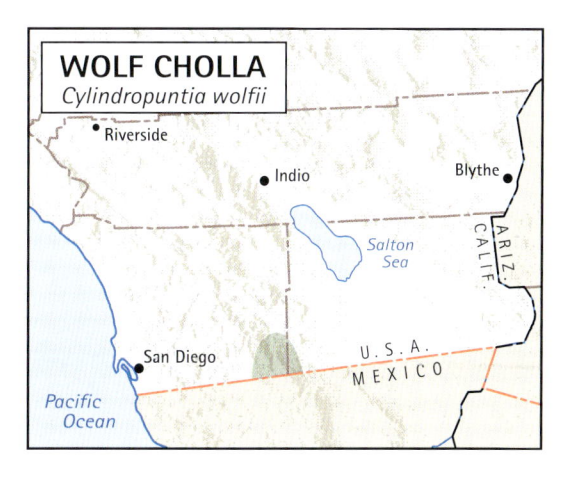

**WOLF CHOLLA**
*Cylindropuntia wolfii*

Cottontop cactus • *Echinocactus polycephalus* var. *polycephalus*   ARTWORK BY SUSAN BAZELL

# *Echinocactus*
## BARREL or COTTONTOP CACTUS

*Echinocactus* means "spiny cactus," but it is not a terribly useful or imaginative name. This is probably due to its description at an early time in the scientific understanding of the scope and diversity of the cactus family. What really distinguishes an *Echinocactus* barrel from any other barrel-shaped cactus is the presence of pale woolly hairs at the crown of the stem and mature fruits that are dry rather than fleshy. In our region, cottontop cactus, *Echinocactus polycephalus,* is also typically branched; this helps set it apart from *Ferocactus* species, which almost always grow as single barrels.

Since it was first described as a genus and published in 1827, *Echinocactus* has had more than 1000 species names assigned to it. In fact, the genus had been a catchall for all globular, ribbed cacti, except for those in the two previously named genera, *Cereus* and *Melocactus.* Today, most botanists now recognize only six species, which are found from central Mexico to Texas, New Mexico, and Arizona. Three species of *Echinocactus* occur in the southwestern U.S., but only one—with two varieties—is native to California and Nevada.

# COTTONTOP CACTUS
*Echinocactus polycephalus* var. *polycephalus*
(eh-kin-oh-KAK-tus pol-ee-SEF-uh-lus)
### Other Common Names
clustered barrel cactus, many-headed barrel cactus, devil's pincushion

# GRAND CANYON COTTONTOP
*Echinocactus polycephalus* var. *xeranthemoides*
(zair-an-them-OY-deez)
### Recent Synonyms
*Echinocactus polycephalus* ssp. *xeranthemoides*
### Other Common Names
cottontop, clustered barrel cactus

*Apical spines arch over cottontop cactus flowers found in Mazourka Canyon in the Inyo Mountains. [Inyo Co.]*

*White woolly hairs obscure the fruits of a cottontop cactus growing in Dedeckera Canyon. [Death Valley N.P.]*

The heavily armed cottontop cactus presents a contrast of textures: its spines are long and rigid, while its fruits, which persist for months atop the cluster of stems, are covered with soft woolly hairs. During midsummer to late summer, when few desert annuals or cacti are still in bloom, cottontop cactus produces fragrant, bright yellow flowers that are held within the spiny armament like caged birds. They don't open widely, but the flowers easily attract cactus bees and other pollinators at a time when sources of pollen are scarce.

Cottontop cactus spines are covered with a fine, transparent, woolly layer that botanists describe as "canescent." During the Mojave Desert's relatively cool, wet winter months the new spines take on a vivid red appearance. The reddish hue becomes dulled as the canescent covering dries or as the red color fades with age.

Cottontop cactus is very slow growing and is rarely found in cultivation because it is difficult to establish. Contrary to some observers' claims that the species has no utilitarian value, cottontop cactus spines were used by Native Americans as fishhooks, needles, and awls for basket weaving. The tiny black seeds, which disperse through a basal pore when ripe, were gathered and ground into a meal.

Packrat midden deposits contain evidence that cottontop cactus has survived in most of its current range for the past 30,000 years, and this long presence suggests it is a resilient species. It can grow in very dry habitats, such as the Ibex Hills that lie in the rain shadow of the Black Mountains in Death Valley National Park. Cottontop cactus prefers rocky slopes composed of either limestone or granitic substrates. It is found in Mojavean creosote bush scrub or open Joshua tree woodland and often grows with blackbrush.

There are two varieties of cottontop recognized by most botanists, and they are distinguished

*Long yellow scales extend beyond the tips of Grand Canyon cottontop's fruits. [Clark Co.]*

chiefly by seed and fruit scale characteristics. The two varieties appear to hybridize where their ranges overlap, which is at the western end of the Grand Canyon in the vicinity of Lake Mead.

**Cottontop cactus** is the more widespread and common variety, occurring from northwestern Sonora, Mexico and western Arizona into California's Colorado Desert. Its range also extends north through most of the Mojave Desert of California and Nevada at elevations up to 4800 feet.

**Grand Canyon cottontop** is found mostly in the Grand Canyon area of northern Arizona at elevations from 1500 to 5500 feet. Within Nevada, it is known from the Gold Butte area in southeastern Clark County. Grand Canyon cottontop is generally—though not consistently—smaller than cottontop and has more numerous spines. This variety has yellow scales on the fruit that protrude beyond the tip of the fruit, whereas cottontop has much shorter scales that dry to brown or black.

## Identifying Characteristics

**Habit:** round to barrel-shaped, branched from base with 5 to 50 heads, clumps up to 4 ft. (1.2 m) across.
**Stems:** gray-green to yellow-green, 4–12 in. (10–30 cm) wide and 12–24 in. (30–60 cm) tall; ribs 11 to 25, narrow.
**Spines:** central 4 per areole; radial 6 to 14 per areole, pink with yellow tips to white or gray, straight or curved, often twisted, stout, ridged; 1.2–3 in. (3–7.5 cm) long; new spines with short, fine woolly hairs, uppermost areoles white-woolly.
**Flowers:** tepals yellow with white-woolly bases, sometimes tinged with red, 2 in. (5 cm) long; flowers 2 in. (5 cm) across; stigma lobes and filaments yellow; blooms June to August.
**Fruits:** dry, heavily covered with white, woolly hairs, 0.5–0.8 in. (1.2–2 cm) long; fruit scales brown to black, 0.2–0.55 in. (5–14 mm) long in var. *polycephalus*; fruit scales yellow, 0.66–1.2 in. (16–30 mm) long in var. *xeranthemoides*; seeds dull, angular, 0.15 in. (3.8 mm) long in var. *polycephalus*; seeds shiny, rounded, less than 0.12 in. (3 mm) long in var. *xeranthemoides*.

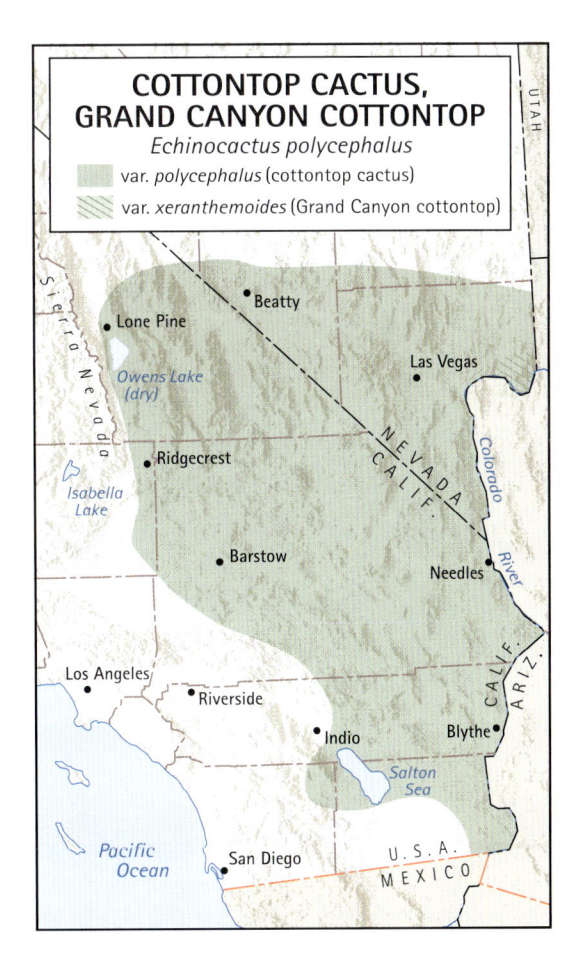

Mojave mound cactus • *Echinocereus mojavensis*   ARTWORK BY E.O. MURMAN

## *Echinocereus*
### HEDGEHOG CACTUS

*Echinocereus* is one of the showiest genera of North American cacti due to its relatively large, colorful flowers. This genus is also popular with cactus growers who admire both the flowers and the typically clustering form of *Echinocereus* species. On most species of hedgehogs, the flowers burst through the epidermis as buds, rather than emerging from areoles as in other cacti. In addition, the funnel-shaped blossoms have green stigmas and remain open all day—two additional flower characteristics that help differentiate hedgehogs from similar-looking cacti. In the absence of flowers, a small hedgehog can be distinguished from *Mammillaria* and *Coryphantha* by its prominently ribbed stems.

*Echinocereus* was first named in 1848 by George Engelmann, who considered it a spiny-fruited relative of the smooth-fruited *Cereus*. *Echinos* is the Greek word for hedgehog, and the scientific name alludes to the spine-covered fruits of this genus. Despite their spines, the ripe fruits of some species are collected and enjoyed for their strawberry-like flavor. Depending on whether numerous varieties are recognized as full species or not, there may be as few as 44 or as many as 60 species of *Echinocereus*. They are found from south-central Mexico east to Kansas and Oklahoma, north to Wyoming, and west to eastern California. About half of the *Echinocereus* species occur in the southwestern U.S., and two occur in California and Nevada.

# ENGELMANN HEDGEHOG
*Echinocereus engelmannii*
(eh-kin-oh-SEER-ee-us ENG-gel-man-ee-eye)

**Recent Synonyms**
*Echinocereus engelmannii* var. *acicularis*, *E. engelmannii* var. *armatus*, *E. engelmannii* var. *chrysocentrus*, *E. engelmannii* var. *howei*, *E. engelmannii* var. *munzii*

**Other Common Names**
calico cactus, strawberry hedgehog cactus

*Clusters of spiny stems and bright magenta flowers characterize Engelmann hedgehog. [Anza-Borrego Desert S.P.]*

Engelmann hedgehog is abundant, easy to recognize, and well known to springtime desert visitors. Its brilliant magenta flowers are among the largest and showiest of any cactus in California and Nevada. This cactus obviously caught the attention and admiration of Charles C. Parry during the United States and Mexican Boundary Survey (1848–1853). Parry collected it in the "Mountains about San Felipe," in southern California and named it in honor of his botanist colleague, George Engelmann.

Like many other common and widespread plants, this cactus is highly variable and has had its share of named varieties, most of which are still too poorly understood to delineate effectively. Lyman Benson recognized nine varieties of *Echinocereus engelmannii*, six of which were listed for California and Nevada. More recent floras recognize two species from these nine varieties (the other being *Echinocereus nicholii* of southern Arizona and Mexico). The purported varieties of Engelmann hedgehog are separated on the basis of their preferred habitat, distribution, and various central spine characteristics, including their "calico" spine colors. To add to the confusion, some populations may have plants assignable to more than one variety.

In contrast to most other hedgehogs—whose flowers emerge from stem tissue just above the areoles—Engelmann hedgehog has flowers that emerge directly from areoles, like most cacti. The flowers each open for three to four successive days, but they are self-incompatible and require pollen from a different plant to produce viable seeds. They are pollinated by leafcutter and other bees. Out-crossing of Engelmann hedgehog is promoted by its protandrous flowers, which have anthers that produce pollen before the stigma becomes receptive. The stigma lobes of Engelmann hedgehog flowers spread apart only after the pollen is gone, and they provide a sticky, bumpy platform for pollen-laden bees arriving from other plants.

Engelmann hedgehog occurs throughout the

*Another name for Engelmann hedgehog—calico cactus—refers to its mottled spines. [Anza-Borrego Desert S.P.]*

*Engelmann hedgehog's self-incompatible flowers require pollen from a different plant. [Anza-Borrego Desert S.P.]*

**Spines:** radial 6 to 14 per areole, 0.3–2 in. (0.8–5 cm) long; central 2 to 7 per areole, 0.5–2.8 in. (1.2–7 cm) long, white, gray, golden-yellow, or reddish brown, usually straight, sometimes curved or twisted; lower central spine longest, flattened, dagger-like.

**Flowers:** tepals bright rose-pink to magenta, darkest near tips; 2.4–3.5 in. (6–9 cm) long; anthers yellow-orange; stigma lobes green; blooms March to May.

**Fruits:** juicy, red or orange, spines deciduous; ripe fruits edible; 1–1.8 in. (2.5–4.5 cm) long.

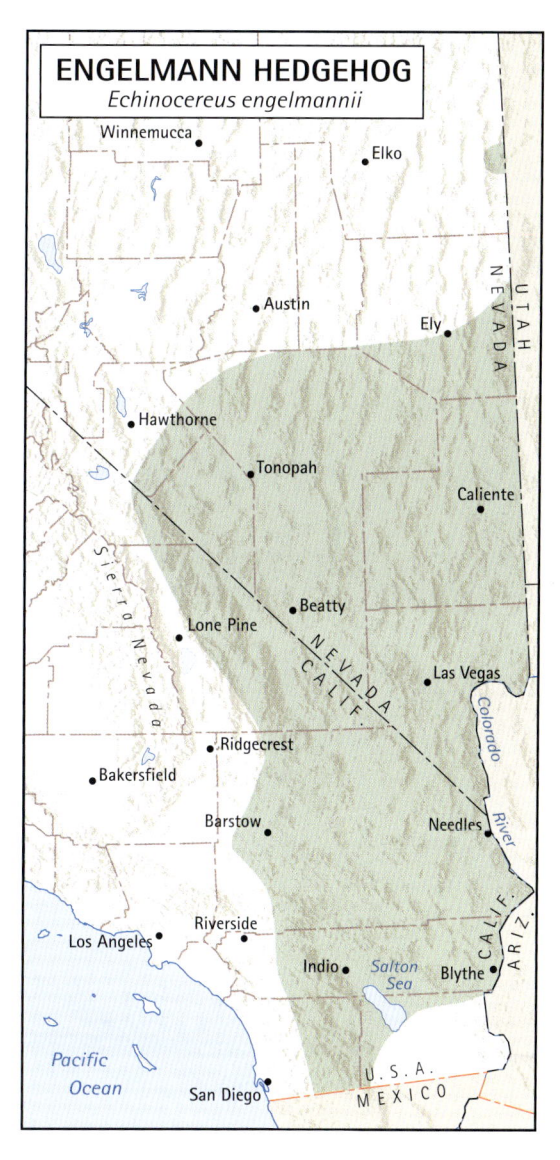

**ENGELMANN HEDGEHOG**
*Echinocereus engelmannii*

Sonoran and Mojave deserts to the southern Great Basin, and it ranges from near sea level in the lower Colorado River Basin to over 7000 feet in the San Bernardino Mountains. It can be seen from Baja California, Mexico north to Mono County, California, east through southern Nevada to southwestern Utah, and south through western Arizona. Engelmann hedgehog is found in habitats ranging from rocky outcrops to sandy washes. It grows in creosote bush scrub of both the Sonoran and Mojave deserts, in chaparral, and up into pinyon-juniper woodlands. It is probably most common on rocky slopes and is frequently found with desert barrel cactus and chollas.

## Identifying Characteristics

**Habit:** open clump, branched from base with 3 to 60 stems, up to 3.3 ft. (1 m) across and 2 ft. (60 cm) tall.

**Stems:** erect, cylindrical, green, 2–3.5 in. (5–9 cm) wide and 5.5–24 in. (14–60 cm) tall; ribs 10 to 13, crests slightly undulate.

# MOJAVE MOUND CACTUS
## *Echinocereus mojavensis*
(eh-kin-o-SEER-ee-us mo-ha-VEN-sis)

**Recent Synonyms**
*E. triglochidiatus*

**Other Common Names**
hedgehog cactus, crimson hedgehog cactus, claret-cup cactus, Mojave kingcup cactus

*Bright red flowers decorate the dense rounded form of a Mojave mound cactus at Cima Dome. [Mojave N. Pr.]*

*The stiff, fleshy flowers of Mojave mound cactus are pollinated by hummingbirds. [Joshua Tree N.P.]*

Mojave mound cactus is the only red-flowered cactus in California and Nevada. It is also the only hummingbird-pollinated cactus in our region and one of just three *Echinocereus* that are pollinated by hummingbirds. Its flower tepals are relatively stiff and fleshy, and they remain open for two to three days, attracting black-chinned and broad-tailed hummingbirds, as well as bees. The funnel-shaped flowers vary in their degree of color saturation, depending on the concentration of red betacyanin pigments dissolved in the cells; they may appear orange-red, pale red, scarlet, or crimson. Mojave mound cactus flowers remain open throughout the night, unlike the blooms of its only relative in the region, Engelmann hedgehog.

Taxonomists have described as many as eight different varieties of Mojave mound cactus, which is testimony to the great variability exhibited by this species. There is significant variation in spine characters, even within local populations that are reputed to be one variety; as a result, many botanists have treated this plant as a "species complex" that is difficult to delineate satisfactorily. A 1989 revision of this species complex by New Mexico botanist David J. Ferguson treated the Mojave mound cactus found in California and Nevada as *E. triglochidiatus* var. *mojavensis* differing from the eastern variety *triglochidiatus* by having more closely spaced areoles, 8 to 10 ribs instead of 5 to 8, and thinner, less angular spines. More recently, plant taxonomists have reverted to the 1886 name for this widespread and variable species—*Echinocereus mojavensis*.

While the species and varieties of Mojave mound cactus that some botanists recognize may be problematic to differentiate, the species as a whole is easily distinguishable from our other native cacti due to two salient features: it grows typically as a dense, spiny mound of stems, and it produces showy red flowers. Young plants consist of small clumps of 10 to 20 stems, while older specimens may consist of several hundred stems that form dense mounds nearly 3 feet high and 5 feet across.

Mojave mound cactus is often found on rocky ledges or steep canyon slopes. An adaptable species, it grows in full sun as well as in partial shade, such as beneath a canopy of pinyon pine, Utah juniper, or mountain mahogany. It occurs on igneous and sedimentary soils from approximately 3000 to nearly 10,000 feet in elevation. Most abundant in the Mojave Desert, it occupies all but the lowest and hottest desert areas of the southwestern United States. It is one of the most widespread of our cactus species, occurring from eastern California to western Colorado and New Mexico. Mojave mound cactus is known in Nevada from the Antelope Mountains of Eureka County south to the Spring Mountains in Clark County and in California from the White-Inyo Range in southern Mono County south to the eastern edge of the Peninsular Ranges in San Diego County.

*Mojave mound cactus flower buds emerge directly through the epidermis, not via areoles. [Joshua Tree N.P.]*

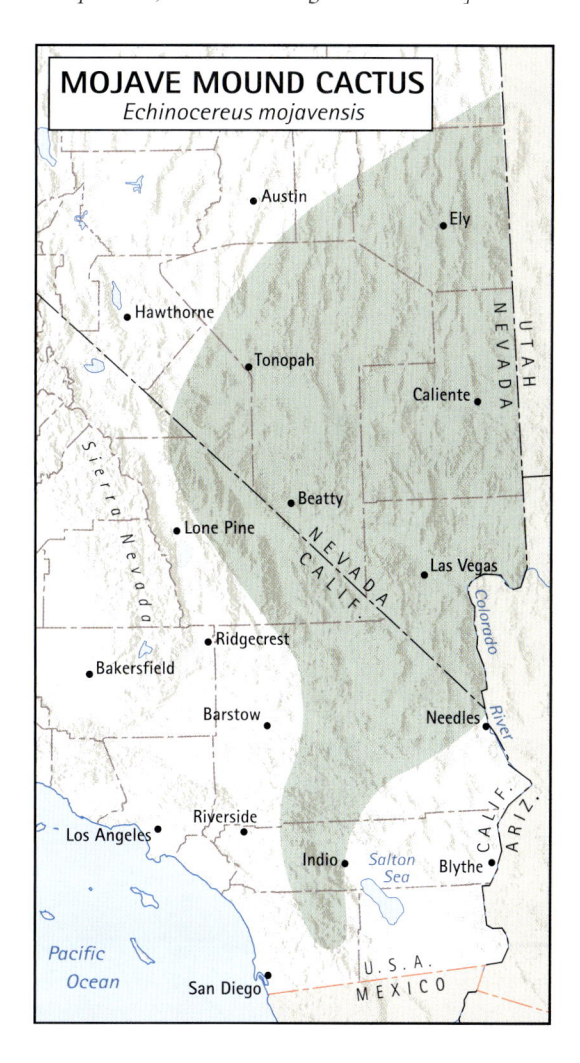

## Identifying Characteristics

**Habit:** small to large compact clumps with 1 to 300 stems, up to 3 ft. high (90 cm) and 5 ft. (150 cm) in diameter.

**Stems:** pale green to bluish green, spherical to cylindrical, 2–6 in. (5–15 cm) wide and 6–12 in. (15–30 cm) tall; ribs 5 to 12, usually undulate.

**Spines:** 1 to 4 central and 5 to 9 radial per areole, but central and radial spines difficult to distinguish; variable, straight to curved, white, gray, black, tan or pinkish, up to 2.5 in. (6.5 cm) long; areoles round, white-woolly.

**Flowers:** tepals red but paler at the base, tips rounded, relatively thick and rigid, 1.5–2 in. (4–5 cm) long; flowers 1.5–2 in. (4–5 cm) across; stigma green; anthers pink to lavender; blooms April to early June.

**Fruits:** oblong to broadly ovoid, green to yellowish, dull red when ripe, spines deciduous; fruits relatively juicy, sometimes with a strawberry fragrance; 1–1.5 in. (2.5–4 cm) long.

**MOJAVE MOUND CACTUS**
*Echinocereus mojavensis*

Desert barrel cactus • *Ferocactus cylindraceus*     ARTWORK BY E.O. MURMAN

# *Ferocactus*
## BARREL CACTUS

Barrel cactus is an iconic plant in many arid regions of the West and probably requires little introduction to desert residents. The genus *Ferocactus* was first described and named in 1922 by American cactologists Nathaniel Britton and Joseph Rose as a segregate from the closely related *Echinocactus*. The name was derived from *ferox,* the Latin word for wild or fierce. This is an appropriate description for these robust, strong-spined cacti, which have a legendary tolerance for drought and high temperatures.

*Ferocactus* is readily distinguished from *Echinocactus*—the other barrel-shaped cactus found in California and Nevada—by the presence of nectar glands on the upper part of the areoles and by the absence of woolly hairs at the stem tips among the flowers or on the fruits. Other characteristics that set *Ferocactus* apart include a ring of hairs that surrounds the stamens and a fleshy fruit that opens at a hole at its base (a basal pore) for seed dispersal. There are 29 species of *Ferocactus,* and they range from southern Mexico throughout Baja California to the southern Mojave Desert and east to Texas. Only two of these species occur in California and Nevada.

# DESERT BARREL CACTUS
## *Ferocactus cylindraceus*
(fair-oh-KAK-tus sil-in-DRAY-see-us)

**Recent Synonyms**
*Ferocactus acanthodes*

**Other Common Names**
California barrel cactus, cliff barrel cactus, spiny barrel cactus, biznaga

*Flowers top the stems of this unusual branched desert barrel cactus. [Anza-Borrego Desert S.P.]*

*The long-lasting flowers of desert barrel cactus attract ground-nesting cactus bees. [Anza-Borrego Desert S.P.]*

Desert barrel cactus is often seen perched on a rocky ledge above a desert wash, where its stout cylindrical profile is easily recognized. This species' common name alludes to its remarkable capacity for water storage. The low surface-to-volume ratio of a barrel cactus—especially a big one—enables this plant to store a large volume of water while exposing a relatively small surface area to evaporative water loss.

Contrary to desert lore, its "water" is of no use to thirsty desert travelers. Edgar M. Baxter, author of *California Cactus* (1935), notably described it as "a mucilaginous, mouth-puckering, greenish yellow liquid that would certainly not be chosen for a drink except under the most extreme conditions." Even in extreme conditions the desperate cactus wrangler would lose more water and energy in the attempt than he would gain in the reward. Native Americans avoided the headache- and diarrhea-inducing barrel-cactus slime, but favored its tasty buds and flowers as well as the fruits, which were parboiled to remove their bitterness. Desert bighorn sheep, wild burros, jackrabbits, and packrats are known to eat the moist tissue of desert barrel cacti.

An individual desert barrel cactus may bloom for 12 to 15 weeks, and during that time it attracts large, solitary, ground-nesting cactus bees as pollinators. Desert barrel cactus blooms most abundantly in May and June, but it may also flower later in the summer, at least in eastern California and Nevada where summer rains are more common than in the western desert. The fruits, which mature six weeks after pollination, resemble tiny pineapples with their rounded scaly sides and dried tepals that remain attached on top.

Desert barrel cactus produces nectar that contains 20 different amino acids, as well as fructose, sucrose, and glucose. This rich nectar comes not from the cactus flowers but from extrafloral nectary glands, also called thorn nectaries, which are located on the areoles. They secrete the greatest amount of nectar during the flowering and fruiting months of May and June, attracting ants in a mutualistic relationship. The ants obtain nectar and moisture from barrel cactus; in turn,

*This columnar barrel cactus is more than 5 feet tall. [San Diego Co.]* PHOTO © JOHN EVARTS

well-fed fighting ants give the cactus protection from herbivorous insects. The nutrients associated with nearby ant nests provide the cactus with a perpetual source of fertilizer.

Some botanists recognize two varieties of barrel cactus in our region, but they are often indistinguishable. Variety *lecontei* occurs at elevations above 2500 feet and has untwisted central spines approximately 2.5 inches long. Variety *cylindraceus* is found below 2500 feet and has central spines that measure from 3 to 6.6 inches long.

Desert barrel cactus is a common inhabitant of both the Sonoran and Mojave deserts. Cold limits its northern distribution, but the relatively pubescent and spiny tip of desert barrel cactus protects this species from temperature extremes and allows it to range farther north and grow higher than any other barrel cactus. The adaptability of desert barrel cactus is also enhanced by its amazing heat tolerance; in a controlled experiment, it was able to tolerate a temperature of 154°F (68°C)—the highest temperature of any California cactus.

Desert barrel cactus occurs at elevations from sea level to 5200 feet. It ranges from northern Mexico to transmontane California—reaching north to the Panamint Range and extending east into southern Nevada, southwestern Utah, and western Arizona. Desert barrel cactus can usually be found in rocky areas within Sonoran and Mojavean creosote bush scrub, where it grows on thin, well-drained soils and on igneous and limestone substrates. It is most common on south- and southwest-facing slopes and often grows with a southern tilt.

## Identifying Characteristics

**Habit:** erect, spheric to cylindric, solitary, unbranched.
**Stems:** pale green, usually 10–16 in. (25–40 cm) in diameter and 1.5–6 ft. (45–180 cm) tall, with 21 to 31 ribs.
**Spines:** 12 to 32 per areole; smallest radial spines bristle-like; central spines 4 per areole, flattened with transverse ridges, central and larger radial spines rigid, curved, red, yellow, or white, longest ones 2–6 in. (5–15 cm) long.
**Flowers:** tepals yellow, outer tepals often with red midline; flowers 1.6–2.5 in. (4–6 cm) across; tepals 1.2–2.5 in. (3–6 cm) long; filaments, anthers, and stigma lobes yellow; blooms May to September.
**Fruits:** nearly round, fleshy and yellow drying to leathery and tan, scaly, 1.2–2 in. (3–5 cm) long.

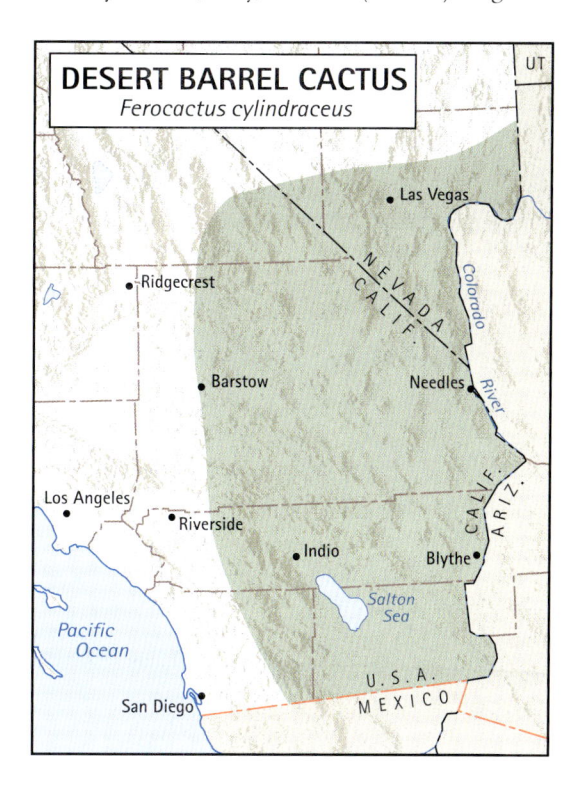

**DESERT BARREL CACTUS**
*Ferocactus cylindraceus*

# COAST BARREL CACTUS
*Ferocactus viridescens*
(fair-oh-KAK-tus veer-ih-DES-sens)
**Other Common Names**
San Diego barrel cactus

*The ribs of coast barrel cactus exhibit a slight helical swirl. [Border Field S.P.]*

*The protandrous flowers of coast barrel cactus encourage cross-pollination. [Torrey Pines S.R.]*

Coast barrel cactus grows in close proximity to several million southern California residents, yet it is not nearly as well known as its larger and more abundant cousin, desert barrel cactus. Less than 1.5 feet tall and often obscured by taller shrubs, coast barrel cactus frequently goes unnoticed in its native habitats. It becomes easier to spot after its red and yellow buds open to reveal bright yellow flowers that resemble upside-down, fringed bells.

Coast barrel cactus, like all other barrel cacti, has protandrous flowers that remain open for several days. Since the anthers release their copious pollen before the stigma of the same flower is receptive, they cannot be self-pollinated like chollas and prickly-pears. A local population of coast barrel cactus—if it is large enough—provides numerous flowers at different stages that are likely to be both pollen producers and pollen receivers. In this way, gene exchange as a result of out-crossing is promoted, and genetic variation for coast barrel cactus is increased.

The ribs of coast barrel cactus are often slightly helically swirled, and the number of ribs at mid-stem is most often 8, 13, 21, or, in especially old and large specimens, 34. These numbers follow the *Fibonacci* sequence, where each number (when listed in ascending order) is the sum of the two previous numbers. Other ribbed cacti, but most notably *Ferocactus* species, adhere to this growth pattern as they produce new growth from the apical meristem at the tip of the stem. This growth

## COAST BARREL CACTUS
### *Ferocactus viridescens*

*Coast barrel cactus's limited distribution occurs where development pressures are high. [Border Field S.P.]*

pattern is common in other spirally arranged plants, such as agaves, and is also evident with pine cones.

The apical meristem of coast barrel cactus receives only 20% to 25% shade from spines and pubescence. In contrast, the spines and pubescence at the tip of a desert barrel cactus provide 65% to 95% shading for its apical meristem. Botanists surmise that protective shading is not as necessary for coast barrel cactus because the species is confined to a moderate coastal climate.

Coast barrel cactus grows on sea bluffs and hill crests, where it prefers southwest-facing slopes among rocks and well-drained, gravelly loam soils. In addition to its occurrence in chaparral and coastal sage scrub plant communities, coast barrel cactus is also found in valley grasslands on the periphery of vernal pools. Its entire population in the U.S. is located within western San Diego County.

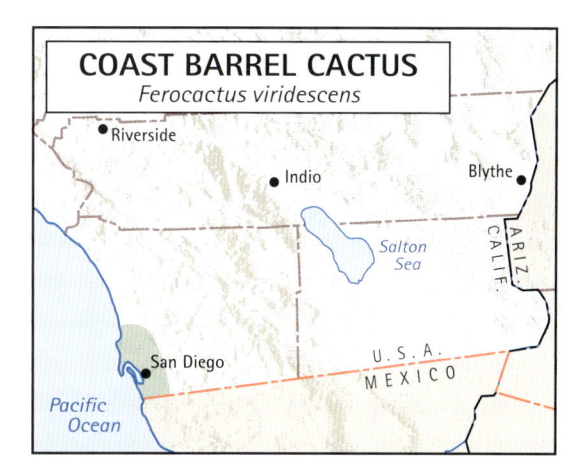

It ranges inland as far as the Escondido area and southward through Otay Mesa and into northern Baja California. Coast barrel cactus used to be very common within its range, but it is currently in decline due to rapid urbanization, as well as from illegal collecting.

### Identifying Characteristics

**Habit:** erect, spheric to short cylindric, solitary.
**Stems:** green to dark green, usually 4–18 in. (10–45 cm) wide and 4–14 in. (10–35 cm) tall, with 13 to 34 ribs.
**Spines:** 10 to 19 per areole; central spines 4 per areole, flattened with transverse ridges; central and larger radial spines rigid, straight or slightly curved, pink or yellow, longest one 1.2–2 in. (3–5 cm) long; smallest radial spines bristle-like.
**Flowers:** tepals greenish yellow; outer tepals with red midline, 1.2–2.5 in. (3–6 cm) long; flowers 1–2 in. (2.5–5 cm) across; filaments, anthers, and stigma lobes yellow; blooms May to July.
**Fruits:** round, bright yellow, fleshy to leathery, scaly, 0.8–1.4 in. (2–3.5cm) long.

Parish club-cholla • *Grusonia parishii* ARTWORK BY E.O. MURMAN

# *Grusonia*
## CLUB-CHOLLA

The gorgeous blossoms of club-chollas command attention. In fact, they are the only feature of these low-growing cacti that draws much notice. Without their flowers, club-chollas are very inconspicuous—and may even appear to be dead. *Grusonia* as a genus was first named and published in 1894 to honor German engineer, plant collector, and horticulturist Herman Gruson (1821–1895). The genus was seldom used in scientific literature until recent genetic research in *Opuntia* warranted the subdivision of that large, variable, and unwieldy genus into smaller genera. Species currently treated in *Grusonia* used to be treated as species of *Opuntia, Cylindropuntia, Corynopuntia,* and several other small genera from Mexico.

The *Flora of North America* recognizes 14 *Grusonia* species, 2 of which occur in the deserts of California and Nevada. The other species occur in the deserts of Mexico and north into Texas, New Mexico, and Arizona. The genus can be distinguished from *Cylindropuntia,* its closest relative, by its low mat-like growth habit and flattened (not rounded) spines with little or no papery sheath.

# PARISH CLUB-CHOLLA
*Grusonia parishii*

(gru-SON-ee-ah pa-RISH-ee-eye)

**Recent Synonyms**
*Opuntia parishii, O. stanleyi* var. *parishii*

**Other Common Names**
dead cactus, devil's cactus, ground mat cholla, horse crippler

*A seemingly moribund patch of spines comes to life when Parish club-cholla blooms. [Red Rock Canyon N.C.A.]*

*The flowers of Parish club-cholla appear elevated and sit on top of a floral tube. [Red Rock Canyon N.C.A.]*

When a person spots a Parish club-cholla for the first time, he is likely to wonder: "Is it alive?" For most of the year, Parish club-cholla resembles a partially decomposed prickly-pear with shrunken pads and a cloak of thick, prominent spines. Indeed, one of its other common names is "horse crippler," which underscores its camouflaged danger. But the life force is deceptively dormant in this fierce-looking little cactus. During late May or June, Parish club-cholla produces yellow and pink funnel-shaped flowers that seem to reach for the sky, and for a short while this cactus becomes an enthralling sight.

Parish club-cholla is uncommon and easy to overlook, which makes its discovery while in bloom all the more exciting. A flower of Parish club-cholla appears bigger than it really is because it sits elevated upon a fleshy stalk-like growth (the floral tube) that encloses the ovary. After pollination by bees, the ovary swells to become a yellow fruit that sports a dense covering of short, yellowish glochids and resembles a miniature spiked club.

This mat-forming cactus is about 6 inches tall, and may spread 2 or 3 feet out from the center, with most new growth occurring around the mat's perimeter or occasionally among old, decomposed stems nearer the center. Its growth form and dense interlacing of flattened spines distinguish this species

*A ripe glochid-covered fruit of a Parish club-cholla protrudes above a mat of spines. [Joshua Tree N.P.]*

## PARISH CLUB-CHOLLA
### *Grusonia parishii*

from any other cactus in our area.

Parish club-cholla grows most often in open Joshua tree woodland on sandy or gravelly flats at elevations from 3000 to 5000 feet. It occurs in a wide swath of the Mojave Desert in eastern California and southern Nevada, as well as in a smaller area of the southern Mojave that is mostly in Riverside County. It also grows in the northwestern Sonoran Desert of Arizona. The range of Parish club-cholla does not overlap with the range of its smaller relative, the sand-cholla, which largely occurs farther to the north and east.

### Identifying Characteristics

**Habit:** small, short clumps forming mats 4–8 in. (10–20 cm) tall.
**Stems:** dark green or reddish, club-shaped, 0.8–1.2 in. (2–3 cm) wide and 2–3.5 in. (5–9 cm) tall; tubercles prominent.
**Spines:** 17 to 22 per areole, mostly in upper portion of each stem segment; 5 to 6 central spines, largest ones flattened basally, stout, reddish becoming gray, up to 2.6 in. (6.5 cm) long; lower spines of each areole bent downward.
**Flowers:** inner tepals yellow to apricot; outer tepals yellowish with red tips and midstripes, 0.6–1 in. (1.5–2.5 cm) wide and 1.5–2 in. (4–5 cm) long; filaments pink to green or pale yellow; style white to pink; stigma white, yellow, or pale green; blooms May to July.
**Fruits:** vase-shaped, fleshy, yellow with dense yellowish glochids, 1.5–3.25 in. (3.5–8 cm) long.

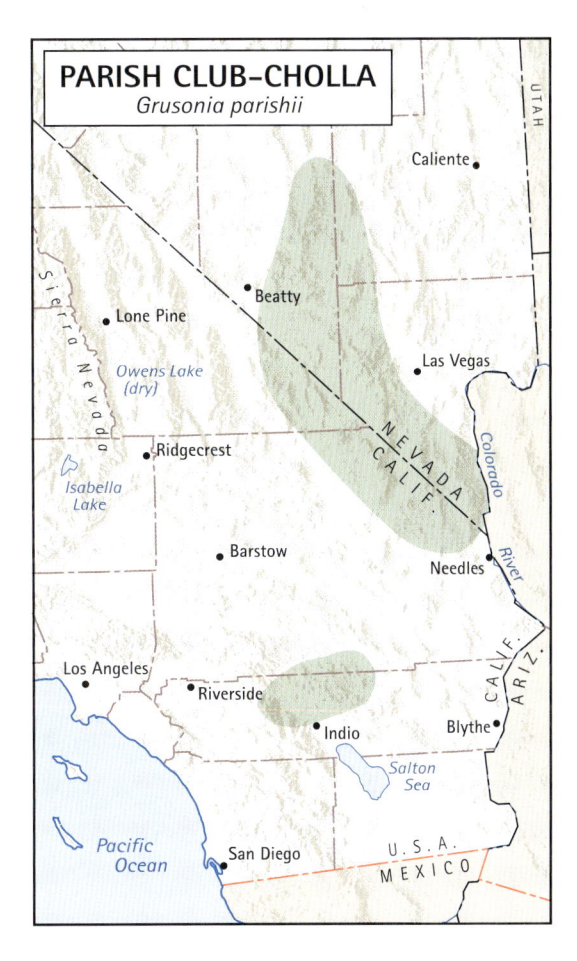

Species Profiles

# SAND-CHOLLA
## *Grusonia pulchella*
*(gru-SON-ee-ah pull-CHEL-uh)*

**Recent Synonyms**
Opuntia pulchella, Micropuntia gracilicylindrica, M. pulchella

**Other Common Names**
beautiful cholla, dwarf cholla

*Sand-cholla produces out-sized flowers for such a small cactus. [White Pine Co.]*

Sand-cholla is known for its capacity to undergo a dramatic physical transformation in a short period of time. Under the right conditions, this plant changes from an inconspicuous, desiccated clump of stems into a robust cactus festooned with brilliant magenta blossoms. Due to its small size and near invisibility when not in flower, club-cholla amazes cactus lovers with its phoenix-like trait of "coming back to life" in the late spring. Sand-cholla, like Parish club-cholla, produces an extraordinarily large and beautiful flower for such a small cactus.

The visible portion of sand-cholla may die back in times of severe drought, but it survives due to its thickened underground stem, or tuber. The tuber is covered with "eyes"—meristematic buds much like those on a potato—that produce new stems. This cactus tends to grow near desert playas and in valleys with silty to sandy soils that do not dry out as rapidly as those on sloping ground with

*Top: A sweat bee forages for nectar and pollen in a sand-cholla blossom near the Snake Range. [White Pine Co.]*
*Bottom: A dime lends a sense of scale to the new growth of this sand-cholla in Fish Lake Valley. [Esmeralda Co.]*

*Due to its thick underground stem, sand-cholla can survive in the driest regions. [White Pine Co.]*

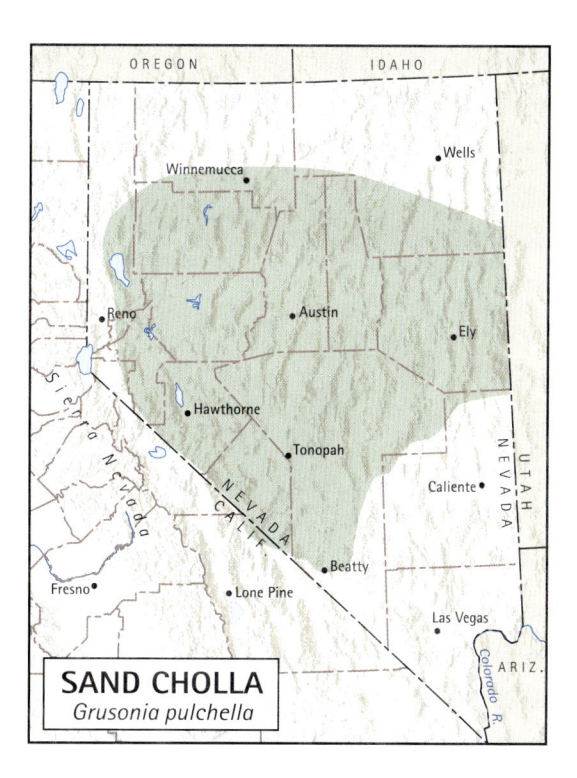

## SAND CHOLLA
*Grusonia pulchella*

County and southwestern Nye County north through much of the state and east into western Utah. It occurs at elevations from 3950 feet up to around 6500 feet and is typically found in the open with sagebrush and saltbush.

### Identifying Characteristics
**Habit:** small, short clumps forming mats 4–8 in. (10–20 cm) tall.
**Stems:** dark green or reddish, cylindrical to club-shaped; 0.2–1 in. (0.5–2.5 cm) wide and 0.4–4 in. (1–10 cm) tall; tubercles prominent.
**Spines:** 8 to 15 per areole, mostly in upper portion of each stem segment, largest ones flattened basally, white to reddish brown becoming gray, up to 2.4 in. (6 cm) long; lower spines divergent or bent downward.
**Flowers:** tepals magenta (rose to purple), 1.5–2 in. (4–5 cm) long; flowers 0.6–1 in. (1.5–2.5 cm) across; filaments green to yellow; style pink; stigma white to yellow; blooms late May to July.
**Fruits:** vase-shaped, reddish, fleshy, smooth with flexible, hair-like glochids; 0.6–1.2 in. (1.5–3 cm) long.

more rocky substrates. As a result, sand-cholla is able to enlarge and produce flowering stems when conditions are wet; during prolonged drought it can shed its small, succulent stems and store water below ground.

Sand-cholla can be distinguished from its closest relative, Parish club-cholla, by its more narrow, round stem-joints and shorter, pink flowers. The bee-pollinated flowers of sand-cholla open widely and are nearly as showy as those of beavertail cactus.

Sand-cholla is a species of the Great Basin and northern Mojave deserts, whereas its relative, Parish club-cholla, is found in the eastern and southern Mojave Desert. Sand-cholla barely gets into California, where it makes its way into northeastern Inyo County. In Nevada it occurs from Esmeralda

Graham fishhook • *Mammillaria grahamii*   ARTWORK BY E.O. MURMAN

# *Mammillaria*
## FISHHOOK or NIPPLE CACTUS

*Mammillaria* is the second largest genus in the cactus family, after *Opuntia*, and one of the most popular genera among succulent enthusiasts. Mammillarias are admired for their small size, diversity of spine shape and color, and attractive flowers. *Mammillaria* was described and named in 1812 by English botanist and etymologist, Adrian Haworth. Although more than 400 species have been named and published, most sources currently put the total number of species between 150 and 175. *Mammillaria* is considered to be one of the more specialized and recently evolved genera of the cactus family. *Mammillaria* species are found in Venezuela, the Caribbean, and Guatemala. From there, they range north into the southwestern U.S., with the vast majority of species occurring in Mexico. Only three species are native to California and Nevada.

The scientific name *Mammillaria* refers to the nipple-like tubercles characteristic of species in this genus. Additional diagnostic features for mammillarias include the way their flowers emerge from the bases of older tubercles to form a ring around the upper stem and the presence of apical spines on the tubercles. Mammillarias may grow as a single stem or in large tight clumps. They can be distinguished from non-flowering plants of *Coryphantha* by their ungrooved tubercles that are round in cross section. Our three mammillarias differ from both *Coryphantha* and *Pediocactus* by having dimorphic areoles and one or more noticeable hooked central spines.

# CALIFORNIA FISHHOOK CACTUS
## *Mammillaria dioica*
(mam-mil-LAIR-ee-uh dy-OH-ih-ka)

**Other Common Names**
coastal fishhook cactus, strawberry cactus, nipple cactus

*California fishhook cactus thrives in both coastal and desert environments. [Anza-Borrego Desert S.P.]*

*This California fishhook cactus flower is male-sterile; its stamens lack pollen. [Anza-Borrego Desert S.P.]*

When it blossoms, California fishhook cactus produces rings of flowers that encircle the tops of its short, plump stems. This display gives a cheerful impression and presents an interesting contrast to the annual wildflowers and grasses that often grow near this cactus. A rocky hillside covered with flowering California fishhook cactus is a beautiful sight—and also one that offers a chance to learn something about cactus flowers.

As you explore a patch of California fishhook cactus in bloom, you may notice some plants with large flowers and, nearby, other plants with flowers that might be only two-thirds as big. This difference in flowers is due to the fact that California fishhook cactus is gynodioecious. This means the species has two flower types: bisexual (perfect) and functionally female (pistillate). The two types are found on different individuals. If you examine the plants more closely, you will find that the larger flowers are bisexual; they have yellow, pollen-producing anthers surrounding the green stigma. The cacti with smaller flowers, however, have blossoms with small anthers and no yellow pollen, which means they are male-sterile, or pistillate. Researchers have discovered that the pistillate flowers of the California fishhook cactus produce more seeds than the perfect flowers. This gynodioecy may represent an evolutionary step away from cacti with perfect flowers—currently found in all but five or six cactus species—to cacti that are truly dioecious, with male and female flowers occurring on separate plants.

California fishhook cactus and desert barrel cactus both grow in the hot environment of the Colorado Desert, and these two species have the highest known heat tolerances of any cacti native to California. In an experiment testing high temperature responses of 14 Sonoran and Mojave desert cacti, researchers found that California fishhook cactus could tolerate a temperature—after acclimating for ten days—of 148°F (64.4°C). This tolerance was higher than all other California species tested, with the exception of desert barrel cactus.

California fishhook cactus can be distinguished from our other two native mammillarias by its pale yellow gynodioecious flowers, single central hooked spine, and white woolly hairs at the tubercle bases. In contrast, common fishhook has many more radial spines, usually two to four central hooked spines, and a seed with a unique corky appendage. Graham fishhook cactus has pink and white flowers with one to three central hooked spines and lacks woolly hairs.

Easy to overlook when not in flower, California fishhook cactus is one of the few cacti that thrives in both cismontane and transmontane areas of California. Although it grows in two very different habitats, it does not range into the higher elevations of the mountains that separate its coastal and desert distributions. Near sea level, it occurs with coast barrel cactus in the coastal sage scrub of San Diego County, and on the lower eastern slopes of the Peninsular Ranges it joins desert barrel cactus in Sonoran creosote bush scrub. It is common in Anza-Borrego Desert State Park from 1000 to over 3000 feet elevation. It is also distributed throughout most of Baja California.

## Identifying Characteristics

**Habit:** erect, spherical to tall cylindrical, solitary or in tight clumps.

**Stems:** green, firm, usually 2–2.8 in. (5–7 cm) wide and 2–12 in. (5–30 cm) tall; axils between tubercles with white wooly hairs.

**Spines:** 14 to 26 per areole; radial spines 11 to 22 per areole, mostly in one plane, white; central spines 3 to 4 per areole, white with red, brown, or black tips; longest central spine hooked, to 0.6 in. (1.5 cm) long.

**Flowers:** tepals white to pale yellow with reddish midline, narrow, 0.4–0.9 in. (1.2–2 cm) long; flowers 0.8–2 in. (2–5cm) across; filaments and anthers yellow; stigma lobes green to greenish yellow; blooms March to June.

**Fruits:** elongate, juicy, red, with floral remnant persistent; 0.8–1.4 in. (2–3.5 cm) long; seeds black.

*A ring of flowers encircles the stem of a California fishhook cactus. [Anza-Borrego Desert S.P.]*

**CALIFORNIA FISHHOOK CACTUS**
*Mammillaria dioica*

# GRAHAM FISHHOOK CACTUS
*Mammillaria grahamii* var. *grahamii*
(mam-mil-LAIR-ee-uh GRAM-ee-eye)

**Recent Synonyms**
*Mammillaria microcarpa, M. milleri*

**Other Common Names**
Arizona fishhook cactus, Graham's nipple cactus

*Graham fishhook cactus, seen here in the Whipple Mountains, is a Sonoran Desert species. [San Bernardino Co.]*

*The bright red fruit of a Graham fishhook cactus resembles a tiny chili pepper. [San Bernardino Co.]*

The vast majority of *Mammillaria* species occur where summer rains comprise a significant portion of the annual rainfall, and Graham fishhook cactus is no exception. The summer monsoonal rainfall pattern of the Sonoran Desert is one of the major factors that initiates blooming of Graham fishhook cactus. The buds on this short cactus are produced at the bases of old tubercles on the upper stem during the summer growing season. They then apparently become dormant until the following summer. About one week after the first summer rainstorm, most of the buds—the first phase—will burst forth with bright pink flowers. Since each flower remains open for only one day, this cactus has a short time to attract the bees that pollinate it. As a result, this cactus seems to "hedge its bets" for effective pollination by delaying the opening of some buds until the next summer rainstorm. An individual Graham fishhook cactus may flower 3 or 4 times per year, with robust individuals producing more than 40 flowers per year. Through the winter months, the plants display their bright red fruits, which are often referred to as *chilitos* (Spanish for "little chiles").

When Graham fishhook cactus is not showing off its bowl-shaped pink flowers, it can be difficult to distinguish from California's other two

*Graham fishhook cactus flowers in response to rain, but the blossoms last only one day. [San Bernardino Co.]*

# GRAHAM FISHHOOK CACTUS
*Mammillaria grahamii* var. *grahamii*

mammillarias. Its areoles usually form more radial spines and have two to three hooked central spines, in contrast to California fishhook cactus, which has fewer radial spines and only one hooked central spine. Common fishhook cactus typically has more than 30 radial spines and four hooked central spines; in addition, it feels flabby when poked with a stick, in comparison to the firmness of Graham fishhook cactus.

Graham fishhook cactus, like its famous distant cousin, the giant saguaro, is abundant in Arizona, absent from Nevada, and rare in California, where it is limited to the state's easternmost extension—the Whipple Mountains area. This species also ranges through southern Arizona, southern New Mexico, the southwestern corner of Texas, and south into Chihuahua and Sonora, Mexico. In the Whipple Mountains, Graham fishhook cactus is found on igneous gravelly slopes and rocky hillsides. It frequently grows within the shade cast by burrobush or paloverde, but also occurs in the open alongside desert barrel cactus and buckhorn cholla. Although Graham fishhook cactus has been verified only in the Whipple Mountains, it could be awaiting discovery in other mountain ranges of eastern Riverside or Imperial counties, or even in the southern Newberry Mountains of Clark County, Nevada.

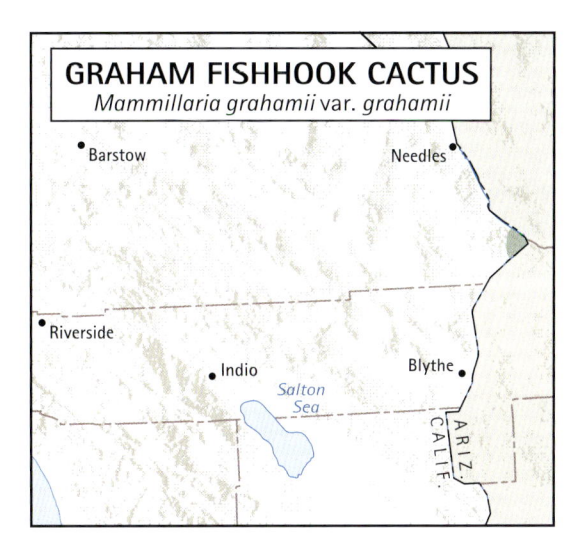

## Identifying Characteristics

**Habit:** erect, spherical to cylindrical, solitary or in tight clumps.
**Stems:** green, firm, usually 1.4–2.7 in. (3.5–6.8 cm) wide and 2–12 in. (5–30 cm) tall.
**Spines:** 20 to 39 per areole; radial spines 17 to 35 per areole, mostly in one plane, white to tan; central spines 3 to 4 per areole, white with red, brown or black tips; 1 to 3 central spines hooked, to 1 in. (2.5 cm) long.
**Flowers:** tepals pale pink to dark rose-pink with whitish margins, narrow, minutely fringed at the tips, 0.6–1.4 in. long (1.5–3.5 cm) long; flowers 0.8–1.8 in. (2–4.5 cm) across; filaments pink, anthers yellow; stigma lobes green to greenish yellow; blooms April to September.
**Fruits:** elongate, juicy, bright red, floral remnant persistent; 0.5–1.2 in. (1.2–3 cm) long.

# COMMON FISHHOOK CACTUS
## *Mammillaria tetrancistra*
(mam-mil-LAIR-ee-uh teh-tran-SIS-tra)

**Recent Synonyms**
*Phellosperma tetrancistra*

**Other Common Names**
corkseed cactus, corkseed mammillaria, corky-seed pincushion, California pincushion, desert fishhook cactus, nipple cactus

*A buprestid beetle in a common fishhook cactus flower. [Granite Mtns., Mojave N. Pr.]* PHOTO © TASHA LA DOUX

*A split-open fruit of a common fishhook cactus shows the corky appendages on its seeds. [Imperial Co.]*

Although widespread in the desert Southwest, common fishhook cactus is inconspicuous, and it can be hard to find one in flower. This cactus is more often spotted due to its characteristic ring of edible crimson fruits. They are known as *chilitos* (Spanish for "little chiles") and hold seeds that resemble miniature black acorns in brown cups. The corky appendage on the seed is unique among *Mammillaria* species, and at one time this species was placed in its own genus named *Phellosperma,* from the Greek words for "cork" and "seed." But botanists have since concluded that this single character is not sufficient reason to place this cactus in a separate genus. The specific name for this cactus is also derived from Greek, with *ankistron* for "fishhook," and *tetra* for "four," referring to its characteristic four central hooked spines (although it frequently exhibits only one, two, or three).

Of the more than 150 species of *Mammillaria*, only common fishhook cactus reaches as far north as southern Nevada. It is Nevada's only fishhook cactus and our region's most widespread *Mammillaria*. Common fishhook cactus has several adaptations that enable it to tolerate drier and colder habitats than any of its close relatives. Its fleshy taproots shrink during drought periods and draw the lower stem down below the ground surface. The nipple-like tubercles also contract, pulling the spine clusters closer together to form more of a barrier that may help prevent water loss and frost damage.

Common fishhook can be distinguished from California's other two mammillarias by several characteristics: its more numerous radial spines are arrayed in two or three ranks; it has up to four central hooked spines; and the fruit contains unique corky seeds. It can also be differentiated by touch—just be sure to use a sturdy, blunt stick instead of your finger. Common fishhook cactus has the consistency of a spine-encrusted, thick-skinned water balloon, in contrast to the firmness of both

*A common fishhook cactus growing in the Palo Verde Mountains displays fruits and barbed spines. [Imperial Co.]*

## Identifying Characteristics

**Habit:** erect, spherical to cylindrical, base usually wider; usually solitary but occasionally in tight clumps.

**Stems:** pale green, flaccid, 1.4–3.1 in. (3.5–8 cm) wide and 2–10 in. (5–25 cm) tall.

**Spines:** 33 to 64 per areole; radial spines 30 to 60 per areole, in 2 to 3 ranks, white; central spines 3 to 4 per areole, white with red, brown, or black tips, longest central spines hooked, to 1 in. (2.5 cm) long.

**Flowers:** tepals pale pink to rose-purple with white margins, narrow, 1–1.4 in. (2.5–3.5 cm) long; flowers 1–1.6 in. (2.5–4 cm) across; outer tepals with fringed margins; stigma lobes green to greenish yellow; blooms April to August.

**Fruits:** elongate, juicy, bright red, floral remnant deciduous and leaving scar; 0.6–1.2 in. (1.5–3 cm) long; seeds black with brown corky appendage.

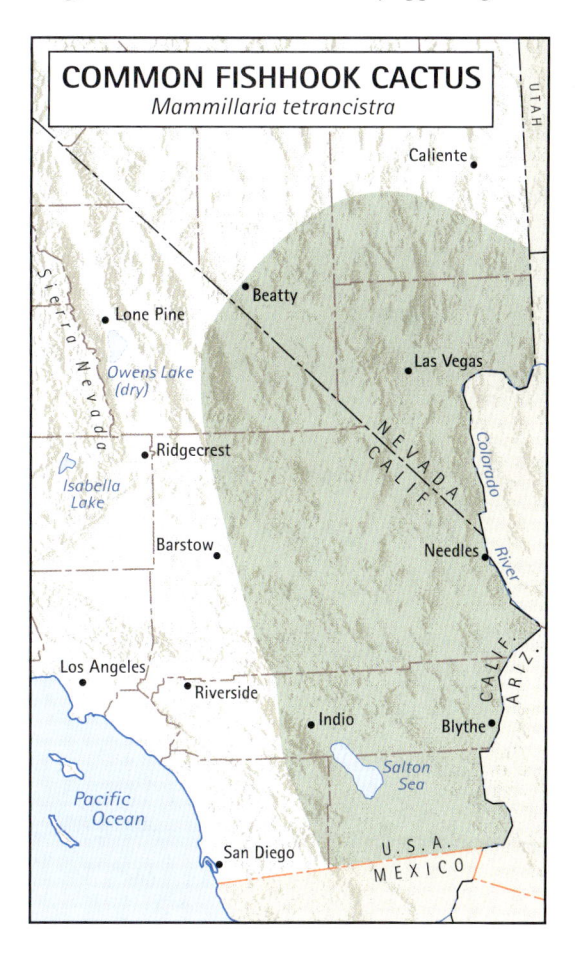

**COMMON FISHHOOK CACTUS**
*Mammillaria tetrancistra*

California and Graham fishhook cacti.

Common fishhook cactus ranges from the Sonoran Desert of Baja California and Sonora, Mexico to southwestern Arizona, southeastern California and north through the Mojave Desert of California to southern Nevada and southwestern Utah. Within our region, common fishhook occurs in California from the Jacumba Mountains north to the Panamint Range. This species extends from Death Valley National Park east to Nevada's Sheep Range and south through Clark County, Nevada. Common fishhook cactus can be found in rocky to sandy soils on bajadas and mountain slopes. It grows at elevations from 450 to 5400 feet and is associated with vegetation types ranging from creosote bush scrub in the Sonoran Desert to Joshua tree woodland in the northern Mojave Desert.

Pancake prickly-pear • *Opuntia chlorotica*     ARTWORK BY E.O. MURMAN

# *Opuntia*
## PRICKLY-PEAR

*Opuntia* is the most abundant and widespread of all cactus genera, as well as the most important economically. Since the 15th century, when Christopher Columbus first carried *Opuntia* specimens from the New World back to Spain, prickly-pear cacti, especially *Opuntia ficus-indica,* have been propagated around the world. *Opuntia* was also one of the original four genera (along with *Cereus, Melocactus,* and *Pereskia*) to be named in a plant family (Cactaceae) that was still formally unnamed until 1789. *Opuntia* was initially illustrated and published in 1700 by Joseph Pitton de Tournefort. But it was the English gardener and botanist Philip Miller who first validly named and described the genus in 1754. The name *Opuntia* allegedly comes from the ancient Greek region Locris Opuntia with its capital city Opus, where a "cactus-like" plant once grew.

There are approximately 180 species of *Opuntia,* and they range from Argentina to British Columbia, including the islands of the Caribbean. Eight native species, four varieties, and several named hybrids occur in coastal, mountain, and desert habitats of California and Nevada. Though prickly-pears are closely related to and have been grouped with the chollas *(Cylindropuntia)* and club-chollas *(Grusonia),* they are easily recognized in our region by their flattened stem segments, or pads, and lack of papery sheaths on their spines. Prickly-pears, like chollas, are highly variable and many species tend to hybridize, making species identification difficult (see "Prickly-pear Hybrids" on page 128). An abbreviated summary of identifying characteristics of prickly-pear species profiled in this book is found in Appendix E "Prickly-pear Species Comparison" on page 222.

# BEAVERTAIL CACTUS
## *Opuntia basilaris* var. *basilaris*
(o-PUN-tee-ya bas-ih-LAIR-iss)
### Recent Synonyms
*Opuntia whitneyana, O. basilaris* var. *ramosa, O. basilaris* var. *aurea*
### Other Common Names
beavertail prickly-pear

# SHORT-JOINT BEAVERTAIL
## *Opuntia basilaris* var. *brachyclada*
(brack-ee-KLADE-uh)
### Recent Synonyms
*Opuntia brachyclada*
### Other Common Names
little beavertail prickly-pear

# BAKERSFIELD CACTUS
## *Opuntia basilaris* var. *treleasei*
(tre-LEASE-eye)
### Recent Synonyms
*Opuntia treleasei*
### Other Common Names
Kern beavertail, Kern cactus, Trelease beavertail prickly-pear

*Of the three* basilaris *varieties, Bakersfield cactus is the only one with spines on its pads. [Kern Co.]*

*Cactus flowers, like these beavertail cactus blooms, owe their color to betalain pigments. [Death Valley N.P.]*

**Beavertail cactus** is undoubtedly one of the most recognizable cacti in the western United States. Its large, brilliant pink to magenta flowers and bluish green, spineless pads distinguish it from any other prickly-pear. Lacking permanent spines, their succulent pads take on a velvety appearance, and this has lured many admirers into handling beavertail cactus; as a result they unwittingly receive a painful lesson about the tenacity of barbed glochids. (Glochids can be removed from clothing with tape and from the skin with tweezers.) The Cahuilla Indians of the Colorado Desert would roll the new fruits in sand to dislodge glochids before roasting the fruits with meat.

Beavertail cactus thrives in some of the hottest and driest parts of the Mojave and Sonoran deserts due to its remarkable tolerance of heat and drought. In growth-chamber experiments, its ability to withstand high temperatures was surpassed only by California fishhook and desert barrel cacti. It survived a temperature of 144°F (62.6°C) if allowed to acclimate to a day/night temperature regime of 122°F/104°F (50°C/40°C). Beavertail cactus, like most other cacti, uses CAM photosynthesis; this allows it to absorb $CO_2$ at night and keep its stomata closed during the day to prevent water loss. During extreme drought, beavertail cactus, like other CAM cacti, is able to photosynthesize at an "idle" by internally recycling $CO_2$ and closing its stomata day and night. When it rains and the soil is rewetted, beavertail cactus is already

*Beavertail cactus survives in some of the hottest and driest desert regions. [Valley of Fire S.P.]*

*The pads of beavertail cactus shrivel in drought conditions. [Palo Verde Mountains Wilderness, Imperial Co.]*

metabolically active and can open its stomata to "accelerate" its photosynthesis, making the most of what may be a brief wet period. The pads of beavertail cactus exhibit a more obvious adaptation to drought; they expand following storms and shrivel following months of drought.

Beavertail cactus occurs on both metamorphic and sedimentary substrates in a broad array of habitats, ranging from sandy valleys in the lower Colorado River Basin to rocky slopes at 9200 feet in the eastern Sierra Nevada. It occurs along the Mexican border from western Arizona to southeastern California and ranges north to the edge of the Great Basin Desert in California and Nevada; in essence, it is found in hot desert areas where winter rainfall equals or exceeds summer rainfall.

Beavertail cactus has no close relatives. Most taxonomists recognize four varieties of *Opuntia basilaris*. Cactus expert Donald Pinkava has described a likely scenario for speciation of prickly-pears and chollas. He proposes that when small, peripheral populations become isolated, they may eventually evolve into separate "daughter species," while the "mother species" persists as a distinct but closely related entity. He theorizes that *Opuntia basilaris* var. *longiareolata,* Grand Canyon beavertail (of southern Utah and northern Arizona), gave rise to *Opuntia basilaris* var. *basilaris*—the common, widespread beavertail to the west. This variety eventually formed two peripheral "daughter species" of its own that we know as *Opuntia basilaris* var. *brachyclada,* the short-joint beavertail, and *Opuntia basilaris* var. *treleasei,* the Bakersfield cactus.

**Short-joint beavertail** differs primarily from beavertail cactus in having small, laterally compressed pads that are densely packed together. It only occurs in the San Gabriel and San Bernardino mountains, where it grows in chaparral and pinyon-juniper woodland at elevations of 3500 to 6000 feet. This cactus is uncommon and easy to overlook because of its 5-inch stature, but its flowers are an immediate eye-catcher. Short-joint beavertail blooms in May. A good place to view it is in the Cajon Pass area and around the nearby community of Wrightwood.

**Bakersfield cactus** is distinguished from the other two varieties in having spines, mostly in the upper areoles. It also has three sets of chromosomes instead of two, as in the other varieties. Some botanists treat it as a distinct species, *Opuntia treleasei*. Bakersfield cactus used to cover extensive areas

*Beavertail cactus's striking pink flowers and bluish pads make it easy to identify. [Lake Mead N.R.A.]*

along the bluffs of the Kern River, throughout the Bakersfield area, and in the foothills of the Tehachapi Mountains south to the Tejon Hills. Today it is confined to approximately 11 populations in the vicinity of Bakersfield, and its survival remains threatened by residential housing developments, commercial development, and conversion of its habitat to agriculture. It is mostly found on sandy soils in valley grassland, saltbush scrub, and foothill woodland from 400 to 1800 feet in elevation. Bakersfield cactus blooms from late April through May, and this is a good time to see this variety at places like Sand Ridge Preserve and along Caliente Creek, east of Bakersfield.

## Identifying Characteristics
**Habit:** shrubs, in dense, low-growing clumps, to 20 in. (50 cm) tall and 6.6 ft. (2 m) across.
**Stems:** thick, bluish green, sometimes tinged

*Short-joint beavertail's pads are smaller than in other* basilaris *varieties. [San Bernardino Co.]*

*Bakersfield cactus, pictured here in the Sand Ridge Preserve, is an endangered species. [Kern Co.]*

## BEAVERTAIL CACTUS, SHORT-JOINT BEAVERTAIL, BAKERSFIELD CACTUS
*Opuntia basilaris*

- var. *basilaris* (beavertail cactus)
- var. *brachyclada* (short-joint beavertail)
- var. *treleasei* (Bakersfield cactus)

purple, elliptic to wedge-shaped; or club-shaped in var. *brachyclada;* 2.6–6.3 in. (6.5–16 cm) wide and 2.8–13.8 in. (7–35 cm) long in var. *basilaris;* 0.6–2 in. (1.5–5 cm) wide and 2–5.1 in. (5–13 cm) long in var. *brachyclada;* or 2–3 in. (5–7.5 cm) wide and 3.5–8 in. (9–20 cm) long in var. *treleasei*.

**Spines:** 8 to 19 areoles per diagonal row in var. *basilaris*, 4 to 6 in var. *brachyclada*, 7 to 8 in var. *treleasei;* 0 spines per areole in vars. *basilaris* and *brachyclada*, 2 to 8 in var. *treleasei*, straight, spreading, yellow, to 1 in. (2.5 cm) long.

**Flowers:** tepals pink to magenta, rarely white, 1–1.6 in. (2.5–4 cm) long; flowers up to 3 in. (7.5 cm) across; style white to pink; stigma lobes dull yellow; filaments red to magenta; some flowers with watermelon-like fragrance; blooms February to June.

**Fruits:** green, drying to tan, glochids but no permanent spines or with few yellow spines in var. *treleasei;* 0.8–1.6 in. (2–4 cm) long.

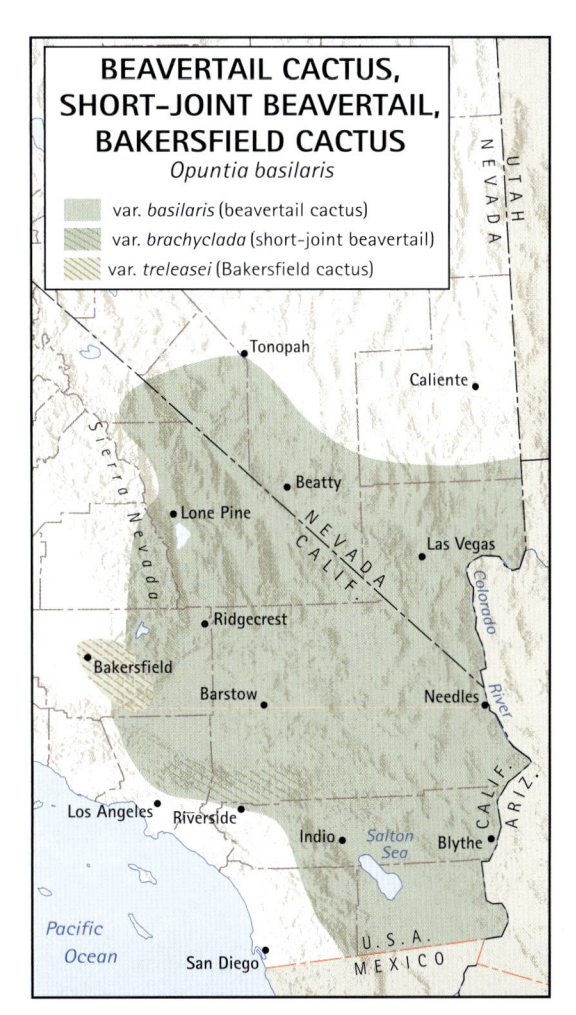

*Blossoms unfold atop the densely packed stems of a short-joint beavertail. [San Bernardino Co.]*

Species Profiles

# PANCAKE PRICKLY-PEAR
## *Opuntia chlorotica*
(o-PUN-tee-ya klor-OTT-i-kuh)
**Other Common Names**
silver dollar cactus, flapjack prickly-pear

*A pancake prickly-pear displays new flowers and buds. [Cima Dome, Mojave N. Pr.]*

Pancake prickly-pear is easy to recognize due to its large stature and its round, flat, bluish green pads that display yellow, downward-pointing spines. Mature specimens have well-developed trunks; they stand over 7 feet tall and may spread equally wide. Unlike many other prickly-pears, pancake prickly-pear tends to occur in populations of widely scattered individuals.

Pancake prickly-pear has been the focus of research by plant physiologist Park Nobel, and his study into the interactions of latitude, climate, and photosynthesis on pad orientation provides fascinating evidence about how this species adapts to its environment. Due to the vertical alignment of their pads, as well as the shading from spines and other pads, most prickly-pears need to maximize their absorption of sunlight. The new pads of pancake prickly-pear are oriented in the most optimal direction during the period when water is available and new growth occurs. In the Sonoran Desert, where summer rainfall is significant, most pancake prickly-pear pads are oriented east-west to take advantage of as much sunlight as possible during their active summertime growth period. But in the Mojave Desert and in California's Colorado Desert, where rain falls predominantly in the winter, pancake prickly-pear puts on new pads in the spring and most of these pads are oriented north-south. In general, pads facing east-west receive more sunlight on a yearly basis than those facing north-south. At latitudes greater than about

*Pancake prickly-pears, like this multi-trunked specimen, may exceed a height of 7 feet. [Joshua Tree N.P.]*

*Pancake prickly-pear's downward-curving spines and bluish pads typify the species. [Joshua Tree N.P.]*

30°N, however, a pad that is oriented north-south will receive twice as much solar radiation during the winter months than those facing in any other direction.

New pad production coincides with the development of flowers in pancake prickly-pear, and those pads that receive the greatest amount of sunlight tend to produce the most flowers. Large, solitary cactus bees are the most important pollinators of pancake prickly-pear flowers. The plant's labyrinth of large pads and spines also provides excellent cover for nesting desert birds and packrats.

Pancake prickly-pear spans nearly 10 degrees of latitude, from 27.5°N in central Baja California to 37°N in Utah. This robust species is usually found at elevations of 2000 to 7800 feet, growing in creosote bush scrub, Joshua tree woodland, and into the lower range of pinyon-juniper woodland. Pancake prickly-pear inhabits grasslands in the eastern part of its range, but in California and Nevada it prefers rocky slopes and flat areas among boulders. Pancake prickly-pear occurs from the western Chihuahuan Desert of New Mexico through most of the Sonoran Desert of Mexico and Arizona to the eastern Mojave Desert of southwestern Utah and southern Nevada and throughout much of southeastern California.

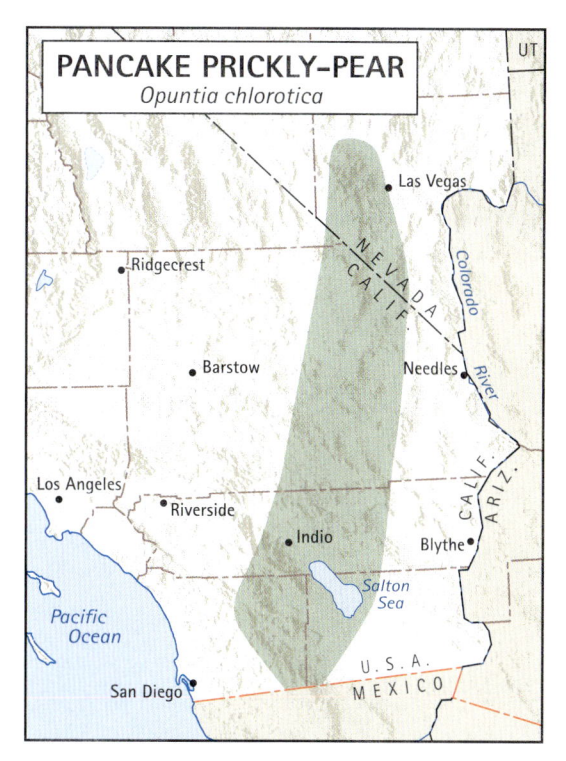

## Identifying Characteristics

**Habit:** erect, shrubby to tree-like, to 8 ft. (2.5 m) tall.

**Stems:** flat, yellowish green to bluish green, broadly oval, 4.5–7.5 in. (11.5–19 cm) wide and 5–8.3 in. (13–21 cm) long.

**Spines:** 7 to 10 areoles per diagonal row, 0 to 7 spines per areole, marginal areoles with additional bristly spines, some lower areoles with 0 spines, straight to weakly curved, deflexed, yellow, 1–1.8 in. (2.5–4.5 cm) long.

**Flowers:** tepals yellow, with reddish orange at base and on outer tepals, 0.7–1.2 in. (1.8–3 cm) long; stigma pale green; anthers pale yellow; blooms May to July.

**Fruits:** barrel-shaped, red to purple, fleshy, spineless, 1.2–2.4 in. (3–6 cm) long.

# ENGELMANN PRICKLY-PEAR
## *Opuntia engelmannii* var. *engelmannii*
(o-PUN-tee-ya ENG-gel-man-ee-eye )

**Recent Synonyms**
*Opuntia charlestonensis, O. littoralis* var. *martiniana, O. phaeacantha* var. *discata*

**Other Common Names**
cactus apple, purple-fruit prickly-pear, *tuna*

*The flowers on this Engelmann prickly-pear are beginning to fade. [Anza-Borrego Desert S.P.]*

Like other desert prickly-pears, Engelmann prickly-pear is pollinated by cactus bees and attracts them with rewards of nectar and pollen. Plant ecologist Janice Bowers observed that flowers of Engelmann prickly-pear may open for either one or two days. Those that open in the morning tend to last one day, remaining open for 5 to 10 hours; those that open in the afternoon close up at night and open early on the second morning, remaining open for a total of more than 12 hours. Though more nectar and pollen are present in fresh flowers, those that open for a second day tend to open earlier in the morning than one-day flowers, making themselves available to pollinating cactus bees for a longer period. Two-day flowers are more common during cooler weather, when cactus bees are less active, and when it is less physiologically stressful for these prickly-pears to open their flowers for a second day.

The deep red, juicy fruits of this species are an important food source for desert tortoises, coyotes, packrats, rabbits, and fruit-eating desert birds. The seeds are dispersed as they pass unharmed through the guts of these animals. Humans find the fruits to be sweet and tasty, as well, and have long used them to make candies, jams, and jellies. The rich red fruits of Engelmann prickly-pear have also served as a source of red dye.

Engelmann prickly-pear is abundant and well known in parts of Arizona, but in California and Nevada, where it is much less common, the species has been something of an enigma. This is because the California and Nevada populations of Engelmann prickly-pear overlap with those of brown-spined prickly pear, a similar-looking relative with which it hybridizes. The result is stands of prickly-pears with traits that are intermediate between the two species. There are, however, various characteristics that distinguish these two from each other. Engelmann prickly-pear is often taller than its relative and grows as a robust, rounded shrub; it also tends to have larger flowers and pads, and shorter spines, than brown-spined prickly-pear. Engelmann prickly-pear often has one short downcurved spine. The reddish brown color of the spine bases of Engelmann prickly-pear is generally confined to the lower tenth of the longest spines, whereas brown-spined prickly-pear spines typically have reddish brown color extending well up from the spine base. The glochids of Engelmann prickly-pear are long and widely spaced, with the longest ones scattered about within each areole. In contrast, the glochids of brown-spined prickly-pear are shorter and compacted into a dense, crescent-shaped tuft with the longest glochids at the center. Engelmann prickly-pear has barrel-shaped fruits that are red inside, while brown-spined prickly-pear

*An Engelmann prickly-pear sprawls along the top of a ridge. [Anza-Borrego Desert S.P.]*

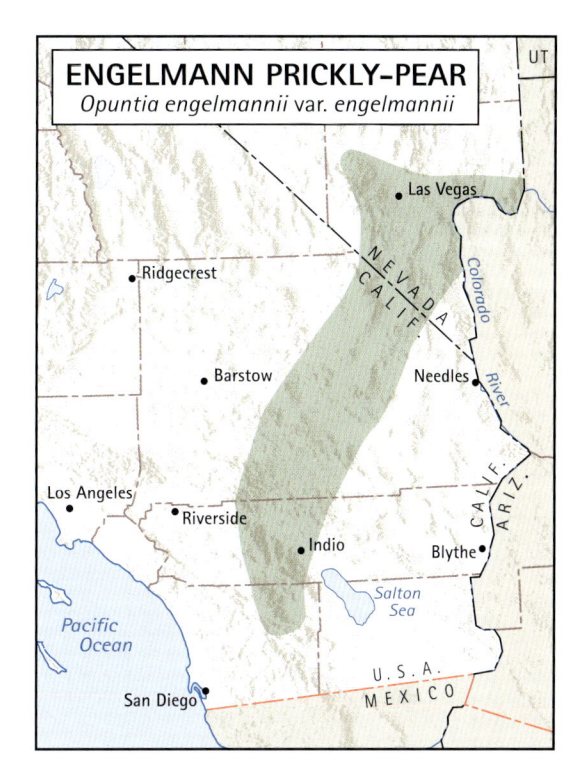

## ENGELMANN PRICKLY-PEAR
*Opuntia engelmannii* var. *engelmannii*

fruits have a longer, narrowed base and are green inside when ripe.

There are five varieties of Engelmann prickly-pear recognized by most botanists, but only one of them occurs in our region. It ranges from southwest Texas and northern Mexico up through most of Arizona and west into southern California and southern Nevada. Engelmann prickly-pear is found on both granitic and limestone-derived soils. It grows at elevations of 2200 to 8000 feet, from the upper edge of Sonoran creosote bush scrub up to pinyon-juniper woodland. In Nevada, Engelmann prickly-pear occurs on the southern slopes of Mt. Charleston, where it was once named *Opuntia charlestonensis*. Good locations to see this cactus in California are on the lower slopes and canyons of the Providence and Clark mountains in the eastern Mojave Desert and in the lower San Felipe Valley near the edge of Anza-Borrego Desert State Park.

## Identifying Characteristics

**Habit:** erect shrub, mound-shaped, 2.5–6.5 ft. tall (0.75–2 m).
**Stems:** green to blue-green, round to obovate, 4.7–8 in. (12–20 cm) wide and 6–12 in. (15–30 cm) long.
**Spines:** 5 to 8 areoles per diagonal row; 0 to 12 spines per areole, but usually 1–5, straight to curved, flattened or angular at base, chalky white but yellow when wet, some with lowermost bases reddish brown, aging gray, the longest 0.8–2 in. (2–5 cm) long.
**Flowers:** tepals yellow, sometimes orange to pink, or with darker bases, 0.7–1.2 in. (1.8–3 cm) long; style white; stigma yellow-green or green; filaments and anthers white; blooms April to June.
**Fruits:** barrel-shaped, red to purple throughout, juicy, spineless, 1.6–2.6 in. (4–6.5 cm) long.

*Glochids and spines grow from the areoles on this Engelmann prickly-pear pad. [Anza-Borrego Desert S.P.]*

Species Profiles 115

# LITTLE PRICKLY-PEAR
## *Opuntia fragilis*
(o-PUN-tee-ya frah-JILL-iss)
**Other Common Names**
brittle prickly-pear, fragile prickly-pear

prickly-pear, it has a low, ground-hugging growth habit, which helps keep it insulated beneath the winter snow pack. These adaptations allow little prickly-pear to inhabit regions where temperatures fall to -40°F (-40°C).

*Of all the prickly-pears, little prickly-pear is the smallest and most cold-tolerant. [Siskiyou Co.]*

On May 18, 1792, while exploring Protection Island between Vancouver and mainland British Columbia, botanist Archibald Menzies wrote, "Among other Plants I collected I was not a little surprizd to meet with the *Cactus opuntia* thus far to the Northward, it grew plentifully, but in a very dwarf state." Menzies was the naturalist for Captain George Vancouver's expedition to the Pacific Northwest and the first to write about this cactus, known today as little prickly-pear, or *Opuntia fragilis*. This species has the broadest range of any of our native cacti and grows farther north than any other cactus, reaching a latitude of 56°N in British Columbia, Canada. It also claims the distinction of being the smallest prickly-pear.

Among all the world's cacti, little prickly-pear has the greatest ability to tolerate cold and acclimate to subarctic conditions. It avoids frost damage by significantly decreasing its cellular water content and shrinking its pads by a third while still retaining its solutes. And like its close relative, porcupine

*Little prickly-pear, growing here on basalt, favors rocky slopes. [Shasta Valley, Siskiyou Co.]*

As its specific name, *fragilis,* implies, little prickly-pear is fragile, and its uppermost pads are easily dislodged. To some, this little cactus may look cute and adorable, but the finely barbed spine tips of little prickly-pear cling tenaciously to nearly anything that touches them. Similar to some of the chollas, little prickly-pear reproduces primarily by vegetative propagation. Its pads are transported to new locations by various means, including rolling downhill, floating downstream, or sticking to the coats of passing mammals.

*The easily detached stems of little prickly-pear carry sharply barbed spines. [Shasta Valley, Siskiyou Co.]*

**LITTLE PRICKLY-PEAR**
*Opuntia fragilis*

Little prickly-pear has the unique distinction of occurring in closer proximity to Canada's Yukon than to Mexico, the center of cactus diversity. It ranges from northern Texas west to Arizona, north through the Rocky Mountains to western Canada, northeast through most of the Midwest and northern Plains states to southern Ontario, Canada. However, the entire distribution within California is limited to the Shasta Valley in central Siskiyou County, where a few populations are found near Big Springs. Throughout its extensive range, little prickly-pear generally prefers rocky outcrops within the numerous vegetation types it occupies. Little prickly-pear occurs up to nearly 10,000 feet in the Colorado Rockies and down to near sea level in Washington and British Columbia. In California, little prickly-pear is found at elevations around 2500 feet in open woodlands of western juniper, where it grows on volcanic rocky outcrops with grasses and widely scattered sagebrush. Rocky sites are important to little prickly-pear because they provide a warm microclimate and good drainage.

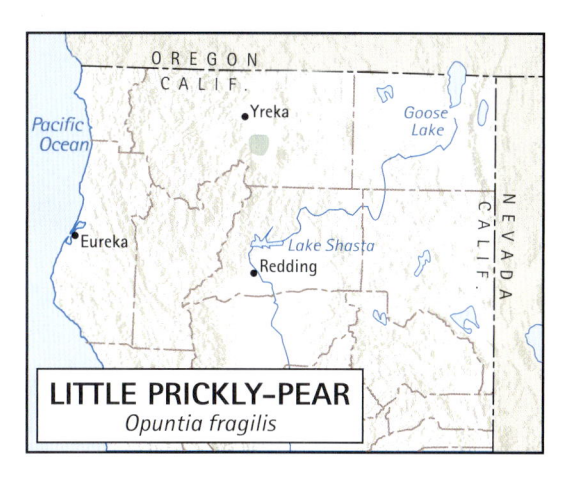

## Identifying Characteristics

**Habit:** low-growing mats; 1–4 in. (2.4–10 cm) tall and 1–3 ft. (30–90 cm) across.

**Stems:** dark green to blue-green; elliptic to broadly oval, somewhat flattened but nearly as thick as wide; 0.6–1.2 in. (1.5–3 cm) wide and 0.6–2.2 in. (1.5–5.5 cm) long.

**Spines:** 3 to 5 areoles per diagonal row; 3 to 8 spines per areole, spreading, straight, sharply barbed, gray with brown tips, the longest (in upper areoles) to 1 in. (2.4 cm) long; glochids inconspicuous.

**Flowers:** tepals pale yellow to pale orange, sometimes with reddish bases, approximately 1 in. (2–2.6 cm) long; style white; stigma lobes green; filaments orange to red; blooms May to July.

**Fruits:** reddish green drying to tan, dry; upper areoles with short spines; 0.4–1.2 in. (1–3 cm) long.

# COASTAL PRICKLY-PEAR
## *Opuntia littoralis*
(o-PUN-tee-ya lit-toe-RAL-iss)
**Other Common Names**
sprawling prickly-pear, short coastal prickly-pear

*Coastal prickly-pear forms thickets in sandy soils near the coast. [Cedar Ridge Park, San Diego Co.]*

fruits, causing fruit deformations and galls. Coastal prickly-pear's spiny but succulent pads and fruits supply food and shelter for brush rabbits, mice, packrats, coyotes, and many birds. Coastal prickly-pear also provides important nesting sites for the shrinking number of coastal cactus wrens.

*Coastal prickly-pear grows with sand verbena on a bluff overlooking the Pacific Ocean. [Torrey Pines S.R.]*

Draw a line around the most urbanized region of southern California, and you have essentially shown the range of coastal prickly-pear. This cactus inhabits a swath of prime real estate along the southern California coast, from near Santa Barbara south to northern Baja California. Named *littoralis* because of its seashore habitat preference, this rather generic-looking prickly-pear has the same distribution as its more robust and distinctive cousin, tall prickly-pear. These two species, along with various prickly-pear hybrids, form dense thickets that can cover acres of coastal bluffs.

Coastal prickly-pear blossoms during the foggy months of May and June, when its large yellow to pale red flowers add a splash of color to the gray-green shades of coastal sage scrub. Numerous native bees visit the pollen-laden flowers, but European honey bees are probably responsible for much of the flower pollination. The cactus fruit midge seems to have a special preference for coastal prickly-pear, and its larvae burrow into the

The low, spreading growth habit of coastal prickly-pear may be an adaptation for growing in sandy, disturbed soils. Land managers at Torrey Pines State Reserve in northern San Diego County take advantage of the soil stabilization qualities of coastal prickly-pear by placing pads in open, erosion-prone areas. Detached pads will readily root from areoles in contact with the soil and eventually grow into clonal adults. Coastal prickly-pear also forms dense colonies; the density of the colony may help it withstand fire as only the outer pads near more flammable plants burn while pads at the colony's center survive.

Despite its lack of any single, highly distinctive character, coastal prickly-pear is identifiable, especially if you can tell it apart from its frequent neighbor, tall prickly-pear. In contrast to tall prickly-pear, coastal prickly-pear is shorter, has fewer areoles per pad, has more elongate pads—often with a broadly tapered tip—and its spines are mostly chalky white, spreading, and straight. The yellow tepals of coastal prickly-pear are relatively broad, and the fruits, both young green and mature red ones, have a narrow base, few glochids, and a shallow umbilicus (the depression at the top of the fruit where the flower was seated). The fruits of tall prickly-pear are more barrel-shaped, have more numerous, longer glochids, and a deep umbilicus. Interestingly, coastal prickly-pear is a more fertile species than tall prickly-pear and will produce viable seeds whether it is self- or cross-pollinated. Coastal prickly-pear and tall prickly-pear can hybridize, and neighboring plants may have characters similar to both of these species.

Coastal prickly-pear is a common hybrid partner with other prickly-pears that overlap its range. (See "Prickly-pear Hybrids" on page 124.)

One of these hybrids is Vasey prickly-pear, *Opuntia* X*vaseyi,* which is the offspring that is produced when coastal prickly-pear crosses with brown-spined prickly-pear. Coastal prickly-pear ranges along the coast from Carpenteria to Ensenada. It occurs as far as 35 miles inland in Los Angeles and Riverside counties and is also found on all of the Channel Islands. It grows most frequently in sandy and rocky soils on south- and west-facing coastal bluffs in coastal sage scrub and chaparral below 1200 feet elevation.

### Identifying Characteristics

**Habit:** shrubs, spreading or sprawling, in clumps 1–3.3 ft. (30–100 cm) tall and up to 30 ft. (9 m) across.
**Stems:** flat, green, elliptic to narrowly obovate, 2.6–5.5 in. (6.5–14 cm) wide and 6–12 in. (15–30 cm) long.
**Spines:** 5 to 7 areoles per diagonal row; 4 to 11 spines per areole, straight to curved, spreading, bone white, some with brown bases, shorter spines to 0.5 in. (1.2 cm) long, and longest ones 0.8–1.6 in. (2–4 cm) long.
**Flowers:** tepals yellow to pale red, 1.4–1.8 in. (3.5–4.5 cm) long; style pink to red; stigma lobes yellow-green to green; filaments orange to yellow; blooms April to June.
**Fruits:** narrowly egg-shaped with shallow umbilicus, dark red-purple throughout, juicy, spineless, 1.4–2 in. (3.5–5 cm) long.

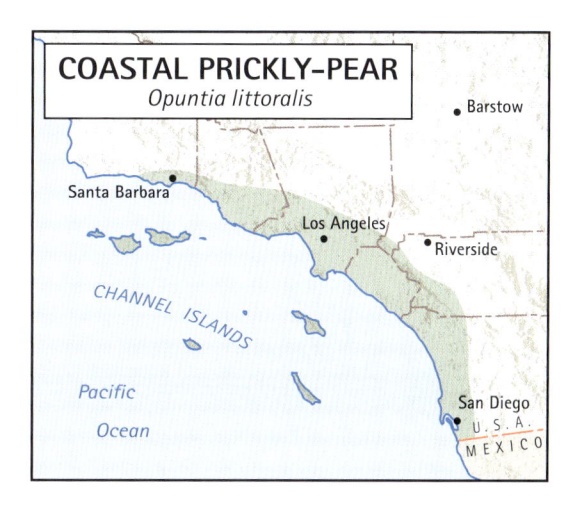

*Coastal prickly-pear hybridizes freely with neighboring prickly-pear species. [Torrey Pines S.R.]*

# TALL PRICKLY-PEAR
## *Opuntia oricola*
(o-PUN-tee-ya o-RIK-o-la)

**Other Common Names**
chaparral prickly-pear, tall coastal prickly-pear

*The depression in the top of this tall prickly-pear's unripe fruit is called the umbilicus. [Torrey Pines S.R.]*

*A tall prickly-pear pad shows flowers, buds, and young fruit. [Torrey Pines S.R.]*

In his 1935 book *California Cactus,* Edgar M. Baxter wrote of an "odd form" of coastal prickly-pear that "grows to eight feet tall . . . Alongside grows the standard form about three feet high." Baxter also observed differences in the fruits of these two dissimilar prickly-pears, noting that "the spines of the tall plants are curved sharply downward." Tall prickly-pear did not get its due recognition until 1964 when it was formally described as a species by Santa Barbara botanist Ralph Philbrick. It had long been treated as a variant of coastal prickly-pear because these two species nearly always occur together (and sometimes with hybrid prickly-pears that exhibit characteristics that are intermediate between the two).

The unusual thing is that these two co-occurring coastal prickly-pear species are readily recognizable and relatively uniform in their appearance, and they do not appear to be hybridizing themselves into extinction. This is partly due to their high degree of asexual vegetative reproduction and to the uncommon occurrence of hybrid progeny. Philbrick demonstrated that tall prickly-pear and coastal prickly pear can hybridize with each other and with local hybrid clones, but the offspring from this cross-pollination produce very few viable seeds. Thus the hybrids tend to remain local, and tall prickly-pear remains—for the most part—reproductively isolated from coastal prickly-pear. Tall prickly-pear, like coastal prickly-pear, may lend some genes to the *Opuntia* X*occidentalis* hybrid complex (see "Prickly-pear Hybrids" on page 124).

Tall prickly-pear has round, yellow-spined pads, yellow flowers, and a tall, robust growth habit. Its fleshy red fruits mature during the dry summer months and provide food for coyotes,

*Tall prickly-pear grows near and resembles coastal prickly-pear but becomes much taller. [Torrey Pines S.R.]*

rabbits, packrats, mice, and birds. Tall prickly-pear can be distinguished from its frequent neighbor, coastal prickly-pear, by the pad and habit features noted above, and by its wider fruit with a deeper umbilicus. Tall prickly-pear prefers well-drained, south-facing slopes below 1500 feet elevation and is often found in disturbed habitats. It grows within approximately 25 miles of the coast in coastal sage scrub, valley grassland, and chaparral habitats from near Ensenada in northern Baja California to the Santa Barbara area. It is also found on all of the Channel Islands.

## Identifying Characteristics

**Habit:** erect, shrubs or small trees, 3.3–9.8 ft. (1–3 m) tall.
**Stems:** dark green, broadly elliptic to nearly round, 4.7–7.5 in. (12–19 cm) wide and 6–10 in. (15–25 cm) long.
**Spines:** 8 to 10 areoles per diagonal row; 5 to 13 spines per areole, straight to curved, spreading, reflexed, translucent yellow or white with yellow tips; longest spines 0.8–1.6 in. (2–4 cm) long;
**Flowers:** tepals yellow, 1–1.6 in. (2.5–4 cm) long; style red with bulbous base; stigma lobes green; filaments orange to yellow; blooms April to May.
**Fruits:** barrel-shaped with deep umbilicus, red to red-purple, pale yellow inside with red seed pulp, juicy, spineless, 1.5–2.4 in. (3.7–6 cm) long.

**TALL PRICKLY-PEAR**
*Opuntia oricola*

# BROWN-SPINED PRICKLY-PEAR
## *Opuntia phaeacantha*
(o-PUN-tee-ya fay-uh-KANTH-uh)

**Recent Synonyms**
*Opuntia phaeacantha* var. *major, O. phaeacantha* var. *mojavensis, O. mojavensis, O. piercei*

**Other Common Names**
desert prickly-pear, Mojave prickly-pear, major prickly-pear, berry prickly-pear, Pierce prostrate prickly-pear

*Green stigma lobes enhance the beauty of brown-spined prickly-pear's yellow flowers. [Riverside Co.]*

Brown-spined prickly-pear displays beautiful color in its spines, flowers, fruits, and pads. The scientific name for brown-spined prickly-pear comes from the Greek words *phaios,* for "dusky" or "gray," and *akantha,* meaning "thorn" or "spine." Although its old spines are dusky gray, the new spines are reddish brown at the base and pale brown or white above; these bicolored spines are a good diagnostic character for this common and variable species.

The new yellow flowers on this cactus often have reddish bases, and in late spring they display a colorful combination of yellow and red tepals, green stigma, green and yellow filaments, and yellow anthers. Flowers of brown-spined prickly-pear, like those of Mojave prickly-pear, are open for only one to two days, starting out yellow and fading to an orange or peach color after five to eight hours. The green-skinned fleshy fruits of early summer ripen to the color of Merlot by summer's end. Brown-spined prickly-pear is colorful even in fall and winter when cold temperatures inhibit the production of green chlorophyll pigments and the underlying purplish betacyanin pigments in its pads become visible.

Like several other widespread prickly-pears and chollas, brown-spined prickly-pear is quite variable, has four or six sets of chromosomes, and is likely to hybridize with similar species in its vicinity. This means it can be challenging to satisfactorily identify. In 1982, Lyman Benson assigned 10 varieties to *Opuntia phaeacantha.* Since then, other cactologists with a better understanding of genetics have placed some of those varieties within the closely related Engelmann prickly-pear and treated others as expressions too variable and indistinct to be considered good varieties. In its typical growth form, brown-spined prickly-pear pads appear aligned next to one another along the ground in one plane, with newer pads arising upwards and outwards.

Brown-spined prickly-pear is the most widespread member of its genus in the southwestern United States and is found in nine states. It ranges from Chihuahua, Mexico north to western Kansas and from central Texas to coastal California. This species spans an elevational range from 300 feet up to approximately 7300 feet and can be found on limestone or metamorphic rocks, as well as in gravelly or sandy soils. It is locally common throughout the mountains of southern Nevada, where it grows in pinyon-juniper woodland and Mojavean creosote bush scrub. In California, brown-spined prickly-pear occurs from the western Colorado Desert through the Mojave; a separate population

*Brown-spined prickly-pear's bicolored young spines are a good diagnostic character. [Mojave N. Pr.]*

*Brown-spined prickly-pear has a broad geographic and altitudinal distribution. [Anza-Borrego Desert S.P.]*

is found in the South Coast Ranges, where it is associated with chaparral. It extends to San Luis Obispo County at the northwest corner of the Cal Poly State University campus—which is farther north and west than any other native California cactus, with the exception of little prickly-pear in Siskiyou County.

## Identifying Characteristics

**Habit:** shrubby, sprawling or prostrate, to 35 in. (90 cm) tall and 8.2 ft. (2.5 m) across.
**Stems:** green, sometimes tinged purple, obovate to nearly round, 2.8–8 in. (7–20 cm) wide and 4–10 in. (10–25 cm) long.
**Spines:** 5 to 7 areoles per diagonal row; 0 to 8 spines per areole, sometimes absent in lower pad segment, stiff, straight to curved, spreading, reddish brown to white, typically darkest at the base, the longest 1–3 in. (2.5–8 cm) long.
**Flowers:** tepals yellow, often with red-orange bases, 1.2–1.6 in. (3–4 cm) long; style white; stigma lobes green; filaments greenish basally with yellow tips; blooms April to July.
**Fruits:** fleshy, green ripening to reddish purple, green internally, spineless, 1.2–2 in. (3–5 cm) long with a narrowed base.

**BROWN-SPINED PRICKLY-PEAR**
*Opuntia phaeacantha*

Species Profiles 123

## MOJAVE PRICKLY-PEAR
*Opuntia polyacantha* var. *erinacea*
(o-PUN-tee-ya paul-ee-uh-KANTH-uh er-in-uh-SEE-uh)
### Recent Synonyms
*Opuntia erinacea, O. erinacea* var. *ursina, O. ursina.*
### Other Common Names
grizzly bear cactus, hairy prickly-pear, old man cactus

## PORCUPINE PRICKLY-PEAR
*Opuntia polyacantha* var. *hystricina*
(hiss-trih-SEE-nuh)
### Recent Synonyms
*Opuntia erinacea* var. *hystricina, O. erinacea* var. *rhodantha, O. hystricina, O. polyacantha* var. *xanthostemma.*

## PLAINS PRICKLY-PEAR
*Opuntia polyacantha* var. *polyacantha*
(paul-ee-uh-KANTH-uh)
### Recent Synonyms
*Opuntia missouriensis, O. polyacantha* var. *juniperina, O. polyacantha* var. *rufispina*
### Other Common Name
starvation prickly-pear, juniper prickly-pear

*Mojave prickly-pear's long, hair-like spines give rise to its other name: grizzly bear cactus. [Death Valley N.P.]*

*Mojave prickly-pear, like other varieties of* Opuntia polyacantha, *is quite variable. [Hiko Range, Lincoln Co.]*

When visitors to the Mojave and Great Basin deserts of California and Nevada see a prickly-pear, they are most likely seeing one of three varieties of *Opuntia polyacantha*. Though the beavertail cactus may be better known to most people, *Opuntia polyacantha* is more widespread and is the most commonly encountered prickly-pear at middle and upper elevations in the two states.

Botanist Bruce Parfitt has extensively studied *Opuntia polyacantha,* and he recognizes five closely related varieties of this prickly-pear. Three of them are found in California and Nevada: Mojave prickly-pear (var. *erinacea*); porcupine prickly-pear (var. *hystricina*); and Plains prickly-pear (var. *polyacantha*). These varieties all have twice the usual number of chromosomes (i.e., are tetraploid) and are therefore apt to be highly variable. Parfitt writes that, "These are weak varieties with many intermediates. All appear to be rather recently derived from a common diploid ancestor." The closest relative appears to be little prickly-pear.

As the lists of recent synonyms suggest, the species as a whole has had a confusing taxonomic history. The variation in the abundance, length, and shape of its spines has led to the naming of numerous expressions as distinct species and varieties, despite the occurrence of intermediate forms within a population. *Opuntia polyacantha* varieties are known to intergrade where their ranges approach each other, so even cactus experts cannot always assign a varietal name to any given specimen. In addition, environmental conditions account for some variation within each variety. For example, Mojave prickly-pears in shady locations tend to have fewer spines than plants in bright light, and those growing at higher, more snow-bound

Old specimens may have abundant chalky white or gray flexuous spines over 6 inches long that sometimes obscure the green surface of the pads. This "long-haired" prickly-pear from the Mojave Desert ranges of California, southern Nevada, and western portions of Arizona and Utah has long been referred to as *Opuntia ursina* or *Opuntia erinacea* var. *ursina*.

Mojave prickly-pear is probably the most common prickly-pear of the middle and upper elevations of desert mountain ranges in California and southern Nevada. This variety spans a remarkable elevational range of approximately 7000 feet. It is found up to 10,400 feet in the White-Inyo Range with pinyon, juniper, mountain mahogany, and sagebrush. It extends down to about 3500 feet in the Turtle Mountains (San Bernardino County), where it mingles with several species of yuccas and chollas and Engelmann hedgehog. Mojave prickly-pear grows in gravelly alluvial soils or perched on limestone or metamorphic rocks.

**Porcupine prickly-pear** has spines of variable lengths that are straight, stiff, and often dark brown. This variety contrasts with Mojave prickly-pear by having fewer spines on its small pads; it may even have no spines at all on the lower portion of the pads. The flowers of these two varieties are identical, though the fruits of porcupine prickly-pear are less spiny.

Porcupine prickly-pear occurs in the Great Basin of eastern California, central and northern

*Mojave prickly-pear grows high up in desert ranges; this one is at 10,400 feet in the White Mountains. [Mono Co.]*

elevations tend to remain shorter with smaller pads. *Opuntia polyacantha* as a species, however, is readily recognizable from our other prickly-pears by its typical low growth form; relatively long, often hair-like spines; and yellow or pink flowers with a green stigma.

**Mojave prickly-pear** is characterized by having long, flexible spines that typically measure 2 to 4 inches in length. The longest spines emerge from closely spaced areoles of the older, lower pads. Mojave prickly-pear has more spines than in other varieties, and each of its areoles has at least one spine. The fruits are very spiny and bur-like. Some populations have bright magenta flowers that, from a distance, look like beavertail cactus blooms.

This variety's long spines resemble coarse hairs and give it an appearance that is the source of one of its other common names—grizzly bear cactus.

*Porcupine prickly-pear has fewer spines and smaller pads than Mojave prickly-pear. [Bodie Hills, Mono Co.]*

Species Profiles

*Porcupine prickly-pear, like this specimen above Bishop, ranges up to 9200 feet in the Eastern Sierra. [Mono Co.]*

*These porcupine prickly-pear blossoms in the Snake Range produce a bounty of pollen. [White Pine Co.]*

Nevada and Utah, east to the Colorado Plateau, and south to western New Mexico and northern Arizona. There is a disjunct population reported from the north side of Clark Mountain in northeastern San Bernardino County, California. Porcupine prickly-pear inhabits a range of soil types in sagebrush scrub, pinyon-juniper woodland, and montane chaparral.

Porcupine prickly-pears in the eastern Sierra Nevada are found at elevations up to 9200 feet. Some of these Sierran cacti have a few short spines above; they also lack spines in the lower areoles of the older pads, like typical porcupine prickly-pears. Others in the area may show the longer, wispy spines characteristic of Mojave prickly-pear, while still others exhibit long, stiff, reddish brown spines more common to porcupine prickly-pear. These cacti exemplify what taxonomists refer to as "morphological intergradation" between two varieties.

**Plains prickly-pear** is a shorter and smaller variety than the other two. Its spines are no longer than about 1.5 inches, and its major and minor spines are distinct with no size gradation between the long, thick spines and short, slender spines. This contrasts to the spines of porcupine prickly-pear that are graded in size and much longer and more numerous. Members of the Lewis and Clark Expedition could attest to Plains prickly-pear's troublesome spines, which punctured their moccasin-clad feet. On July 15, 1805, at a spot just above the Great Falls of the Missouri River in Montana, Meriwether Lewis wrote that "The prickley pear is now in full blume and forms one of the beauties as well as the greatest pests of the plains."

Plains prickly-pear has a huge range, occurring from New Mexico north into Alberta and Saskatchewan, Canada, and east to the Dakotas and central Kansas. Its range extends westward into northeastern Nevada, where Plains prickly-pear can be found in the northern Schell Creek Range of central White Pine County and the Toano Range of eastern Elko County.

### Identifying Characteristics

**Habit:** shrubby, sprawling, low-growing clumps, to 20 in. (50 cm) tall and 6.6 ft. (2 m) across; prostrate and up to 10 in. (25 cm) tall in var. *polyacantha*.
**Stems:** green, elliptic to obovate, 2–4 in. (5–10 cm) wide and 4–8 in. (10–20 cm) long in var. *erinacea*; 2–3.2 in. (5–8 cm) wide and 3.2–4 in.

green; filaments white to pale yellow, or red in pink-flowered forms; blooms May to July.
**Fruits:** green, drying to tan, densely spiny and bur-like in var. *erinacea,* stout and less spiny in var. *polyacantha,* least spiny in var. *hystricina;* 0.6–1.2 in. (1.5–3 cm) long.

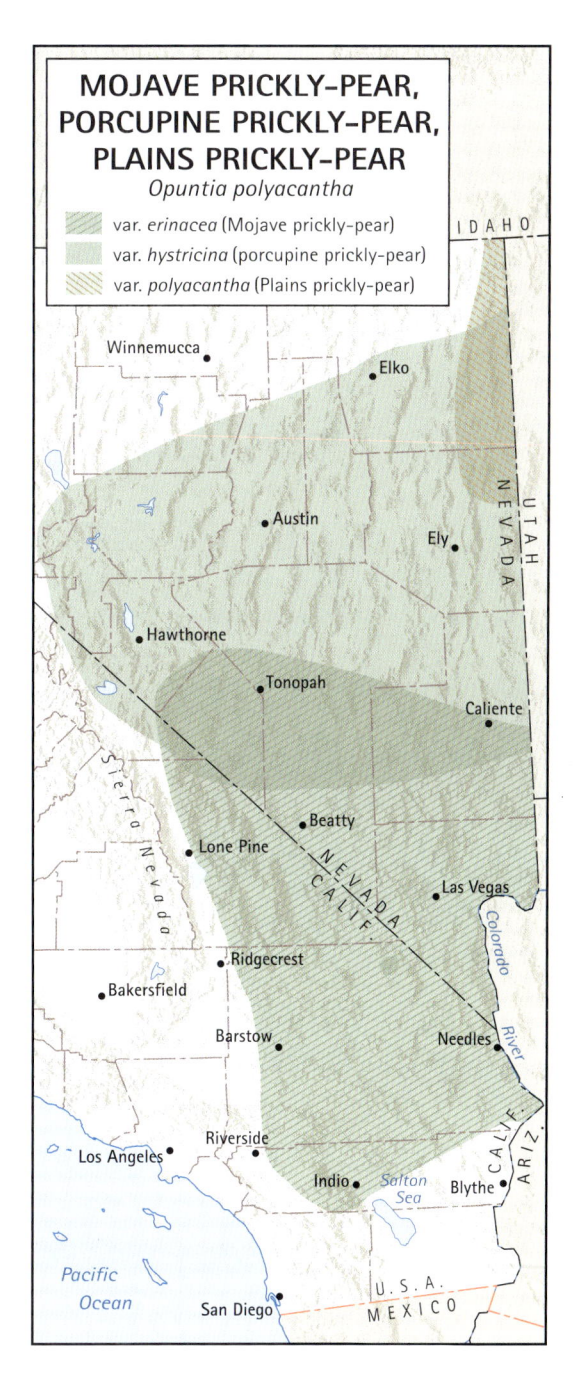

*Plains prickly-pear ranges across the Great Plains and also extends west into eastern Nevada. [Humboldt N.F.]*

**MOJAVE PRICKLY-PEAR, PORCUPINE PRICKLY-PEAR, PLAINS PRICKLY-PEAR**
*Opuntia polyacantha*
- var. *erinacea* (Mojave prickly-pear)
- var. *hystricina* (porcupine prickly-pear)
- var. *polyacantha* (Plains prickly-pear)

(8–10 cm) long in var. *hystricina;* obovate to round, 1.6–4.3 in. (4–11 cm) wide and 1.6–4.7 in. (4–12 cm) long in var. *polyacantha.*

**Spines:** 8 to 14 areoles per diagonal row in var. *erinacea,* 8 to 10 in var. *hystricina,* 6 to 11 in var. *polyacantha;* 1 to 18 spines per areole in var. *erinacea,* 0 to 6 in var. *hystricina,* 0 to 10 in var. *polyacantha;* straight and stiff or flexible and descending, yellow, brown or (usually) pale gray, the longest usually 1.6–3.5 in. (4–9 cm) long, but up to 7 in. (18 cm) long in var. *erinacea;* straight and stiff, yellow-gray to (usually) dark brown, the longest 2–3.2 in. (5–8 cm) long in var. *hystricina;* major spines usually 1 to 3 per areole, mostly deflexed, or erect at stem tip, thick, gray to light brown, 0.8–1.6 in. (2–4 cm) long, minor spines 0 to 5 per areole, deflexed, slender, white, to 0.4 in. (1 cm) long in var. *polyacantha.*

**Flowers:** tepals yellow to orange, or bright pink, 1–1.6 in. (2.5–4 cm) long; style white; stigma lobes

Species Profiles 127

# PRICKLY-PEAR HYBRIDS

## CURVE-SPINED PRICKLY-PEAR or SEARCHLIGHT PRICKLY-PEAR
*Opuntia Xcurvispina*
(o-PUN-tee-ya ker-vi-SPINE-uh)

*Curved-spined prickly-pear, seen here in the McCullough Range, is found between 3000 and 5000 feet. [Clark Co.]*

*Top: Curve-spined prickly-pear is a hybrid between pancake and brown-spined prickly-pear. [Clark Co.] Bottom: There are only three known locations for curve-spined prickly-pear. [Clark Co.]*

Opuntia Xcurvispina is a hybrid between pancake prickly-pear, *O. chlorotica,* and brown-spined prickly-pear, *O. phaeacantha*. It is a shrubby cactus, 1.6 to 5 feet (0.5–1.5 m) tall, that is intermediate in growth habit between the tall, single-trunked pancake prickly-pear and the low, spreading brown-spined prickly-pear. Opuntia Xcurvispina, as its scientific name implies, has spines that are twisted and weakly curved. The longest spines are usually deflexed, though less than in pancake prickly-pear. They measure approximately 2 inches (4–6 cm) long and have reddish brown bases and yellowish tips (similar to brown-spined prickly-pear). The pads are broadly oval, but widest near the tip with an extended marginal crescent of crowded areoles and glochids. The flowers, which open from May to June, have yellow tepals, yellow filaments, a greenish white stigma, and a white style with a broad base.

The only known locations where *Opuntia*

*This western prickly-pear hybrid in Caspers Wilderness Park has an erect growth habit. [Orange Co.]*

*A hybrid that involves at least three parents, western prickly-pear typically has large pads. [Orange Co.]*

Xcurvispina grows are in the southern Mc-Coullough Range west of Searchlight, Nevada, the east side of California's New York Mountains, and a small region of northwestern Arizona. Curve-spined prickly-pear occurs at elevations from about 3000 to 5000 feet in Joshua tree woodland and pinyon-juniper woodland.

## WESTERN PRICKLY-PEAR
### *Opuntia Xoccidentalis*
(o-PUN-tee-ya ox-ih-den-TAL-iss)
**Recent Synonyms**
*Opuntia engelmannii* var. *occidentalis*,
*O. occidentalis*

*Opuntia Xoccidentalis* is a hybrid that probably involves at least three parents. Two of the likely parents are coastal prickly-pear *(O. littoralis)* and the hybrid of Engelmann prickly-pear and brown-spined prickly-pear *(O. engelmannii* var. *engelmannii* X *O. phaeacantha)*; tall prickly-pear *(O. oricola)* may be the third parent. Western prickly-pear has been treated in the past as a variety of *Opuntia engelmannii* and also as a species, but it has always been a source of confusion for taxonomists. This variable hybrid complex has a sprawling to erect growth habit and may stand over 5 feet (1.5 m) tall. It has 3 to 6 spines per areole—fewer than coastal prickly-pear—and they are often absent from the lower portion (10%) of the pads. The spines have brown bases and yellowish tips, and the ephemeral leaves are awl-shaped and relatively long. The pads of western prickly-pear get quite large, measuring 7.5 to 14 inches (19 to 35 cm) long, and because of this trait it was long assumed that Indian-fig cactus *(Opuntia ficus-indica)* was one of the hybrid's parents. The flower of *Opuntia Xoccidentalis* has tepals that are mostly yellow, yellow or white filaments, a green stigma, and a pink or white style.

Western prickly-pear forms extensive stands in coastal sage scrub and chaparral, where it grows with coastal prickly-pear, Vasey prickly-pear, and other plants of these communities. It occurs from the Channel Islands and the southern California coastal plain eastward to the foothills of the San

Gabriel Mountains and from San Diego County to Santa Barbara County at elevations below 1300 feet. At locations that are closer to the inland edge of its range, this hybrid may look less like coastal prickly-pear and more like brown-spined prickly-pear.

## VASEY PRICKLY-PEAR or APRICOT PRICKLY-PEAR
*Opuntia Xvaseyi*

*(o-PUN-tee-ya VAY-see-eye)*

**Recent Synonyms**
*Opuntia covillei, O. littoralis* var. *austrocalifornica, O. littoralis* var. *vaseyi*

*Opuntia Xvaseyi* is a hybrid between coastal prickly-pear *(O. littoralis)* and brown-spined prickly-pear *(O. phaeacantha)*. This hybrid was first described as a species and later treated as two separate varieties of coastal prickly-pear by Lyman Benson. This hybrid prickly-pear, like both of its parents, tends to sprawl and spread, but may reach a height of 3 to 4 feet (1.2 m). It has 1 to 6 spines per areole, but they appear in the upper two-thirds or less of each

*Top: Vasey prickly-pear grows in coastal sage scrub, chaparral, and disturbed grassy areas of California. [Orange Co.] Bottom: Spines only grow from areoles in the upper two-thirds of the pads on Vasey prickly-pear. [Orange Co.]*

*The parents of this common but unnamed hybrid are brown-spined and Engelmann prickly-pear. [Joshua Tree N.P.]*

pad only. Its spines are generally flattened, unlike those of coastal prickly-pear, and it has crescent-shaped tufts of glochids along the upper edge of the areoles. Vasey prickly-pear often occurs with western prickly-pear, but the two hybrids are not difficult to tell apart. Vasey prickly-pear has narrow pads about half the size of those on western prickly-pear, and it is generally shorter, with fewer spines. Compared to other prickly-pears, the flowers of Vasey prickly-pear are small, with tepals that are dull red, orange, or yellow; they have yellowish orange filaments, yellow anthers, and a pink style with greenish stigma lobes.

This hybrid prickly-pear is found in coastal sage scrub, chaparral, and disturbed grassy areas. It ranges from the southern California coast inland to the western foothills of the Transverse and Peninsular ranges, from Ventura County south to San Diego County.

*Opuntia X demissa* is a name that has been used in the past for the cactus resulting from the cross between coastal prickly-pear *(O. littoralis)* and tall prickly-pear *(O. oricola)*. But it, too, may involve either Engelmann prickly-pear, brown-spined prickly-pear, or their unnamed hybrid progeny, in addition to tall prickly-pear. In any case, the hybrids between coastal prickly-pear and tall prickly-pear do not consistently resemble each other, and *Opuntia X demissa* is not treated in recent floras.

In addition to those named and described in floras and discussed above, other prickly-pear hybrids from California and Nevada include the following:

*Opuntia phaeacantha* X *Opuntia engelmannii* var. *engelmannii*: common in many areas, and seen in the lower San Felipe Valley east of Highway S2, at the edge of Anza-Borrego Desert State Park and in the Wonderland of Rocks area of Joshua Tree National Park.

*Opuntia phaeacantha* X *Opuntia ficus-indica*: documented to date only from a location east of San Luis Obispo, California, near the northern extension of brown-spined prickly-pear.

*Opuntia phaeacantha* X *Opuntia polyacantha* var. *erinacea*: documented near the Grand Canyon and may also occur near Spring Crest along Highway 74 on the north slope of the Santa Rosa Mountains, California.

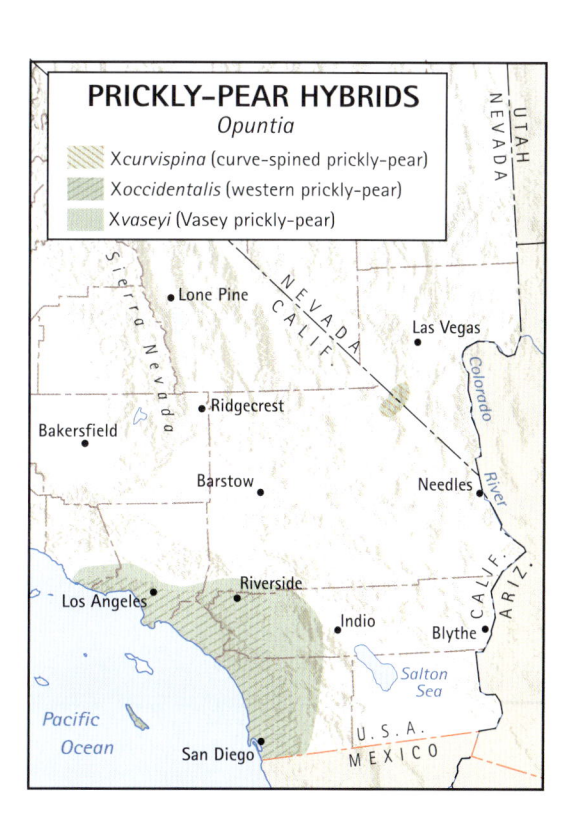

Mountain cactus • *Pediocactus simpsonii*     ARTWORK BY SUSAN BAZELL

# *Pediocactus*
## PLAINS CACTUS

The species of *Pediocactus* are mostly endemic to small areas and are very popular among cactophiles due to their beauty and rarity. Britton and Rose described this genus, commonly referred to as Plains cactus, in 1913. They gave it the scientific name *Pediocactus* from the Greek word *pedion,* meaning a "plain," in reference to the location of its members in the western Great Plains and the intermountain West. Other previous names for the genus, such as *Navajoa, Puebloa,* and *Utahia,* also allude to the scenic areas *Pediocactus* inhabits.

*Pediocactus* are solitary or clustered low-growing cacti that vary widely in flower and spine characteristics. These cacti may have flowers of yellow, pink, magenta, or white and central spines that are rigid, flexible, hair-like, stout, twisted, curved, straight, or absent altogether. The seemingly disparate members of *Pediocactus* are unified by similarities in their fruiting structures: all have floral remnants that fall away early from the developing fruit (leaving a lid-like cap) and dry fruits that open along a vertical slit when ripe. Genetic analyses also show that the members of *Pediocactus* are clearly related, yet not closely related to their traditional cohort, *Sclerocactus*. The nine species of *Pediocactus* are found from southwestern South Dakota to central Nevada, north to Montana, and south to northern New Mexico. Only the most variable and wide-ranging species, *Pediocactus simpsonii,* occurs in our region.

# MOUNTAIN CACTUS
## *Pediocactus simpsonii*
(pee-dee-oh-KAK-tus SIMP-sun-ee-eye)

**Recent Synonyms**

*Pediocactus simpsonii* ssp. *bensonii*, *P. simpsonii* ssp. *idahoensis*, *P. simpsonii* var. *hermannii*, *P. simpsonii* var. *indraianus*, *P. simpsonii* var. *minor*, *P. simpsonii* var. *robustior*

**Other Common Names**

mountain ball cactus, Simpson hedgehog cactus, hedgehog thistle, snowball cactus

*When not in flower, a small mountain cactus can easily blend into gravelly soil. [White Pine Co.]*

Mountain cactus lives up to its name since it grows at higher elevations than any other cactus in North America. It is also widespread and remarkably adaptable, yet distinctly difficult to spot. Its small stature, ability to retract into the soil, and cryptic appearance allow mountain cactus to blend with its rocky substrate and become nearly invisible, especially during the 11 months of the year when not in flower. Cactus expert Lyman Benson wrote of *Pediocactus* species that, "Even when their approximate location is known, days of searching may be consumed in finding the plants."

In the spring, mountain cactus swells up from winter moisture, emerges from the gravelly soil, and produces small, beautiful flowers with a sweet, jasmine-like fragrance. Flowering mountain cactus may sit perched above the ground or remain nestled beneath the soil surface with its flowers displayed just above ground level. Mature round and spiny mountain cacti range in size from that of a tangerine to a cantaloupe, with flowers that are white, pink, or pale yellowish orange. Flowering occurs in late April to May at lower valley elevations and from June to July in higher, snow-bound mountain habitats.

Mountain cactus may be difficult to distinguish from beehive cactus, our region's other widespread, mountain-inhabiting cactus, especially when not in bloom or with fruits. The tepals of mountain cactus are broader, and they lack the fringed margins exhibited by beehive cactus tepals. Mountain cactus flowers arise from the areole very close to the tubercle tip, while the flowers of beehive cactus are borne near the base of the upper tubercles at the end of a longitudinal groove. The unique fruit of mountain cactus is also helpful in separating it from beehive cactus. The fruit has a flat, lidded tip with a circular scar, which marks where the floral remnant fell off. In addition, the radial spines of mountain cactus splay out to the

*Mountain cactus ranges up to 11,800 feet in elevation; no other North American cactus grows higher. [White Pine Co.]*

*Mountain cactus swells up in spring from winter moisture and produces beautiful, fragrant blossoms. [White Pine Co.]*

Nevada to north-central New Mexico, Colorado, and Wyoming, and it continues north into central Idaho and southwestern Montana.

### Identifying Characteristics

**Habit:** mostly round, sometimes egg-shaped or with tip depressed, solitary or occasionally clustered, basal half sometimes buried.

**Stems:** green to gray-green 1–6 in. (2.5–15 cm) wide and 1–6 in. (2.5–15 cm) tall; tubercles distinct; areoles oval to round, hairy.

**Spines:** 16 to 46 per areole, smooth; radial spines 15 to 35 per areole, white, narrow, widely spreading, to 0.5 in. (1.3 cm) long; central spines 1 to 11 per areole, basal half white to yellow, tips reddish brown, rigid, straight to slightly curved, longest spines to 0.8 in. (2 cm) long.

**Flowers:** tepals white, pink, pale yellow, or pale orange; inner tepals 0.5–1 in. (1.2–2.5 cm) long; flowers up to 2 in. (5 cm) across; stigma lobes yellow to green, occasionally orange; blooms April to July.

**Fruits:** short-cylindrical with flat tip, green drying to reddish brown, spineless; 0.25–0.4 in. (6–11 mm) long.

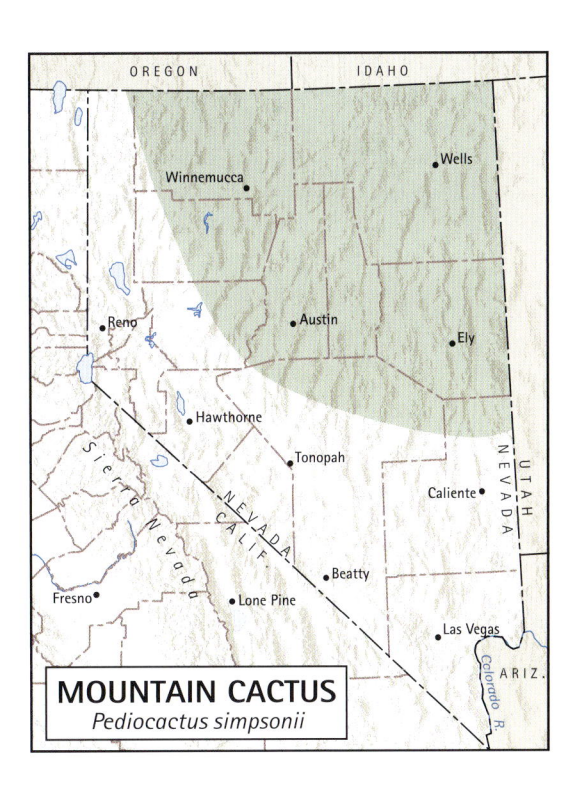

side more than those of beehive cactus and are generally shorter and narrower. The tubercles of mountain cactus are also shorter than those of beehive cactus.

Like other widespread cactus species, mountain cactus is quite variable in its overall size, spination, and flower color. Although some botanists recognize three varieties, mountain cactus is treated in the *Flora of North America* as one "exceedingly variable species" because it shows a continuous range of variation throughout its distribution.

Mountain cactus is found on calcareous soils in sagebrush scrub at elevations as low as 4600 feet. It also grows among limestone and metamorphic outcrops in pinyon-juniper woodland and coniferous forest dominated by limber pine. It even occurs in alpine habitats as high as 11,800 feet in the ranges of central Nevada. Mountain cactus extends eastward from central and northern

**MOUNTAIN CACTUS**
*Pediocactus simpsonii*

Johnson pineapple cactus • *Sclerocactus johnsonii*   ARTWORK BY E.O. MURMAN

# *Sclerocactus*
## EAGLE-CLAW or FISHHOOK CACTUS

When Nathaniel Britton and Joseph Rose formally described this genus in 1922, they gave it the descriptor *sclero,* which is Greek for "hard, cruel or obstinate," and wrote that this name referred to "the formidable hooked spines, which hold on in a most aggravating manner." In contrast to their intimidating spines, *Sclerocactus* have relatively large and brilliantly colored flowers. Another interesting trait of *Sclerocactus* species is their change in morphology from juvenile to adult plants: young plants are generally round with prominent tubercles and few, short central spines, but adults are more elongate, with tubercles organized into ribs, and they possess more numerous, longer central spines.

Taxonomists recognize between 14 and 18 species of *Sclerocactus;* the number is not firm because they do not agree on the composition of this genus in regards to species of five related genera. *Sclerocactus* are found from northern Mexico and Texas north to Colorado and west to eastern California. Five species occur in Nevada, and two of these reach California's Mojave Desert.

Two species of *Sclerocactus* from Nevada's Great Basin Desert are listed as sensitive by the Nevada Natural Heritage Program and by the Bureau of Land Management. One-third of *Sclerocactus* species are listed as rare or endangered by the federal government and are managed by the U.S. Fish and Wildlife Service. Many *Sclerocactus* are becoming increasingly rare because they have limited ranges, do not reproduce dependably, are difficult to propagate, and are collected illegally by unscrupulous growers.

# BLAINE FISHHOOK CACTUS
## *Sclerocactus blainei*
(skler-oh-KAK-tus BLAIN-eye)

**Recent Synonyms**
*Sclerocactus schlesseri, S. spinosior* ssp. *blainei*

**Other Common Names**
Blaine pincushion, Desert Valley fishhook cactus, Schlesser pincushion, devil's claw

*Blaine fishhook cactus grows in mottled clay soil and is well camouflaged when not in bloom. [Lincoln Co.]*

*Bright pink flowers and long, ribbon-like spines are characteristic of Blaine fishhook cactus. [Lincoln Co.]*

This pink-flowered marvel is hard to miss when in bloom yet practically invisible when not flowering. The rough-textured mottled soil acts as the ideal camouflaging background for plants growing in the open. In addition, this cactus's long, pale, ribbon-like spines resemble the dried leaves of galleta grass, with which it grows.

Blaine fishhook cactus, like other species in the genus, shows high variability in its spine characters, both between populations and between younger and older plants. These variations "have made *Sclerocactus* a notoriously difficult group for species-level identification," according to botanists Kenneth Heil and J. Mark Porter. Porter theorizes that the small populations of Blaine fishhook cactus—and *Sclerocactus* species in general—are relics of a wider distribution in the past. They are now more restricted in their interbreeding, which has led to greater variation between populations and the eventual evolution of new species.

Blaine fishhook cactus was first described in 1985 by Stanley Welsh and Kaye Thorne. It has been treated as a subspecies of Engelmann fishhook cactus (*Sclerocactus spinosior*)—a cactus native to southwest Utah—and it is also similar to Great Basin fishhook cactus (*Sclerocactus pubispinus*). Blaine fishhook cactus is treated here as indistinct from Schlesser pincushion (*Sclerocactus schlesseri*), but some botanists consider the narrower-stemmed Schlesser pincushion a separate species. Blaine

The colorful eroded badlands and gray cryptobiotic soils found in parts of Lincoln and Nye counties, Nevada, provide the rare Blaine fishhook cactus with perfect conditions for its survival. It thrives in the unusual gravelly clay calcareous soils along some desert washes and flats.

fishhook cactus differs from both Great Basin and Engelmann fishhook cactus in having a ribbon-like upper central spine nearly 3 inches long and 1/10-inch wide, as well as larger flowers. All central spines other than the upper ribbon-like one may be hooked, which is another characteristic that separates Blaine fishhook cactus from other fishhook cacti of the Great Basin. The pubescent spines of younger plants become more papery and flattened as the plants age.

Blaine fishhook cactus is known only from approximately 10 sites in Nye and Lincoln counties and from several locations in adjacent Iron County, Utah. This rare cactus is vulnerable to poaching and is advertised on at least one European website as "a particular prize among specialist collectors." It occurs at elevations from 4800 to 6000 feet in sagebrush scrub communities and in valleys dominated by shadscale and galleta grass.

*A rare species that is vulnerable to poaching, Blaine fishhook cactus was first described in 1985. [Lincoln Co.]*

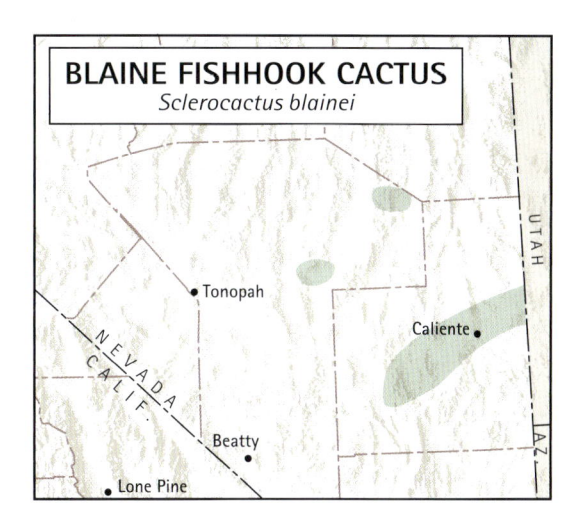

## BLAINE FISHHOOK CACTUS
*Sclerocactus blainei*

### Identifying Characteristics

**Habit:** egg-shaped to spherical, usually solitary or with few stems.

**Stems:** green to dark green, 0.8–3.1 in. (2–8 cm) wide and 1.2–6 in. (3–15 cm) tall; ribs 6 to 13, but with prominent tubercles.

**Spines:** 7 to 23 per areole; radial spines 6 to 16 per areole, white, spreading, pubescent when young; central spines 1 to 7 per areole, white, red, brown, or black, curved to strongly hooked, sometimes flattened, 0.4–2.8 in. (1–7 cm) long; main upper central spine ribbon-like, widest, tipped white or dark, 1.4–2.8 in. (3.5–7 cm) long; lateral and main lower central spines tan to black, usually hooked; spines dense but not obscuring the stem.

**Flowers:** outer tepals reddish brown with pink to dark red margins; inner tepals lavender, pink, or reddish purple, 0.6–0.8 in. (1.5–2 cm) long, widely spreading; flowers 0.8–1.6 in. (2–4 cm) across; filaments reddish; stigma lobes yellow; blooms in May.

**Fruits:** barrel-shaped, dry, scaly, spineless, pale red, to 0.6 in. (1.5 cm) long; opening along 2–4 vertical slits that form before fruits dry.

# JOHNSON PINEAPPLE CACTUS
*Sclerocactus johnsonii*
(skler-oh-KAK-tus JOHN-sun-ee-eye)

**Recent Synonyms**
*Echinomastus johnsonii, Neolloydia johnsonii*

**Other Common Names**
pineapple cactus, pygmy barrel cactus, beehive cactus

*Johnson pineapple cactus is armored with spines that are strongly curved but not hooked. [Mud Hills, Clark Co.]*

*Each Johnson pineapple flower stays open for 5 to 7 days, which is longer than most cactus blossoms. [Clark Co.]*

Johnson pineapple cactus was first described as a species of *Echinocactus* by Charles C. Parry in 1871. Parry named this handsome species for Joseph E. Johnson (1817–1882) of St. George, Utah, a horticulturist and friend to Dr. Parry. Although Johnson pineapple cactus is treated under the genus *Echinomastus* in *Flora of North America*, it is recognized here as a species of *Sclerocactus;* recent genetic studies have shown that *Sclerocactus johnsonii* is more closely related to other *Sclerocactus* species than it is to species in the genus *Echinomastus.*

Johnson pineapple cactus can be distinguished from Mojave fishhook cactus, the only other *Sclerocactus* within its range, by its shorter, unhooked spines, obvious tubercle protrusions along the ribs, and fruits that open along a single lengthwise split. Johnson pineapple cactus differs from other Nevada fishhook cacti by its lack of hooked spines.

In California, Johnson pineapple cactus is located on alluvial fans and hills and grows only in rocky, limestone soils; in Nevada, it occurs on both limestone and granitic substrates. Johnson

By late April, when the desert annuals of Death Valley have begun to wither up and blow away, the large pink flowers of Johnson pineapple cactus are just coming into bloom in the adjacent Funeral Mountains. The showy funnel-shaped flowers of Johnson pineapple cactus are maroon at the inside of their bases and have yellow anthers that contrast beautifully with the red filaments and lower tepals. Unlike most cactus flowers, which open for one to three days, Johnson pineapple cactus flowers may remain open for five to seven successive days; as a result, they can look a bit haggard after being buffeted by the Mojave Desert winds.

*The rocky limestone soil on this alluvial fan offers good habitat for Johnson pineapple cactus. [Death Valley N.P.]*

pineapple cactus grows mostly in open areas of Mojavean creosote bush scrub at elevations from 1700 to 4600 feet. It is found with a variety of desert shrubs, as well as chollas, beavertail, and Engelmann hedgehog cactus.

Although Johnson pineapple cactus is native to four states, its distribution is more limited than its relative, Mojave fishhook cactus. In California, Johnson pineapple cactus extends from the Funeral Mountains south to the Kingston Range and then east to the Muddy Mountains of Clark County, Nevada. It also occurs in southwestern Utah and farther south in western Arizona. Some populations of Johnson pineapple cactus with yellow flowers are found in the Black Mountains and Newberry Mountains in southern Nevada. This yellow-flowered form, recognized by some botanists as *Sclerocactus johnsonii* var. *lutescens,* has been called chartreuse pineapple cactus or yellow beehive cactus.

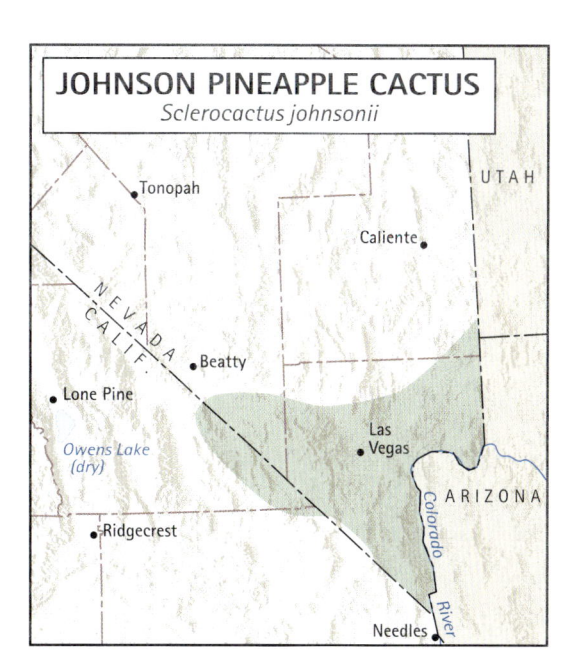

## Identifying Characteristics

**Habit:** erect, barrel-shaped to cylindrical, solitary or with few stems.

**Stems:** pale green, firm, 2.8–6 in. (7–15 cm) wide and 4–10 in. (10–25 cm) tall; ribs 13 to 21, but each tubercle distinct.

**Spines:** 13 to 25 per areole; radial spines 9 to 16 per areole, pale pink to gray, spreading; central spines 4 to 9 per areole, pink to reddish, aging gray to black, spreading, straight to strongly curved (but not hooked), to 1.6 in. (4 cm) long, mostly obscuring the stem.

**Flowers:** outer tepals mauve to pale pink; inner tepals rose to magenta, or yellow, dark red at tepal bases, 1.6–2.6 in. (4–6.5 cm) long, widely spreading; flowers 2–3 in. (5–7.7 cm) across; filaments reddish; stigma lobes yellowish green; blooms March to May.

**Fruits:** nearly round to oblong, dry, scaly, spineless, green to brown, to 0.7 in. (1.8 cm) long.

# TONOPAH FISHHOOK CACTUS
*Sclerocactus nyensis*
(skler-oh-KAK-tus nye-EN-sis)

**Recent Synonyms**
*Pediocactus nyensis*

**Other Common Names**
Nye fishhook cactus, Nye pincushion

*Most of the time, the diminutive Tonopah fishhook cactus is hard to spot—until it blooms. [Esmeralda Co.]*

Tonopah fishhook cactus is Nevada's only endemic cactus species and is one of the rarest and smallest cacti in our region. This diminutive spiny wonder seems to erupt from gray-brown gravelly volcanic tuff to produce a bright pink flower that stands out like a beacon to all bees (and botanists) in the vicinity. The volcanic tuff in which it grows is inhospitable to all but the hardiest desert plants, but Tonopah fishhook cactus somehow looks right at home in this environment. Young plants barely protrude above the gravel surface; they are made visible only by their green tubercles topped with woolly areoles and radiating spines. Older plants perch like spiny domes on the open gravelly slopes or occasionally beneath the meager shade of a four-wing saltbush.

*Sclerocactus nyensis* was named for one of its home counties (Nye) by German botanist Fritz Hochstätter in 1992. It is most closely related to grama grass cactus, or toumeya, *(Sclerocactus papyracanthus)*, from the Chihuahuan Desert, and Mojave fishhook cactus, with which it sometimes occurs.

Tonopah fishhook cactus somewhat resembles a small young Mojave fishhook cactus because of its many hooked spines and pink flowers, but its spines are shorter and less numerous and its flowers and fruits are much smaller than those of Mojave fishhook cactus. Tonopah fishhook cactus differs from our other two rare Nevada fishhook cacti in having six to eight central spines (in older, larger plants), fewer ribbon-like spines, and an indehiscent fruit. The barrel-shaped fruits of Tonopah fishhook cactus dry without opening along regular slits and hold unusual furrowed seeds that resemble tiny raisins.

Tonopah fishhook cactus is currently known from only three populations, which are located southwest, south, and southeast of Tonopah in Esmeralda and Nye counties. The size of these populations is subject to large fluctuations depending on the vagaries of precipitation, germination, and insect infestation. Fishhook cacti are susceptible to attack by cactus longhorn beetles, parasitic moths, and probably other insects. Unfortunately, cactus poachers also seek this species out, and at least one of its populations has been negatively impacted by gold-mining activities.

Tonopah fishhook cactus grows in sparsely vegetated shadscale scrub and sagebrush scrub where the northeastern Mojave Desert transitions into the Great Basin. It is found in both pale and dark volcanic soils at elevations from 4900 to 5800 feet. In some places it occurs with Mojave fishhook cactus, beavertail cactus, and silver cholla.

*A young Tonopah fishhook cactus may barely protrude from the volcanic tuff in which it grows. [Esmeralda Co.]*

*This is the habitat of Tonopah fishhook cactus, a rare species and Nevada's only endemic cactus. [Esmeralda Co.]*

## Identifying Characteristics

**Habit:** egg-shaped, spherical, or short cylindrical, solitary or with few stems.

**Stems:** green to pale green, 1.6–4 in. (4–10 cm) wide and 2–4.7 in. (5–12 cm) tall; ribs 12 to 15 on older plants, tubercles evident on younger plants.

**Spines:** 14 to 22 per areole; radial spines 10 to 14 per areole, white, straight, flat, less than 0.8 in. long (2 cm); central spines 4 to 8 per areole; 3 to 5 lower and lateral main spines red to reddish brown, usually hooked, 0.8–2.4 in. (2–6 cm) long; main upper central spines 1 to 2, occasionally 3, white, straight, flat, usually not hooked, 1–1.8 in. (2.5–4.5 cm) long; spines dense, partially obscuring the stem.

**Flowers:** outer tepals greenish purple with purple to magenta margins; inner tepals rose-purple to magenta, 1.2–1.6 in. (3–4 cm) long; flowers 0.8–1 in. (2–2.5 cm) across; filaments green to yellow; stigma lobes greenish yellow; blooms April to May.

**Fruits:** barrel-shaped, dry, spineless, green to pale red, to 0.8 in. (2 cm) long; indehiscent or opening along irregular slits.

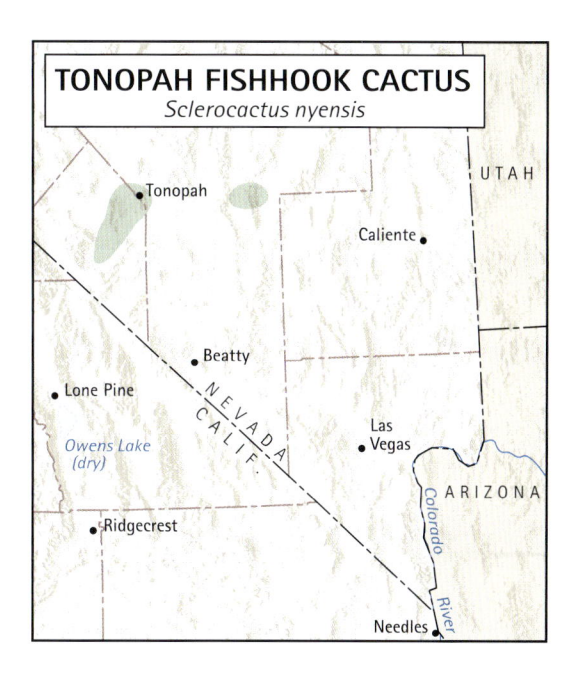

### TONOPAH FISHHOOK CACTUS
*Sclerocactus nyensis*

# MOJAVE FISHHOOK CACTUS
## *Sclerocactus polyancistrus*
(skler-oh-KAK-tus paul-lee-ann-SIS-trus)
### Other Common Names
hermit cactus, pineapple cactus, Mojave eagle-claw cactus, red-spined fishhook cactus, long-spined fishhook cactus, devil-claw cactus

*Mojave fishhook cactus is also known as hermit cactus due to its propensity to grow as a lone individual. [Inyo Co.]*

*The largest species in its genus, Mojave fishhook cactus has a showy flower with a spicy fragrance. [Inyo Co.]*

Mojave fishhook cactus is a favorite of many cactus enthusiasts because of its unique beauty and rarity. The large bright rose-purple flowers that arise from the stem tips are captivating, and they emit a wonderful spicy fragrance. Mojave fishhook cactus—the largest species of the genus—is roughly the size and shape of a pineapple, and its sinuous red and white spines give this cactus a shaggy appearance. Its occurrence in widely scattered populations of lone individuals explains how it received one of its other common names—hermit cactus. Although Mojave fishhook cactus is currently not listed as rare or endangered, its limited distribution and popularity among illegal collectors have kept it on watch-lists of public agencies and our two states' native plant societies.

Mojave fishhook cactus was first observed and collected in 1854 by John M. Bigelow, who encountered "this elegant and striking species" during the Pacific Railroad Survey "at the headwaters of the Mohave" (northeast of present-day Barstow). Bigelow described and named this cactus with George Engelmann in their account of the survey, "The Report of the Botany of the Expedition," published in 1856.

An important aspect of the ecology of Mojave fishhook cactus (and of *Sclerocactus* species in general) is its strong susceptibility to rot as a result of damage from infestation by cactus longhorn beetles and parasitic pyralid moths or from herbivory by small mammals. Cactus longhorn beetles, for example, lay their eggs at the base of the stem of a Mojave fishhook cactus. The emergent larvae bore into and feed on the succulent stem tissue. They eventually create a pupal cell near the cactus base, and the plant often dies. Cactus skeletons that are intact are a sure sign of death caused by insect larvae, but cactus carcasses that are torn apart exhibit the effects of herbivory, mostly by desert packrats. Seedlings and juveniles of Mojave fishhook cactus are often found at the base of their decaying parent

*A Mojave fishhook cactus in the Inyo Mountains displays the long curving spines typical of the species. [Inyo Co.]*

## Identifying Characteristics

**Habit:** erect, barrel-shaped to elongate cylindrical, solitary or with few stems.

**Stems:** green, firm, 2–3.5 in. (5–9 cm) wide and 4–15.8 in. (10–40 cm) tall; ribs 13 to 17, well-developed with no visible tubercles.

**Spines:** 19 to 27 per areole; radial spines 10 to 15 per areole, white, straight, short, spreading to form a circle, 0.8–2.4 in. (2–6 cm) long; central spines 9 to 12 per areole, pink to reddish, aging white, straight to curved or twisted, 5 to 8 hooked, longest spines to 3.5 in. (9 cm) long, mostly obscuring the stem.

**Flowers:** tepals rose-purple to magenta with dark red to dull green at tepal bases; inner tepals 2–2.4 in. (5–6 cm) long; flowers funnel-shaped, 2 in. (5 cm) across; filaments greenish yellow; stigma lobes yellowish green; blooms April to June.

**Fruits:** barrel-shaped, green ripening to red, with few white-fringed scales, spineless, irregularly dehiscent at the base; 1–2 in. (2.5–5 cm) long.

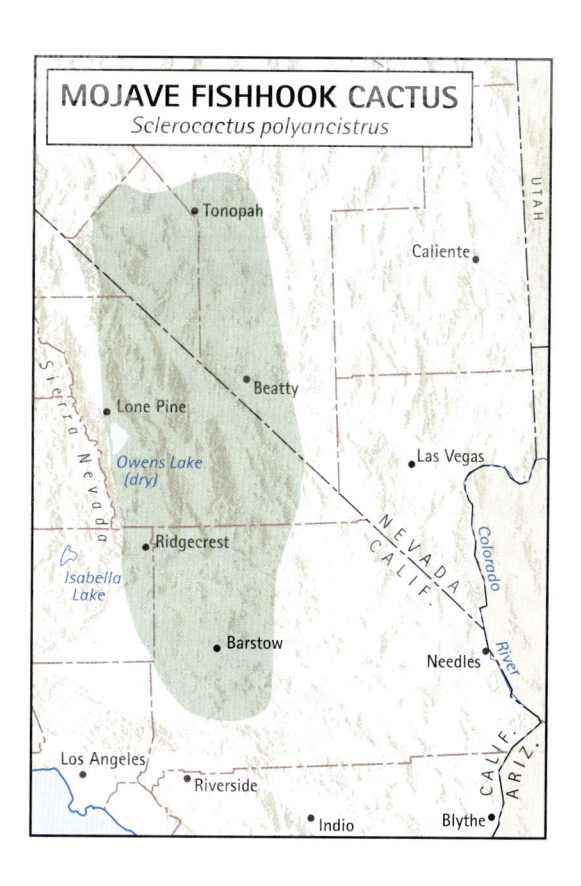

cacti. The carcasses provide young plants with some protection from excessive temperatures, light, and renewed herbivory, thus helping to offset the original deadly impacts from insects or small mammals.

In California, Mojave fishhook cactus can readily be distinguished from Johnson pineapple cactus by its long hooked spines and by its more developed, continuous ribs that are without obvious tubercle bumps. Within its Nevada range, Mojave fishhook cactus can be separated from Tonopah fishhook cactus by its larger flowers, larger fruits, and longer radial spines. Mojave fishhook cactus can be differentiated from the much smaller Blaine fishhook cactus by its lack of tubercles and by the irregular way its fruit opens.

The heart of the Mojave Desert is where Mojave fishhook cactus makes its home. In California, this species of *Sclerocactus* ranges from the southwestern edge of the Mojave Desert north to the White-Inyo Range and east into Nevada. In Nevada, it grows from northwestern Esmeralda County east to near Tonopah in western Nye County and south through the Nevada Test and Training Range in Nye County. This cactus grows on rocky limestone soils as well as gravelly alkaline soils. Mojave fishhook cactus is most common at elevations from 2500 to 4000 feet in Mojavean creosote bush scrub and Joshua tree woodland, but it is also found up to 7000 feet in pinyon-juniper woodland.

**MOJAVE FISHHOOK CACTUS**
*Sclerocactus polyancistrus*

# GREAT BASIN FISHHOOK CACTUS
## *Sclerocactus pubispinus*
(skler-oh-KAK-tus pube-ih-SPINE-us)

**Other Common Names**
Great Basin eagle-claw cactus

*Great Basin fishhook cactus occurs in low-density populations, which can make it hard to find. [Lincoln Co.]*

*Like other fishhook cacti, Great Basin fishhook cactus reveals itself best when it blooms. [Lincoln Co.]*

Great Basin fishhook cactus is probably the most elusive of Nevada's fishhook cacti, not only because it is rare, but also because it blends in so well with its soil substrate. Dome-shaped plants protrude a few inches above their gravelly soil sanctuary and reveal themselves best during the spring blooming season when they put forth bronze and pale-yellow flowers. Great Basin fishhook cactus—like its much larger southern cousin, Mojave fishhook cactus—occurs in low-density populations, which makes it difficult to find. But the reward of locating such a beautiful, small, camouflaged cactus is well worth the effort.

Named *Echinocactus pubispinus* by George Engelmann for its pubescent spines, Great Basin fishhook cactus has short white hairs on the spines of younger plants only. Older, larger plants typically lack pubescent spines, an age-related trait that Engelmann was unaware of. Mature plants of Great Basin fishhook cactus also tend to have longer, more hooked spines, and their prominent tubercles are coalesced into ribs to a greater degree than those of younger plants. A relatively large Great Basin fishhook cactus typically has four central spines: the lowermost is darkest and usually hooked; the two lateral spines are sometimes hooked and may also be dark red to brown but fade to white; and the upper central spine is white and ribbon-like.

In Nevada, different species of *Sclerocactus* occur together only in very few instances, so the challenge of identifying Great Basin fishhook cactus in the field (as well as other fishhook cacti) is not as great as the challenge of finding it in the first place. For example, its range does not overlap with Blaine fishhook and Engelmann fishhook cacti; Blaine fishhook cactus is found further south and west in Nevada, and Engelmann fishhook, native to southwestern Utah, is not known from Nevada.

Without flowers, Great Basin fishhook cactus looks similar to both Blaine fishhook and Engelmann fishhook cacti, and studies of their chloroplast DNA show these three are closely related species. However, they are morphologically distinct enough to be treated as separate species. In comparison to Great Basin fishhook cactus, both Blaine fishhook and Engelmann fishhook cacti have longer, wider upper central spines. Blaine fishhook cactus also has more (up to six) hooked spines per areole and its flowers are larger. The color of the flowers of these two cacti differs from that of Great Basin fishhook, as well. Blaine fishhook cactus has pink flowers while the blossoms of Engelmann fishhook cactus are reddish purple.

Great Basin fishhook cactus ranges from the southern Snake Range of White Pine and adjacent Lincoln counties north to the Toano Range of Elko County. This species extends into adjacent western Utah, but is known in Nevada from less than a dozen locations within 16 miles of the Utah border. It grows in calcareous soils alongside sagebrush, rabbitbrush, and ephedra and occurs both in the open and beneath shrubs. Great Basin fishhook cactus is found in sagebrush scrub on valley floors to open areas of pinyon-juniper woodland in the foothills at elevations from 4500 to 6200 feet.

## Identifying Characteristics

**Habit:** hemispheric, egg-shaped, or cylindrical, usually solitary.
**Stems:** pale green, 1.6–6 in. (4–15 cm) wide and 1.2–6 in. (3–15 cm) tall; ribs 13 to 14, with prominent tubercles.
**Spines:** 7 to 22 per areole, pubescent in juvenile plants; radial spines 6 to 16 per areole, white or with dark tips, spreading, straight to slightly curved; central spines 1 to 6 per areole, white to reddish brown, usually hooked, 0.4–2.2 in. (1–5.5 cm) long; main upper central spine white or with dark tip, flat, straight or twisted, generally to 1 in. (2.5 cm) long.
**Flowers:** outer tepals pale red to yellowish brown with paler margins; inner tepals pale yellow to bronze with darker midlines and paler margins, 0.6–1 in. (1.5–2.5 cm) long; flowers 0.8–1.6 in. (2–4 cm) across; filaments cream, green, yellow, red-violet, or pink; stigma lobes greenish yellow; blooms late April to early June.
**Fruits:** barrel-shaped, dry, spineless with few scales, green or pink, to 0.5 in. (2 cm) long; opening along 2 to 4 vertical slits.

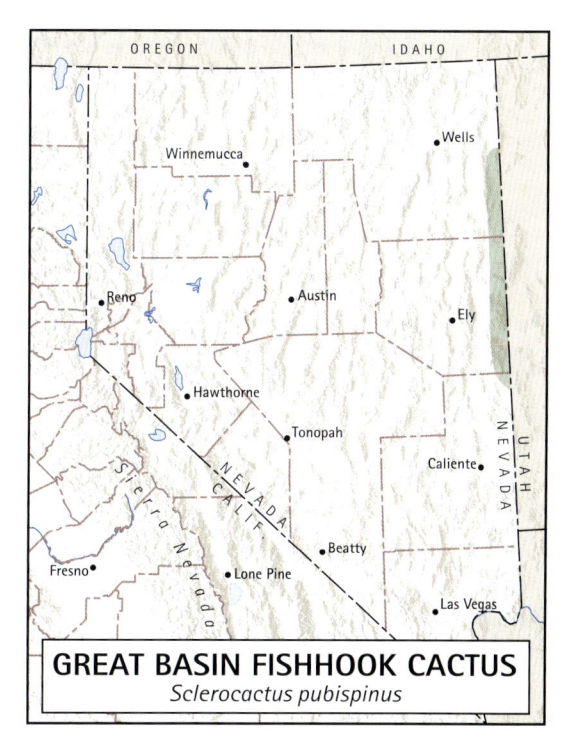

**GREAT BASIN FISHHOOK CACTUS**
*Sclerocactus pubispinus*

*Great Basin fishhook's scientific name,* pubispinus, *refers to pubescent spines on young plants. [Lincoln Co.]*

# Agavaceae

*Mojave yuccas and Joshua trees are scattered across a basin in the Gold Butte area near the Virgin Mountains. [Clark Co.]*

× ¾

Shaw agave • *Agave shawii* ARTWORK BY E.O. MURMAN

# *Agave*
## CENTURY PLANT or MESCAL

*Agave* has a long and noble history and was first described as a genus by Swedish taxonomist Carolus Linnaeus in his *Species Plantarum* in 1753. The genus name, *Agave,* comes from the Greek word for illustrious or noble, and it alludes to the ornamental and utilitarian qualities of these plants. Noted agave expert Howard Scott Gentry proclaimed that the "uses of agave are as many as the arts of man have found it convenient to devise."

Native Americans cultivated *Agave* and carried many species to new locations. In the 18th and 19th centuries, numerous *Agave* species were also shipped from Mexico and the Caribbean to Europe to be planted in public gardens and private greenhouses as botanical novelties for the upper classes. This translocation of agave species added to the ambiguity of species origins and complicated efforts by European botanists who were trying to describe and name them. One hundred twenty years after Linnaeus's initial attempt at classifying *Agave* species, Sir Joseph Hooker, Director of the Royal Botanic Gardens at Kew, England, remarked that, "Of all cultivated plants none are more difficult to name accurately than species of *Agave.*"

*Agave* as a genus is readily identifiable and can be distinguished from yuccas by an inferior ovary and thick, succulent, spine-tipped leaves that—at least in our region—have spiny teeth along the leaf margins. Nearly all *Agave* bloom once and then die, though many produce clonal rosettes. There are approximately 250 species of *Agave,* ranging from tropical South America north to the southwestern U.S. and east to Florida. Three species with several varieties occur in California and Nevada.

# DESERT AGAVE
*Agave deserti* var. *deserti*
(ah-GAH-vee DES-ert-eye)
**Other Common Names**
century plant, mescal

# SIMPLE DESERT AGAVE
*Agave deserti* var. *simplex*
(SIM-plex)
**Recent Synonyms**
*Agave deserti* ssp. *simplex*
**Other Common Names**
century plant

proceed together for a period of 8 to 20 years, like a boiler building up a head of steam until enough pressure is developed to open the valve, or the apical meristem, and send high an ephemeral superstructure, the inflorescence." Plant physiologist Park Nobel reported that the effort to bloom for desert agave is equal to the photosynthetic production for an entire year, and this effort requires the transfer of 40 pounds of water to the inflorescence, which grows nearly 3 inches a day.

Only about 2% of desert agaves in a given population bloom in any single year, and years with fewer blossoms alternate with years of higher flower production. Their yellow, nectar-rich flowers

*The flowering stalk of desert agave grows at the rate of nearly 3 inches per day. [Anza-Borrego Desert S.P.]*

*Like 75% of* Agave *species, desert agave is monocarpic; it blooms once and then dies. [Anza-Borrego Desert S.P.]*

The desert agave, like 75% of *Agave* species, is monocarpic, meaning it flowers once and then dies. But when it flowers, it really goes all out. Agave expert Howard Scott Gentry described it this way: "Growth and accumulation of reserves

attract bats, bees, and hummingbirds. A desert agave inflorescence may be nearly 15 feet tall and produce 65,000 seeds, but seedlings are very rare and only about one in a million seeds will grow into a mature plant. The seedlings that do survive

*Only about 2% of desert agaves within a given population will bloom in any single year. [Anza-Borrego Desert S.P.]*

have spent their early years in the shelter of a desert shrub or bunchgrass. These "nurse plants" cast shade that reduces the high summertime temperatures lethal to agave seedlings, and they also help protect young plants from herbivores.

Two varieties of desert agave occur in California, and like several agaves, they are sometimes referred to as "century plants." This term is a misnomer, however, since the species does not need 100 years to flower. Instead, desert agave is associated with a different form of longevity. Offsets from the underground stem (rhizome) of an original plant, called ramets (also known as pups), are produced every year and receive water and nutrients from the parent plant for as long as 15 years. Over time, a mature plant often becomes surrounded by these younger offspring. The oldest plants eventually bloom and die, typically before an individual reaches 20 to 25 years of age, and then they slowly decay. As the older plants at the middle

*The handsome leaves of desert agave are tipped with formidable spines. [Anza-Borrego Desert S.P.]*

Species Profiles 153

*The roasted leaves and stalks of agave were an important Native-American food. [Anza-Borrego Desert S.P.]*

*Bees, bats, and hummingbirds feed on the nectar that is secreted by desert agave flowers. [Anza-Borrego Desert S.P.]*

die out, they leave behind colonial rings that can be 20 feet across. Agaves at the edge of the rings will produce their own ramets and continue the cycle. Some agave rings can be hundreds of years old.

Many parts of desert agave were highly valued by Native Americans for food or as a source of fiber for making cord, cloth, and sandals. A number of tribes roasted agave leaves and stalks in large earthen pits—often called mescal pits—and these sites are scattered throughout the range of the species. Cooked desert agave inflorescences were pounded into "mescal cakes" and traded with the Apaches and Utes to the north. Young agave inflorescences, like the palatable flowering stalks of its close relative, asparagus, were prized for their rich taste and nutritional value. In addition, the cooked rosette could be eaten like a giant artichoke, and the flower seeds were pounded to make flour.

Desert bighorn sheep as well as packrats and other rodents eat the young inflorescences, and packrats also use desert agave colonies for nest sites.

**Desert agave** has a perianth tube less than ¼ inch long, with stamens attached at the top of the tube and rosettes that tend to produce copious offsets. This variety is the most common one and is abundant in Anza-Borrego Desert State Park and the western Colorado Desert; it also occurs in northern Baja California. Desert agave is found on well-drained soils in broad sandy washes or on rocky slopes, from elevations of about 300 feet to over 5000 feet. Hot summertime temperatures limit the survival of seedlings at low elevations, and the upper elevational limit is apparently due to cold intolerance and, in some cases, to an excess of shade from other plants.

*Desert agave is not found in Nevada, and in California it occurs in the Colorado Desert. [Anza-Borrego Desert S.P.]*

**DESERT AGAVE, SIMPLE DESERT AGAVE**
*Agave deserti*

- var. *deserti* (desert agave)
- var. *simplex* (simple desert agave)

**Simple desert agave** has a perianth tube greater than ¼ inch long, with stamens attached within the tube and rosettes that are usually solitary. Simple desert agave is known from the Providence and Ivanpah mountains of the Mojave National Preserve, the Whipple Mountains, southwestern Arizona, and northwestern Mexico. It occurs on rocky slopes from the upper creosote bush scrub zone into lower pinyon-juniper woodland. McKelvey agave *(Agave mckelveyana)*, a similar species with slightly smaller leaves, occurs in western Arizona where California, Nevada, and Arizona meet and may hybridize with simple desert agave.

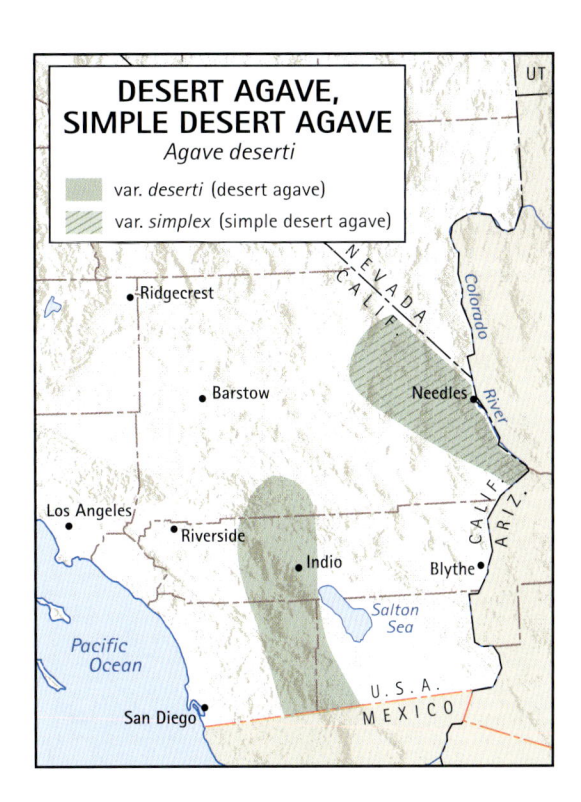

## Identifying Characteristics

**Habit:** usually tightly clumped but sometimes solitary with open rosettes in var. *deserti*; usually solitary with more compact rosettes in var. *simplex*.

**Leaves:** 10–16 in. (25–40 cm) long and 2–3 in. (5–8 cm) wide in var. *deserti*; 10–24 in. (25–60 cm) long and 1.8–4 in. (4.5–10 cm) wide in var. *simplex*; gray-bluish, glaucous, often banded; lanceolate with regularly spaced marginal teeth to 0.5 in. (5–13 mm) long; concave above, spine-tipped.

**Inflorescence:** stout; 6.5–13 ft. (2–4 m) tall in var. *deserti* with wide, triangular bracts; 13–20 ft. (4–6 m) in var. *simplex*; 6 to 15 short branches in upper ¼ of inflorescence.

**Flowers:** yellow; 1.5–2.5 in. (3–6 cm) long, perianth tube 0.1–0.2 in. (3–5 mm) long with filaments arising from top of tube in var. *deserti*; or 0.2–0.4 in. (5–10 mm) long with filaments arising from middle of tube in var. *simplex*; 12–48 flowers per cluster; blooms late March to July.

**Fruits:** dry capsules with thick walls, 1.5–2.3 in. (3.5–5.5 cm) long and 0.5 in. (1.5–1.8 cm) wide; seeds black.

# SHAW AGAVE
*Agave shawii* var. *shawii*
(ah-GAH-vee SHAW-ee-eye)

**Other common names**
coastal century plant

*Succulent leaves with spines on margins and tips distinguish agaves from yuccas in our region. [Cabrillo N.M.]*

Shaw agave is an especially colorful succulent that is quite rare in California but increasingly grown in cultivation for its ornamental value. From its glossy, dark green rosette of leaves with reddish orange or purple marginal teeth, up to the purple bracts and yellow flowers, Shaw agave produces an impressive spectrum of color. Even as the rosette slowly dies following flowering, its leaves fade to brilliant shades of orange before withering to light brown and finally to gray. Imprints of the large marginal teeth from neighboring leaves are visible on both leaf surfaces, an attractive feature that Shaw agave shares with many other agaves.

Like golden cereus cactus, Shaw agave used to be more common in San Diego County before much of its preferred habitat, maritime coastal sage scrub, was lost to development. During the 1950s, Shaw agaves were harvested in San Diego in an attempt to use their leaf fibers commercially. This enterprise was unsuccessful, however, since the leaf fibers were found to be relatively short and fragile.

Shaw agave reportedly grows for 20 to 40 years before giving rise to a thick-branched inflorescence up to 13 feet tall. It usually flowers in the spring and early summer, and in the rare event of heavy summer rains, this species may occasionally flower in the fall. The tubular yellow flowers of Shaw agave are visited by bees, bats, and hummingbirds. The beacon-like flowering stalk of Shaw agave provides useful territorial perches for northern mockingbirds, hummingbirds, flycatchers, and other birds. The gray dried stalks may stand for years after flowering and dying.

Shaw agave now occurs naturally in California in only a few locations: Point Loma, at Border Field State Park, and on a bluff in Carlsbad. Fortunately, this agave is much more common

*The thick-branched inflorescence on Shaw agave can reach 13 feet tall. [Rancho Santa Ana Bot. Gar., Claremont]*

*Cabrillo National Monument is one of two sites in the U.S. where Shaw agave occurs naturally. [San Diego Co.]*

along the coast of northern Baja California, which is the main reason it is not listed as an endangered species. Shaw agave has been reintroduced at Torrey Pines State Reserve and at Cabrillo National Monument; it is reproducing in both places and looks very much at home perched on a high sandy bluff by the Point Loma lighthouse. A larger variety, *Agave shawii* var. *goldmaniana*, occurs farther inland and farther south on the Baja California peninsula.

## Identifying Characteristics

**Habit:** clumped or solitary, rosette elongate, erect or decumbent.
**Leaves:** dark green, glossy, rigid, ovate, flat to slightly concave above; 8–20 in. (20–50 cm) long and 3–4 in. (8–10 cm) wide; teeth red, purple, orange or brown, curved or straight, variable in size.
**Inflorescence:** stout; 6–13 ft. (2–4 m) tall with fleshy, purplish red bracts; 8 to 14 branches in upper ½ to ¼ of inflorescence.
**Flowers:** yellow, greenish yellow, or reddish; 2.4–4 in. (6–10 cm) long; 35–75 per cluster; blooms February to May, but variable.
**Fruits:** dry capsules oblong, 2.2–2.8 in. (5.5–7 cm) long; seeds black.

**SHAW AGAVE**
*Agave shawii* var. *shawii*

Species Profiles 157

# UTAH AGAVE
*Agave utahensis* var. *utahensis*
(ah-GAH-vee you-tah-EN-sis)
**Other Common Names**
Utah century plant

# IVORY-SPINED AGAVE
*Agave utahensis* var. *eborispina*
(ee-bor-ih-SPINE-uh)

# CLARK MOUNTAIN AGAVE
*Agave utahensis* var. *nevadensis*
(nev-a-DEN-sis)
**Other Common Names**
pygmy agave

Utah agave occurs farther north than any other agave and is among the most cold-tolerant species in the family. This small agave is found at elevations up to 6200 feet in the mountains of the northeastern Mojave Desert, where it grows predominantly on limestone ridges and outcrops.

Unlike its relatives in more hospitable southern climes, Utah agave has evolved the ability to survive the windblown snow and subzero temperatures of winter.

Although most agaves and cacti grow where winter temperatures are moderate, a hardy few, such as Utah agave, can tolerate temperatures down to -9.4°F (-23°C) before suffering freeze damage. However, these plants will escape damage only if the temperatures decrease gradually over a few weeks, allowing them to acclimate to winter-season temperatures. The gradual transition to colder overnight temperatures in the fall enables Utah agave to undergo several physiological changes within its leaf tissues. Two crucial changes include the loss of water in the leaf cells and an increase in cellular sugars, both of which inhibit the formation of damaging ice crystals within the leaf cells.

There are three varieties of Utah agave in Nevada and California, and they differ from one another by the color and length of the spines at

*Nevada and Calif. have 3 varieties of* Agave utahensis: *Utah (shown), ivory-spined, and Clark Mountain. [Clark Co.]*

*The 3 varieties have an inflorescence that can be 10 times the height of the rosette. [Red Rock Canyon N.C.A.]*

*The color and length of the apical spines are different in each variety; this is ivory-spined agave. [Desert N.W.R.]*

their leaf tips and, to a lesser degree, by marginal spine size and leaf width. These characters are variable and may overlap somewhat within a population, but the different varieties tend to segregate geographically. Some botanists lump the varieties together under *Agave utahensis* or treat them as subspecies of Utah agave; still others place them in a species complex that includes Kaibab agave (*Agave utahensis* ssp. *kaibabensis*), a larger subspecies that is found around the Grand Canyon in northern Arizona. Regardless of how one classifies the Utah agaves, they are remarkable little plants that send up an inflorescence that can be 10 times the height of the rosette.

**Utah agave** has the smallest marginal spines (about .1 inch or 2.5–4 mm) and shortest apical spines (less than 1.5 inches or 2–4 cm) of any variety. Its apical spines are generally gray to brown. It occurs in the Gold Butte Wilderness Study Area east of Lake Mead and the southern Spring Moun-

*In addition to a long apical spine (up to 7 inches), ivory-spined agave has large marginal teeth. [Desert N.W.R.]*

Species Profiles 159

*Ivory-spined agave occurs farther north than any other member of the genus* Agave. *[Desert N.W.R.]*

tains of Nevada, as well as southwestern Utah and northwestern Arizona.

**Ivory-spined agave** is easily recognized by its long, stout, ivory-colored apical spine and impressive marginal teeth, which measure .25 to .5 inch long (6–12 mm). The prominent apical spine may be more than 7 inches long (10–20 cm). Ivory-spined agave occurs farther north and west than any other member of the genus *Agave*. In Nevada, ivory-spined agave can be found from the Pahranagat Range of western Lincoln County south through the Spotted Range, Sheep Range (where it was first discovered), and Las Vegas Range to the northeastern part of the Spring Mountains. In

*Top: Clark Mountain agave, like all* A. utahensis, *survives subzero temperatures. [Red Rock Canyon N.C.A.] Bottom: The west slope of the Nopah Range has California's only stands of ivory-spined agave [Inyo. Co.]*

160   Cacti, Agaves, and Yuccas of California and Nevada

*Clark Mountain agave, seen here below Clark Mountain, is the most common of the varieties. [Mojave N. Pr.]*

**UTAH AGAVE, IVORY-SPINED AGAVE, CLARK MOUNTAIN AGAVE**
*Agave utahensis*

- var. *utahensis* (Utah agave)
- var. *eborispina* (ivory-spined agave)
- var. *nevadensis* (Clark Mountain agave)

California, it is known only from the west slope of the Nopah Range.

**Clark Mountain agave** is distinguished from the other varieties by its brown to white apical spine that is 1.5–3 inches long (4–8 cm) and marginal teeth about .25 inch long (4–6 mm). It is found in the Kingston, Clark, Ivanpah, and New York mountains of eastern California, and the Spring, Mormon, and Muddy mountains of Nevada. This variety is the most common of the three.

## Identifying Characteristics

**Habit:** clumped or solitary, relatively small and compact.
**Leaves:** gray-green, rigid, linear-lanceolate, flat to slightly concave above, convex below; 4.7–12 in. (12–30 cm) long and 0.4–1.25 in. (1–3 cm) wide; teeth brown aging to gray, curved or straight, 0.4–1.5 in. apart (1–4 cm); apical spine gray, 0.8 to 1.5 in. (2–4 cm) long in var. *utahensis;* or white, stout, 4–8 in. (10–20 cm) long in var. *eborispina;* or brown to whitish, slender, 1.5–3 in. (4–8 cm) long in var. *nevadensis.*
**Inflorescence:** narrow, 5–13 ft. high (1.5–4 m) with 40 to 80 very short branches in upper ⅔ to ½ of inflorescence.
**Flowers:** yellow or greenish yellow; 0.9–1.3 in. (2.3–3.2 cm) long; 2–12 per cluster; blooms April to July.
**Fruits:** dry capsules oblong with beaked tips; 0.4–1 in. (1–2.5 cm) long.

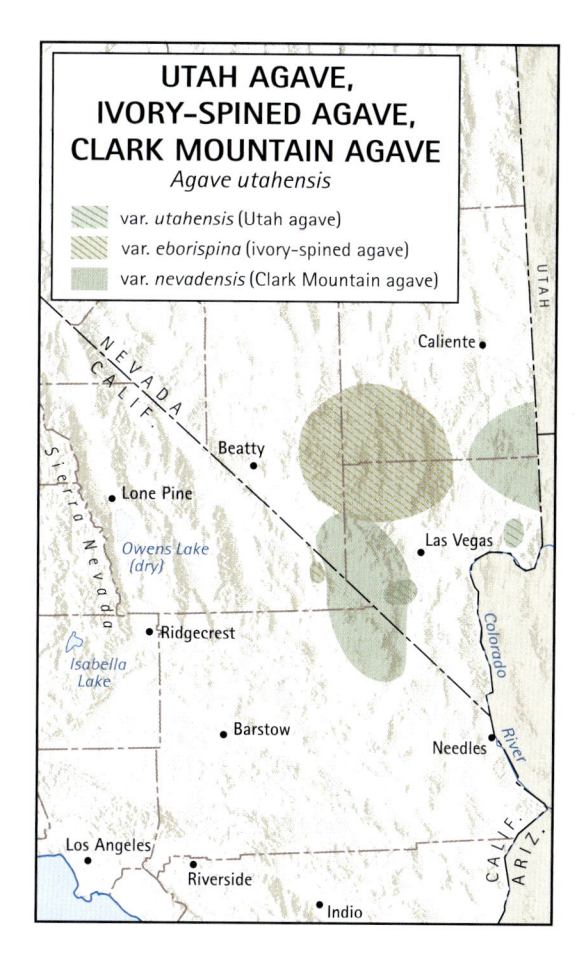

Chaparral yucca • *Hesperoyucca whipplei*     ARTWORK BY E.O. MURMAN

# *Hesperoyucca*
## CHAPARRAL YUCCA

Although it was described as a genus in 1892, *Hesperoyucca,* which means "Western yucca," was treated throughout most of the last century as a small section in the much larger genus *Yucca.* As early as 1893, American botanist William Trelease recognized that flower and fruit characters warranted the separation of *Hesperoyucca* from *Yucca.* Susan Delano McKelvey, lilac and yucca expert and cousin of Franklin Delano Roosevelt, wrote in her two-volume *Yuccas of the South Western United States* (1938 and 1947) that there was justification for separating *Hesperoyucca* "since a number of flower and fruit characters differ from those in all other sections." Nonetheless, McKelvey treated *Yucca* in a broad sense that included *Hesperoyucca.* The recent *Flora of North America* describes *Hesperoyucca* as a distinct genus based on flower and fruit differences and on recent genetic evidence. DNA sequence data actually indicate a closer relationship between *Hesperoyucca* and *Hesperaloë* from southern Texas than between *Hesperoyucca* and *Yucca. Hesperoyucca* is also more closely related to *Agave* than *Yucca* is.

There are three *Hesperoyucca* species: one each from California, Arizona, and Mexico. This genus differs from *Yucca* in having larger flowering stalks, fruits that split open when mature, and minutely serrate leaves from a stemless basal rosette. *Hesperoyuccas* differs from *Nolinas* in having spine-tipped leaves and much larger flowers and fruits. Another important distinction between *Hesperoyucca* and these other two genera is that it is monocarpic—each rosette flowers only once and then turns brown and dies.

# CHAPARRAL YUCCA
## *Hesperoyucca whipplei*
(HESS-per-oh-yuk-uh WHIP-pull-eye)

**Recent synonyms**
*Yucca whipplei, Y. whipplei,* ssp. *caespitosa, Y. whipplei* ssp. *intermedia, Y. whipplei* ssp. *parishii, Y. whipplei* ssp. *percursa*

**Other Common Names**
Our Lord's candle, Whipple yucca, Spanish bayonet, Quixote plant.

*A coastal slope is studded with flower-covered stalks of chaparral yucca. [Santa Monica Mountains, Ventura Co.]*

Chaparral yucca is one of those species that always seems to stand out. Its large hemispherical rosettes composed of numerous gray-green leaves offer a distinct visual contrast to most plants it grows with. The sharp unyielding leaf tips pose a menace to passing hikers and equestrians. Chaparral yucca rosettes grow for six to seven years before sending up a stout inflorescence 8 to 16 feet high that holds hundreds of white, sweetly fragrant flowers. These almost luminescent flower-clad stalks can be visible from miles away. Chaparral yuccas die after producing their one-and-only inflorescence, but the dried flower stalks can persist for several years, and they are a familiar sight on sunny slopes of southern and central California's coastal ranges.

Each chaparral yucca produces several hundred flowers during its bloom, yet fewer than 10% develop into mature seed-bearing fruits. This may seem curious, since its pollinator, the California yucca moth, is relatively abundant. If such a small percent of fruits ripen, why do chaparral yuccas expend the energy needed to put forth so many flowers? Scientists offer several plausible hypotheses: more flowers means there will be a greater amount of pollen available for dissemination; an abundance of flowers increases the probability of pollination if pollinators are scarce in a

*A highly variable species, chaparral yucca occurs from coastal California to the Sierra Nevada. [Sequoia N.P.]*

given season; and large numbers of flowers provide the potential for heavy fruit production when resources are especially plentiful.

Chaparral yucca's prodigious flowering stalk offers a smorgasbord to four diurnal, host-specific moths: one is its true pollinator, and the other three are "cheater" yucca moths. The first moth species to arrive on the scene when chaparral yuccas begin to flower is usually *Prodoxus marginatus*, a non-pollinating, or so-called cheater yucca moth. Using her ovipositor, the female moth injects her eggs into the flower ovaries; the eggs hatch into larvae that feed exclusively on the pulpy portions of the developing fruits. This species relies solely on chaparral yucca for survival—and it is therefore also dependant on its cousin, *Tegeticula maculata*, the California yucca moth, whose pollinating activity is essential to the reproduction of chaparral yucca. The California yucca moth also oviposits its eggs into the ovaries of newly opened flowers, but unlike the cheater moths, it then pollinates the flowers using special tentacles evolved specifically for this job. The larvae of California yucca moths feed on the developed seeds within the mature fruits. Two other species of cheater yucca moth rely on chaparral yucca: *Prodoxus cinereus*, whose larvae tunnel and feed within the middle to lower portions of the flowering stalk while the stalk is still elongating, and *Prodoxus aenescens*, whose larvae use the middle and upper portions of the inflorescence. These two stalk-inhabiting yucca moth species have larvae that spend one to several years in diapause (dormancy) within the old stalks before emerging as adult moths. (For more information, see "Yuccas and Yucca Moths" on page 22).

Five subspecies of chaparral yucca have been recognized in the past based on their growth form and range, but most botanists now treat this plant as a highly variable species that exhibits different forms in different habitats. Some forms have enormous solitary rosettes and others form clumps of smaller rosettes. Not surprisingly, chaparral yucca is found in a variety of vegetation types, including oak woodland and coastal sage scrub, as well as in Sonoran and Mojavean creosote bush scrub.

Chaparral yucca is California's northernmost representative from the Agave family. It ranges throughout most of cismontane California from the Coast Ranges of Monterey and San Benito counties south to northern Baja and east to southern Fresno County in the western foothills of the Sierra Nevada. Chaparral yucca also extends to the western edge of the Mojave and Sonoran deserts, where it typically grows in dense clumps rather than solitary rosettes.

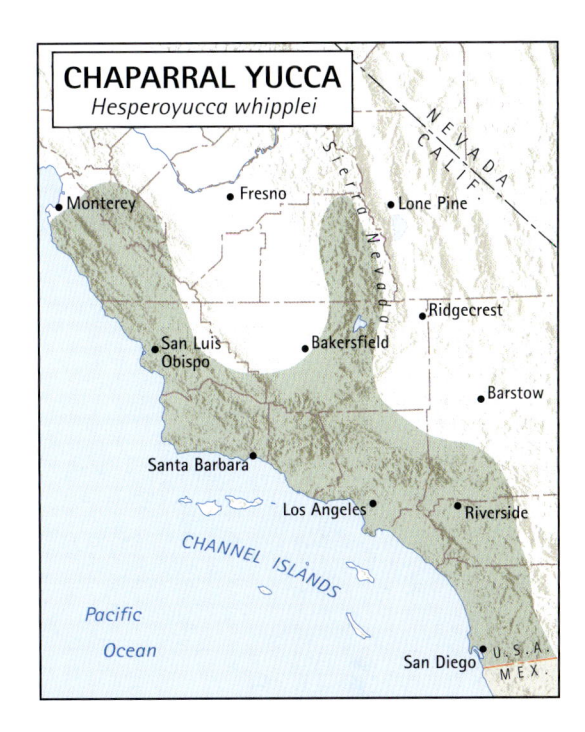

## Identifying Characteristics

**Habit:** trunkless; rosettes dense, hemispherical, solitary or colonial from below-ground branching.
**Leaves:** green, gray-green or bluish green, flaring at base, linear, flat to somewhat 3-angled, finely striated with pale yellow, finely toothed margins; 8–36 in. (20–90 cm) long and 0.3–1 in. (0.8–2.5 cm) wide; sharply spine-tipped.
**Inflorescence:** dense panicle to 16 ft. (5 m) tall with numerous short branches.
**Flowers:** white to cream-colored, suffused with purple outside, pendant, somewhat round; 1.2–2 in. (3–5 cm) long and nearly as wide; blooms April to June.
**Fruits:** woody capsules 1.2–2 in. (3–5 cm) long and about 1 in. (2.5 cm) wide.

× ½

Mojave yucca • *Yucca schidigera*  ARTWORK BY E.O. MURMAN

# *Yucca*
## SPANISH BAYONET

The name for the genus *Yucca* comes from the word *yuca,* which was used by the Carib Indians to refer to cassava *(Manihot esculenta).* The buds of yucca are sometimes roasted and eaten as a starchy food in the same way as cassava roots, so it too was called "yuca." Like its close relative *Agave, Yucca* was first described by Swedish taxonomist Carolus Linnaeus in 1753. *Yucca* has been treated as part of the Lily family (Liliaceae), the Agave family (Agavaceae), and more recently, the Asparagus family (Asparagaceae). However it is categorized, *Yucca* is consistently placed in the same family as its more species-rich cousin, *Agave.*

There are approximately 40 species of *Yucca,* occurring from the southeastern U.S. coastal region and the southwestern U.S. deserts to the Caribbean and south to Guatemala. Five species are found in California and Nevada, and 28 throughout North America. Yuccas, unlike agaves, have flowers that are fleshy and whitish, with a superior ovary. Their leaves are less succulent than agave leaves and display margins that are either fibrous or finely serrate, but not spine-toothed. Another important distinction is that yuccas are polycarpic (can bloom more than once), while the agaves of California and Nevada are monocarpic.

# BANANA YUCCA
## *Yucca baccata* var. *baccata*
(YUK-ah BAK-ah-tah)

**Recent Synonyms**
*Yucca baccata* var. *vespertina*

**Other Common Names**
Datil yucca, blue yucca, Spanish bayonet, fleshy-fruited yucca

*Banana yucca's large flowers help distinguish it from its close relatives. [New York Mountains, Mojave N. Pr.]*

No other yucca in California or Nevada has a bigger flower than banana yucca. Moreover, its attractive bluish leaves and purplish white pendant blossoms make it a desirable plant for horticulture. Banana yucca has also been appreciated for its utilitarian qualities: Native Americans of the Southwest used it as a source of food, fiber, and soap.

American botanist John Torrey gave this yucca its specific name, *baccata,* meaning "having berries," in reference to its fleshy or pulpy fruits. Its common name refers to the resemblance of the shape and size of its fruit to that of a banana. Paleobotanists hypothesize that large, indehiscent, fleshy fruits, such as those of banana yucca and Mojave yucca, evolved to enhance seed dispersal by Pleistocene megafauna, such as giant bears and ground sloths. These large fruit-eating mammals became extinct in North America about 10,000 years ago, but not before exerting long-term selective pressure on the palatability of yucca fruits. The nutritious fruits are eaten nowadays—and the seeds dispersed—by rabbits and rodents.

Development from a flower bud to fruit takes about 10 weeks. Once the flower tepals separate enough to reveal the large stigma-capped ovary, banana yucca moths *(Tegeticula baccatella)* fly to the luscious, fragrant flowers to mate. The female moth then deposits pollen into the ovary's stigmatic groove and her eggs into the ovary wall, thereby insuring pollination of the flower and the production of seeds that are an essential food source for the next generation of yucca moth larvae.

In most cases, banana yucca can easily be distinguished from its close relative, Mojave yucca, by its shorter stature, more bluish curved leaves, and larger flowers and fruits. Its flowers remain more closed and are more pendulous than those of Mojave yucca. In California and Nevada, banana yucca is replaced by Mojave yucca at lower, drier elevations around 2600 feet. (A second variety, *Yucca baccata* var. *brevifolia,* has more numerous branches on taller stems and is found only in Arizona and New Mexico.) Banana yucca and Mojave yucca are the only two *Yucca* species known to hybridize, which happens on rare occasions in locales where they co-mingle in the eastern Mojave of California and southern Nevada. Overall, the hybrid plants resemble small Mojave yuccas, but they have bluish leaves closer in hue to those of banana yucca.

Banana yucca can withstand temperatures as low as −20°F (−29°C), and this exceptional cold-hardiness allows it to occur at elevations as high as 7500 feet. In California and Nevada, banana yucca is most common in pinyon-juniper woodland or Joshua tree woodland at elevations between 4000 and 6000 feet. It is usually less abundant than Mojave yucca or Joshua tree, but one may encounter all three of these yuccas in close proximity in

*Banana yucca is very cold-hardy and has a broad distribution in the Southwest. [Red Rock Canyon N.C.A.]*

some parts of the eastern Mojave Desert. Banana yucca grows from the eastern Mojave Desert of California through southern Nevada and southern Utah to southeastern Colorado. Farther south, it extends through Arizona and New Mexico to west Texas and into northern Chihuahua, Mexico. This vast range—the largest of any yucca species that occurs in California and Nevada—includes parts of the Mojave, Great Basin, Sonoran, and Chihuahuan deserts.

## Identifying Characteristics

**Habit:** trunkless or with short, usually prostrate trunk; rosettes clumped or solitary, less than 8 ft. tall (2.5 m).
**Leaves:** gray-green or blue-green, rigid, erect, sword-shaped, concave above, convex below, 12–40 in. (30–100 cm) long and 1–2 in. (2.5–5 cm) wide; curling marginal filaments white to brown.
**Inflorescence:** erect, narrow panicle 20–31.5 in. (50–80 cm) tall, shorter to slightly taller than rosette.
**Flowers:** pendant, cream-colored inside, usually suffused with purple outside; not opening widely; 2–5 in. (5–13 cm) long and nearly as wide; blooms April to June.
**Fruits:** green, pendant, elongate, 4–9 in. (10–23 cm) long.

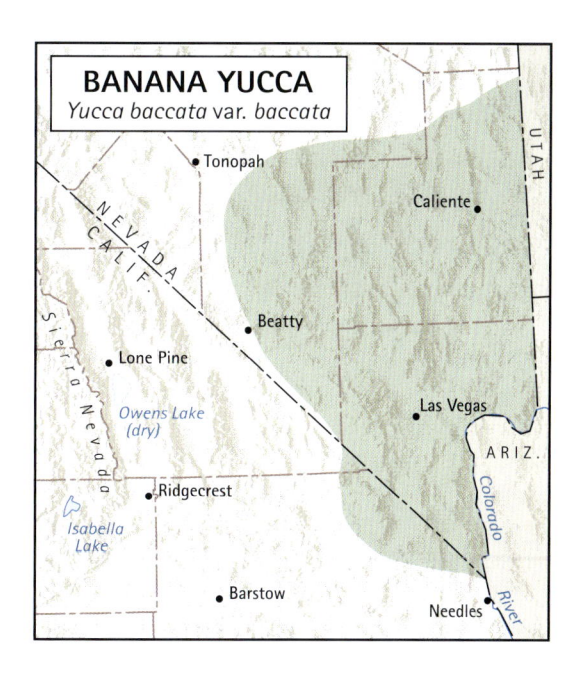

**BANANA YUCCA**
*Yucca baccata* var. *baccata*

# JOSHUA TREE
## *Yucca brevifolia*
(YUK-ah brev-i-FOL-ee-ah)

**Recent Synonyms**
*Yucca brevifolia* var. *herbertii*

**Other Common Names**
tree yucca

*Joshua trees require one or two centuries to achieve the stature of the specimen seen here. [Mojave N. Pr.]*

*Tolerant of cold, Joshua trees range to 7200 feet in elevation, but flourish at 4000 to 6000 feet. [Inyo N.F.]*

Joshua tree can tolerate lower temperatures than the more cold-sensitive saguaro. While most people assume that the Joshua tree is strictly Mojavean, it does venture outside this desert in a few places: the Great Basin just southeast of Tonopah, Nevada; alongside saguaros in the northwestern Sonoran Desert of west-central Arizona; and amid chaparral near Lake Isabella in California's Kern County.

The bizarre growth habit of Joshua tree is what gives it a "strange and singular appearance," as noted in 1844 by explorer John C. Frémont. But it is this same growth habit and leaf arrangement that enables Joshua tree to survive so well in its desert habitat. The uppermost leaves of a branch-tip rosette are arranged vertically and are able to capture light at low sun angles without shading the leaves below. The lower leaves are horizontally splayed so they can receive light when the sun is at higher angles. This leaf arrangement, in part, gives Joshua

The Joshua tree is to the Mojave Desert what the giant saguaro is to the Sonoran Desert—an instantly recognizable symbol of the American Southwest. These two desert icons have other similarities as well: they grow slowly, achieve their prominent stature after one or two centuries, and survive their tenuous first years best when protected by nurse plants. To some extent, Joshua trees and saguaros are probably both limited to their current distribution by low temperatures, although the

*These Joshua tree woodlands at Cima Dome are among the most extensive stands of the species. [Mojave N. Pr.]*

tree the capacity to be light-saturated, which in turn allows it to photosynthesize at its maximum rate, even when the sunlight is only one-quarter of the maximum midday amount. In contrast, the widespread creosote bush needs three to four times as much sunlight to reach its maximum photosynthetic rate. Since Joshua trees are so efficient at photosynthesis, they can put on 80% of their growth from January through May, when light levels are not at their peak but air temperatures and soil moisture are most favorable.

Some botanists recognize two varieties of Joshua tree, based on leaf size, height, branching patterns, and range. *Yucca brevifolia* var. *brevifolia* occurs in the western and southern Mojave. It has the largest leaves and tallest stature, and it branches only after producing an inflorescence at its branch tip. In contrast, the so-called dwarf Joshua tree, or Jaeger Joshua tree *(Yucca brevifolia* var. *jaegeriana),* shows true dichotomous branching, where each branch divides prior to flowering. It occurs in the northern and eastern part of the species range, and

*An icon of the Mojave Desert, the Joshua tree even lends its name to a famous national park. [Joshua Tree N.P.]*

*In some areas, such as the Antelope Valley (shown), many Joshua trees have been lost to development. [Kern Co.]*

its leaves and trunk are relatively short, giving it a more compact appearance.

Joshua tree has recently been recognized as the only yucca to have two host-specific pollinators: *Tegeticula antithetica* and *Tegeticula synthetica*. *Tegeticula antithetica* was recently described as a species after an intriguing study by Olle Pellmyr and Kari Segraves indicated that yucca moths from the eastern Mojave and western Sonoran deserts were morphologically and genetically distinct from those in the western Mojave and warranted recognition as a separate species. The range of *Tegeticula antithetica* coincides with the range of *Yucca brevifolia* var. *jaegeriana*, while the range of *Tegeticula synthetica* aligns with the range of *Yucca brevifolia* var. *brevifolia*. The ranges of these two yucca moth species do not overlap, and this fact lends support to those botanists who recognize two varieties of Joshua tree.

*A Joshua tree's leaf arrangement encourages light saturation during peak growth periods. [Red Rock Canyon N.C.A.]*

*The flowers on Joshua trees have two host-specific pollinators, which is unique among yuccas. [Mojave N. Pr.]*

Flowering in Joshua trees usually occurs from early March to May, beginning first at lower, warmer elevations. This "tree yucca" generally grows in coarse gravelly soils and is a component in a number of plant communities. It is found with a diverse array of plants, ranging from saguaros and poppies to sagebrush and pines. It occurs at elevations from 2000 to 7200 feet, but the most extensive stands—true Joshua tree woodlands—are found between 4000 and 6000 feet. The northern portions of Joshua Tree National Park contain many fine examples of Joshua trees. The shorter variety, Jaeger Joshua tree, forms dense, extensive stands on Cima Dome in the Mojave National Preserve and in Yucca Valley within Nevada's Desert National Wildlife Refuge.

*Many botanists categorize the smaller Jaeger Joshua tree as a separate variety. [Whitney Pockets, Clark Co.]*

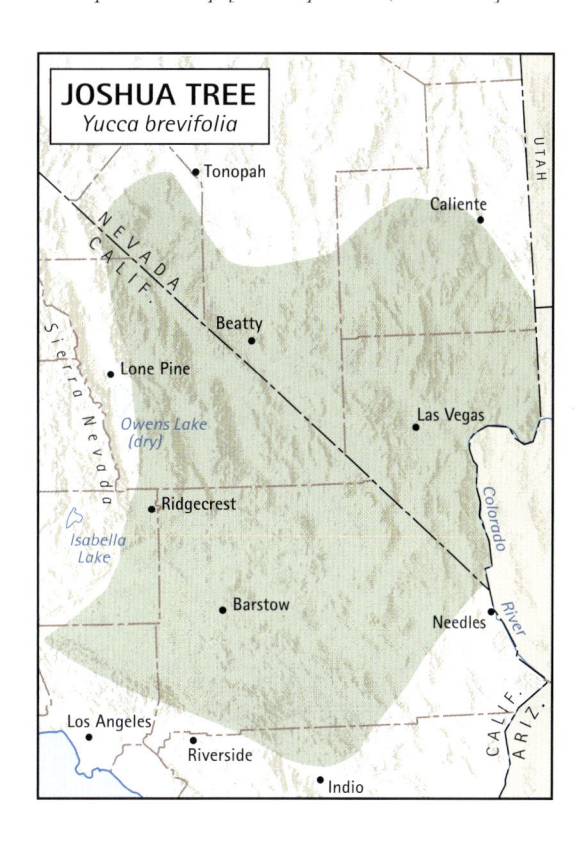

## Identifying Characteristics

**Habit:** trees; solitary or occasionally colonial; branched 13 to 30 ft. (4–9 m) tall and occasionally to 45 ft. (13.7 m).
**Leaves:** pale to dark green, rigid, concave above, convex below; 6–14 in. (15–35 cm) long and 0.3–0.6 in. (0.7–1.5 cm) wide, spine-tipped margins finely serrated.
**Inflorescence:** erect panicle 12–20 in. (30–50 cm) long.
**Flowers:** pale green to cream-colored; fleshy, bell-shaped, 1.6–2.8 in. (4–7 cm) long and nearly as wide; blooms March to May.
**Fruits:** pale green, pendant; 2.4–3.3 in. (6–8.5 cm) long.

**JOSHUA TREE**
*Yucca brevifolia*

# HARRIMAN YUCCA
*Yucca harrimaniae*
(YUK-ah HAIR-i-man-ee-eye)

**Recent Synonyms**
*Yucca gilbertiana, Y. harrimaniae* var. *gilbertiana, Y. harrimaniae* var. *sterilis*

**Other Common Names**
Harriman's Spanish bayonet, narrow-leaf yucca

*Harriman yuccas produce short, dense stalks of nocturnally fragrant flowers in late spring. [Cathedral Gorge S.P.]*

buds and outer tepals are suffused with purple. The nocturnally fragrant flowers attract the high plains yucca moth, which also pollinates two other *Yucca* species from southern Utah and northern Arizona.

A short inflorescence is one of the distinguishing features of Harriman yucca, and the lowest flowers on this stalk are usually situated below the leaf tips of the rosette. Most of the plants produce a raceme with flowers borne on short lateral stalks attached directly to the main stalk, but some plants produce a narrow panicle with short branches of flowers. Utah yucca, its cousin to the south, has a much taller inflorescence. The leaves of Harriman yucca are widest near the middle and slightly concave above; they are a little broader and more rigid than those of Utah yucca. Compared to banana yucca, with which it may grow, Harriman yucca has shorter, narrower, more flexible leaves. In addition, its fruits mature into persistent woody capsules, which are very different from the fleshy elongate fruits of banana yucca.

Harriman yucca was named in honor of philanthropist Mary Averell Harriman (1851–1932). Her husband, railroad tycoon Edward Henry Harriman, is known for organizing and financing the Harriman Alaska Expedition of 1899, which included many prominent naturalists, such as John Burroughs, John Muir, and George Bird Grinnell. Botanist William Trelease, Director of the Missouri Botanical Garden, was also a member of the expedition. On the return trip from Alaska, their train was detained due to a washout in central Utah, and Trelease naturally went out collecting plants; he brought back a new yucca specimen, which he described in 1902 as *Yucca harrimaniae*.

In our region Harriman yucca has a limited distribution. It grows in east-central Nevada, predominantly in sandy, calcareous soils in sagebrush scrub and pinyon-juniper woodland. Harriman yucca often occurs in small, widely scattered colonies at elevations between 4000 and 8200 feet. In Nevada it is found from the Quinn Canyon Range of eastern Nye County eastward through central Lincoln County to the lower slopes of the Snake Range in White Pine County. A good place to see this yucca is Cathedral Gorge State Park, where

Harriman yucca is Nevada's smallest yucca, but this handsome species commands attention from mid-May through June when it displays a densely flowered stalk of bright blossoms. Its flowers are creamy white to pale yellow-green, and the

*Harriman yuccas often form widely scattered colonies in sandy, calcareous soils. [Cathedral Gorge S.P.]*

it is locally common. This species also extends southeastward from Nevada through central and southern Utah to the Four Corners region and north through western Colorado.

## Identifying Characteristics

**Habit:** rosettes small, open, usually stemless but occasionally with stems to 12 in. (30 cm) tall; forming dense to open colonies.

**Leaves:** pale green to blue-green, rigid, linear-lanceolate, widest near the middle with brown marginal stripes and peeling white filaments; 8–20 in. (20–50 cm) long and 0.7–1.7 in. (1.8–4.3 cm) wide.

**Inflorescence:** erect raceme 14–35 in. (35–90 cm) tall, occasionally with short branches above.

**Flowers:** broadly bell-shaped to globe-like, pendant; tepals pale yellow-white to pale yellow-green, often with purple tinge, 1.5–2.4 in. (4–6 cm) long and 0.6–1.3 in. (1.6–3.4 cm) wide; blooms May to June.

**Fruit:** capsules erect, cylindrical but constricted at middle; 1.2–2 in. (3–5 cm) long; splitting lengthwise into thirds when ripe.

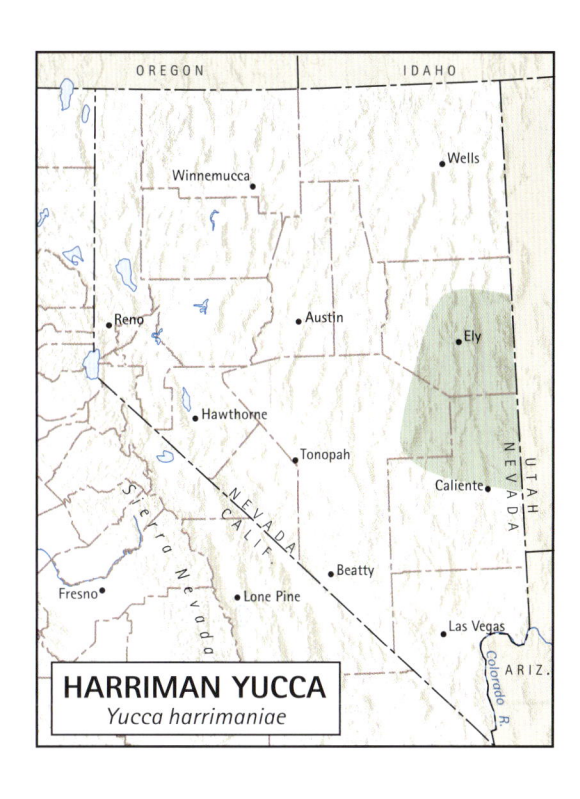

**HARRIMAN YUCCA**
*Yucca harrimaniae*

# MOJAVE YUCCA
## *Yucca schidigera*
(YUK-ah shi-DIG-er-ah)

**Recent Synonyms**
*Yucca mohavensis*

**Other Common Names**
Spanish dagger

*Mojave yucca's leaf fibers were utilized by Native Americans. [Little Chuckwalla Mountains, Riverside Co.]*

*A thick skirt of brown dead leaves covers the trunk of Mojave yucca. [Valley of Fire S.P.]*

From basket-weavers to industrial chemists, humans have discovered a myriad of uses for Mojave yucca. Native Americans roasted Mojave yucca's edible fruits, cut up its roots and stems for soap and shampoo, and stripped its leaves for fibers that could be fashioned into twine, nets, hats, hairbrushes, shoes, baskets, and other items. Mojave yuccas and many other *Yucca* species produce steroidal saponins that act as natural detergents. Saponins are both fat- and water-soluble and have anti-fungal, anti-bacterial, and blood cholesterol-lowering properties, giving Mojave yucca extract a broad range of commercial applications. Mojave yucca is farmed in Mexico, and the trunks are sent to processing plants where they are pulped and the juice is evaporated to produce a yucca extract powder rich in saponins. More recently, this yucca has become an important source of products designed to control odors around pets, livestock, and landfills; it is also used widely as a natural foaming agent for root beer.

A variety of animals, past and present, have used Mojave yucca. Ground sloth dung preserved at Gypsum Cave near Las Vegas reveals that now-extinct giant Shasta ground sloths ate Mojave yucca's green fleshy fruits during the Pleistocene epoch, more than 11,000 years ago. Yucca moths have co-evolved with Mojave yucca and the relationship between them is a classic example of obligate mutualism: the yuccas depend on the coastal sage scrub, chaparral, and oak woodland in the western portion of its range and from creosote bush scrub into lower pinyon-juniper woodland in transmontane California and Nevada. Mojave yucca occurs from southern Nevada and western Arizona south and west into southern California's Transverse and Peninsular ranges and south into north-central Baja California.

## Identifying Characteristics

**Habit:** rosettes open, robust, forming colonies with trunks to 15 ft. (4.5 m) tall.
**Leaves:** dark green or yellow-green, rigid, erect, sword-shaped, markedly concave above; 12–51 in. (30–130 cm) long and 1.2–2 in. (3–5 cm) wide; curling marginal filaments white to brown.
**Inflorescence:** erect, dense panicle 12–24 in. (30–60 cm) tall.
**Flowers:** pendant, tepals spreading, white to cream-colored; 1.2–2 in. (3–5 cm) long and nearly as wide; blooms March to May.
**Fruits:** green, pendant, fleshy, 2–4 in. (5–10 cm) long.

*Mojave yucca occupies a remarkable range of habitats, from desert slopes to seaside bluffs. [Torrey Pines S.R.]*

moths for pollination, and the moths rely on the yucca's fruits for the survival of their larvae. (For more information, see "Yuccas and Yucca Moths" on page 22).

The trunk of Mojave yucca is covered by a skirt of brown, reflexed, dead leaves. At the top, it is crowned by dark green, stiff, succulent leaves, which are arrayed to maximize solar gain. The cream-colored fleshy flowers are produced from March to May and are occasionally suffused with purple on the outside.

Mojave yucca can be found from fog-shrouded sea bluffs near San Diego to sun-baked desert slopes west of Las Vegas. This tall robust yucca is unusual because it thrives in the hot Mojave Desert as well as in the cooler, equable environment of coastal southern California. Few other native plants share the same broad distribution and ecological range. Mojave yucca is found in

# UTAH YUCCA
## *Yucca utahensis*
(YUK-ah you-tah-EN-sis)

**Recent Synonyms**
*Yucca elata* var. *utahensis*

**Other Common Names**
Utah soaptree

*In Nevada, Utah yucca grows in the scenic country of the far northeastern Mojave Desert. [Valley of Fire S.P.]*

*Utah yucca is pollinated by a moth that is not host-species specific—a rare trait in yuccas. [Valley of Fire S.P.]*

One of Utah yucca's most scenic habitats is the red-rock country of Nevada's far northeastern Mojave Desert. In this spectacular setting of smooth red sandstone and golden sands, Utah yucca stands out, displaying its rosettes of yellow-green leaves with their white, shredding leaf margins. Utah yucca's white, fragrant flowers do not appear dependably every year, but that only makes their fleeting beauty all the more special.

Utah yucca was first collected near St. George, Utah in May 1934 by Susan Delano McKelvey, who formally described and named the species in 1947. Utah yucca is considered by some botanists as a short variety of the 15-foot-tall soaptree yucca, *Yucca elata*. Recent genetic research confirms that these two yuccas are distinct species, but are closely related. In addition to its much shorter stature, Utah yucca has slightly smaller fruits, shorter, wider leaves, and a more restricted home range than soaptree yucca. Utah yucca can be distinguished from the more northerly Harriman yucca by its longer, narrower leaves and taller inflorescence.

Utah yucca is one among very few yucca species that is pollinated by a yucca moth that is not strictly host species-specific. The yucca moth *Tegeticula superficiella,* named for its habit of laying eggs superficially just below the ovary wall, also pollinates alpine yucca *(Yucca baileyi)* and Kanab yucca *(Yucca angustissima* var. *kanabensis),* both from southwestern Utah and northwestern Arizona.

Utah agave's general attractiveness, relatively pliable, forgiving leaves, and cold-hardiness to −10°F (−23°C) should make it popular for ornamental landscaping. Native Americans harvested the leaves for their fibers, which were used in making cordage and weaving mats, baskets, and sandals. The roots and leaves contain saponins and can be pounded and mixed with water to make a frothy soap.

*Utah yucca prefers sandy soils and grows in portions of Arizona, Utah, and Nevada. [Valley of Fire S.P.]*

Utah yucca is not found in California, and its Nevada distribution is limited to northeastern Clark County and southeastern Lincoln County. Elsewhere, this species occurs in northwestern Arizona and southwestern Utah. Utah yucca prefers sandstone soils and sandy washes and grows in Mojavean creosote bush scrub and Joshua tree woodland. A good place to view this handsome yucca is at Valley of Fire State Park and the Whitney Pockets outcrops south of the Virgin Mountains.

### Identifying Characteristics

**Habit:** rosettes open, forming small colonies with short stems, but often without a noticeable trunk, or procumbent (lying on the ground); clumps 3.3–9.2 ft. (1–2.8 m) across.

**Leaves:** yellow-green, flexible, linear-lanceolate tapering to a short spine, with curling, white marginal filaments; 8–28 in. (20–70 cm) long and 0.3–0.9 in. (0.7–2.2 cm) wide.

**Inflorescence:** erect panicle 3–5 ft. (1–1.5 m) tall, with lateral branches (below panicle tip) less than 8 in. (20 cm) long.

**Flowers:** bell-shaped, pendant; tepals creamy white, 1.5–2 in. (4–5 cm) long and 0.8–1 in. (2–2.5 cm) wide; blooms late April to June.

**Fruit:** capsules erect, green drying to tan, 2–2.4 in. (5–6 cm) long, splitting lengthwise when ripe.

# Nolinas, Ocotillo, and Non-Native Species

*Twilight illuminates these flower stalks of Parry nolina in the Little San Bernardino Mountains. [Joshua Tree N.P.]*

# *Nolina*
# NOLINA

Nolinas, also known as beargrasses, are frequently confused with yuccas. They look like yuccas and share many of the same habitats, but they are not in the Agavaceae family. Although generally less well known than agaves and yuccas, nolinas are every bit as stunning in their growth forms and flower production. Nolinas were placed in at least six different plant families in the past, and today the genus *Nolina* is treated as part of the Nolinaceae, which also includes two closely related genera, *Dasylirion* (desert spoon) and *Beaucarnea* (ponytail palm). There are approximately 30 species of *Nolina,* and they are found from the south Atlantic and southwestern U.S. to central Mexico. The four species that occur in California and Nevada are described below.

Nolinas differ from yuccas and agaves by having relatively long, pliable, strap-shaped leaves and tiny flowers that are functionally unisexual—that is, having either fertile stamens or a receptive stigma, but not both on the flowers from one plant. Nolinas may put forth gnarled branching trunks to 8 feet high or just produce a ring of leaf rosettes that sprout from horizontal underground stems. Many species, including two in California, are rare and endemic to relatively small areas.

## BIGELOW NOLINA
### *Nolina bigelovii*
*(no-LY-nah BIG-eh-lov-ee-eye)*
**Other Common Names**
Bigelow beargrass

*Widely distributed, Bigelow nolina is Nevada's only native nolina. [Newberry Mountains, Lake Mead N.R.A.]*

Bigelow nolina could be considered a refined distant cousin of Mojave yucca, a species that often shares the same mountainous desert habitat. Unlike the robust, stiff, and unforgiving leaves of Mojave yucca, Bigelow nolina has slender grayish green leaves that are flexible and a taller, narrower inflorescence. Each plant has 50 to 100 strap-shaped leaves in rosettes that vary from 30 inches (75 cm) to over 7 feet (220 cm) in diameter. These plants occur as single or colonial rosettes, branching at ground level or with trunks to 8 feet (2.5 m) tall draped with dried leaves. The leaves are 20 to 60 inches (50–150 cm) long, mostly 0.75 to 1.2 inches (2–3 cm) wide, and are distinguished from those of all other *Nolina* species by having filiferous margins. The tiny white flowers bloom from May to June and are held on an inflorescence that is typically 6 to 9 feet (1.9–2.8 m) tall 13 to 22 inches (33–55 cm) wide.

Bigelow nolina is the most widespread nolina in our region and Nevada's only native representative of the genus. It occupies rocky upland slopes in the northwestern Sonoran Desert of Arizona and Mexico, the Colorado Desert of southeastern California, and the southern Mojave Desert of California and Nevada. It occurs with several cholla species, Mojave yucca, and various shrubs that are common in creosote bush scrub. Bigelow nolina is usually found at elevations from 2000 to 4100 feet. A great place to see Bigelow nolina

*Chaparral nolina occurs only at scattered locales in cismontane California. [Santa Ana Mountains, Orange Co.]*

is east of Christmas Tree Pass in the Newberry Mountains northwest of Laughlin, Nevada, within the Lake Mead National Recreation Area. Bigelow nolina is known to be highly variable from one population to another.

## CHAPARRAL NOLINA
*Nolina cismontana*
(no-LY-nah sis-mon-TAN-uh)
**Recent Synonyms**
*Nolina parryi*
**Other Common Names**
chaparral beargrass

It is an amazing sight when chaparral nolinas bloom en masse, especially when a steep brushy slope is punctuated by dozens of their pale-green and golden flowering stalks. Each inflorescence is impressive in size, measuring 4 to 10 feet (1.3–3.1 m) tall, 4 to 16 inches (10–40 cm) wide and approximately 1.25 inches (2–3.5 cm) in diameter at the base. Chaparral nolina is intermediate in size between the smaller Dehesa nolina and the larger Parry nolina. It has fewer, narrower leaves than those of Parry nolina and a narrower inflorescence. Newly sprouted rosettes are about the size of those of Dehesa nolina, but they lack the blue cross-banding of that species. Chaparral nolina rosettes consist of 30 to 90 leaves that are 20 to 55 inches (50–140 cm) long and approximately 0.5 to 1.2 inches (1.2–3 cm) wide.

For years, chaparral nolina suffered from a case of mistaken identity when it was treated as *Nolina parryi* (Parry nolina) by California botanist Carl Munz and others. In 1988, nolina expert James Dice renamed and described the nolina of the coastal mountains as *Nolina cismontana*. As its scientific name, *cismontana*, implies, this species is found only in the cismontane region of southern California. Parry nolina occurs only on the desert

*Deshesa nolina is known from only 12 locations, including this area near Syquan Peak. [San Diego Co.]*

side of the Transverse and Peninsular ranges.

Chaparral nolina is limited to scattered populations ranging from the Ojai Valley area and Simi Hills in Ventura County south to the vicinity of Viejas Mountain near the community of Alpine in San Diego County. A few of the larger concentrations of chaparral nolina are found in the Santa Ana Mountains. Good places to see this species are the Trabuco Canyon area and at O'Neill Regional Park in Orange County. Like many chaparral plants, this nolina resprouts quickly and blooms profusely following fires. Chaparral nolina grows in chaparral on sandstone and shale soils, and its habitat is threatened by the spread of housing developments.

## DEHESA NOLINA
*Nolina interrata*
(no-LY-nah in-ter-ROT-uh)
**Other Common Names**
Dehesa beargrass, buried nolina

The rare Dehesa nolina resembles a large bunchgrass more than it looks like other nolinas in California. This fire-adapted species has an underground trunk that branches and sends up rosettes with only 10 to 50 leaves. Since Dehesa nolina branches below ground, what appears to be a small colony of plants is actually multiple branches of the same plant. The leaves may be 1 to 5 feet long (30–150 cm), but are usually about 3 feet long (85–105 cm) and 0.5 to 1.4 inches wide (1.2–3.5 cm). The attractive bluish green leaves often show a grayish cross-banding. As a species of the fire-prone chaparral plant community, Dehesa nolina sprouts readily and seems to flower prolifically following a burn. Although it rarely blossoms in the absence of fire, Dehesa nolina is capable of flowering when it is only 3 years old, in contrast to the other nolinas in our region that require 8 to 20 years of growth before blooming. The small-flowered inflorescence of this elusive plant measures 20 to 70 inches (50–180 cm) tall and 4 to 20 inches (10–50 cm) wide.

Dehesa nolina is known from only 12 populations: 9 are located east of El Cajon in San Diego County and 3 in northwestern Baja California. It grows with chaparral yucca, manzanita, California buckwheat, chamise, and other chaparral shrubs and is restricted to gabbro substrates that are rich in iron and magnesium. Although the largest populations are protected within ecological preserves managed by the California Department of Fish and Game and the Nature Conservancy, other populations are threatened by housing developments and illegal collecting.

## PARRY NOLINA
*Nolina parryi*
(No-LY-nah PEAR-ee-eye)
**Recent Synonyms**
*Nolina bigelovii* ssp. *parryi, N. wolfii, N. parryi* ssp. *wolfii*
**Other Common Names**
giant nolina, Parry beargrass

The pre-dawn silhouette of a large Parry nolina in flower is a memorable sight. When gathering twilight illuminates the spindle-shaped inflorescences, they can glow like giant white candles suspended above the surrounding vegetation. The massive flowering stalks of Parry nolina, which are produced from April to June, may reach over

10 feet (1.4–3.8 m) tall and are usually about 1 to 2 feet (28–70 cm) across, and some may be over 4 feet (130 cm) wide. The multitude of blossoms attracts pollinating moths in the genus *Mesepiola*, a less specialized cousin of the yucca moth, as well as bees and numerous other insects. The plant's finely serrated green leaves measure 20 to 55 inches (50–140 cm) long and 0.8 to 1.5 inches (2–4 cm) wide; rosettes consist of 60 to 220 leaves.

Parry nolina, the largest and most commonly observed nolina in California, was named in honor of its collector, the peripatetic botanist Charles C. Parry (1823–1890). With its twisted trunk and head tuft of long narrow leaves, it would seem to fit perfectly in the zany world of a Dr. Seuss story. Like Bigelow nolina, Parry nolina is highly variable among populations, with short-stemmed plants common in some regions and tall plants predominant in others. The population of Parry nolina in the Kingston Range of northeastern San Bernardino County is known for its enormous solitary rosettes of relatively broad rigid leaves growing from short unbranched trunks; at one time the Kingston Range plants were even treated as a distinct subspecies named Wolf nolina. In contrast, the populations in Joshua Tree National Park have somewhat shorter leaves, but many plants have tall branched trunks with numerous rosettes.

Parry nolina, like chaparral nolina, is endemic to California. It occurs from the desert slopes of the Laguna Mountains in San Diego County north to the Kern Plateau in the southern Sierra and eastward to mountainous areas of the Mojave Desert and western Colorado Desert. Found from 4000 feet up to 6900 feet, Parry nolina occurs at higher elevations than other nolinas. It grows in well-drained granitic soils, often among granite boulders. This captivating nolina is found in a broad range of plant communities and is associated with plants such as Joshua tree, Mojave yucca, desert bitterbrush, and pinyon pine. Impressive specimens can be seen along the road to Keys View in Joshua Tree National Park and in the Kingston Range.

*A Parry nolina in the Kingston Range displays the huge rosette typical of this population. [San Bernardino Co.]*

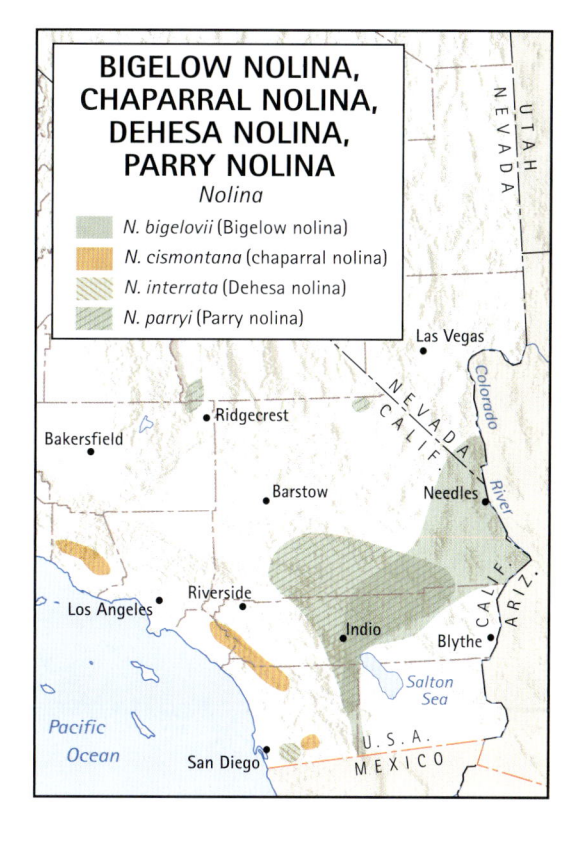

# OCOTILLO
## *Fouquieria splendens* ssp. *splendens*
(foo-kee-AIR-ee-uh SPLEN-denz)

**Other Common Names**
coachwhip, candlewood, Jacob's staff, vine cactus

Many visitors to the Colorado Desert become enamored with the spindly but beautiful ocotillo, which is neither a cactus nor an agave. Ocotillo is 1 of only 11 species in a very old plant family (Fouquieriaceae) that has only 1 genus, *Fouquieria*. This plant family is centered in Mexico, and ocotillo is the only one of its species that ranges north into the United States.

For much of the year this unusual plant survives as a cluster of 15-foot-long spiny branches that are whipped by the dry desert winds. In the spring its slender, splayed branches are tightly clad with bright green leaves and topped with flaming-red tubular flowers. The blooms attract tourists, photographers, and—more importantly for the ocotillo—pollinating hummingbirds. Ocotillo flowers are critical springtime fueling stations for hummingbirds migrating north from their wintering grounds in Mexico. Five species of hummingbirds, as well as verdins, Scott's orioles, and other birds, feed on nectar at the base of the tubular flowers and in the process pass pollen from one flower to another.

Ocotillo's spiny branches, water-storing stems, shallow roots, and desert habitat have led many people to mistake it for a bizarre type of cactus. But a cactus it is not. The ocotillo "to the casual observer, appeared as curious as it is puzzling to the scientific botanist," wrote George Engelmann, the well-known botanist who described ocotillo and numerous other desert plants of the Southwest.

Ocotillo is drought deciduous: when its shallow root system is unable to retrieve adequate soil moisture, it drops its leaves. It can also rapidly leaf out, sometimes within two to three days after a soaking rain. A network of water storage cells surround the leaf buds directly beneath the thin epidermis, and each of these cells contains the oil and sugar ingredients that enable leaves to burst forth in short order—as long as enough water is available.

Ocotillo has two types of leaves: primary and secondary. Primary leaves are the first leaves produced on young shoots, and they grow rapidly in response to a thorough wetting of the soil. When a primary leaf drops, the petiole falls away and leaves behind tough lower outgrowth, which becomes a conical spine. Secondary leaves emerge in clusters containing two to eight leaves; they lack petioles and arise from buds in the axils between the spines and the stem. Even a moderate wetting of ocotillo branches can stimulate the growth of new secondary leaves. An individual stem will produce primary leaves only once, but secondary leaves may grow and drop off as many as six times a year, depending on rainfall patterns.

Ocotillo spines are unusual, or, as Engelmann put it, "quite unique." They are formed from an

*In spring, migrating hummingbirds rely on the nectar-rich flowers of ocotillos. [Anza-Borrego Desert S.P.]*

*Within days of a rain, previously leafless ocotillos can be covered in new green leaves. [Anza-Borrego Desert S.P.]*

outgrowth of the outer stem cortex and epidermis and are not stiffened petioles, as is often assumed. Spines offer protection from potential ocotillo browsers, including rabbits and packrats and other rodents. Bad-tasting chemical compounds in the outer surfaces of an ocotillo, such as saponins, tannins, and resins, also help prevent herbivory as well as retard water loss. No spines or chemicals protect ocotillo's shallow roots, however, and pocket gophers relish them as an excellent source of starchy food. In the absence of severe, prolonged drought and weak roots caused by pocket gopher activity, an ocotillo may survive for as long as 200 years.

Large old specimens growing in nutrient-rich sites may produce up to 75 branches and attain heights from 25 to 30 feet. Most ocotillos of the Colorado Desert are shorter, in the 10- to 15-foot range, but they can still put forth an abundance of showy red flowers. Ocotillos occur from central Texas to the western edge of California's Colorado Desert and also in a few spots at the southern tip of Nevada. They grow in Sonoran creosote bush scrub, often with desert agave, desert barrel cactus, and teddy-bear cholla.

**OCOTILLO**
*Fouquieria splendens* ssp. *splendens*

## Non-Native Naturalized Cacti and Agaves

In California, several species of non-native cacti and agaves have escaped from cultivation and have become established in the surrounding vegetation, where they are referred to as "naturalized" plants. Cacti and agaves that have naturalized in our region are species used by humans as sources of food or for ornamental horticulture. In habitats that offer the right conditions, naturalized species and cultivars thrive, spread, and even occasionally hybridize with a close relative that is a native. The most common cacti and agaves that have become naturalized in native plant communities and disturbed areas are described below.

**Indian-fig cactus** *(Opuntia ficus-indica)* may be more familiar to many Californians than any of our native cacti. Its huge pads, abundant orange or red fruits, and tree-like stature make Indian-fig cactus easy to recognize. This cactus forms a woody trunk and may grow to 20 feet (6 m) tall and 10 feet (3 m) wide. Its oblong pads measure 4 to 10 inches (10–25 cm) wide and 8 to 24 inches (20–60 cm) long. The form of Indian-fig cactus seen most often in native plant communities has sizeable spiny pads, yellow flowers, and large globular fruits, which ripen from green to orange.

This utilitarian cactus has been transported around the world since the 16th century. It was first brought to California by Spanish Franciscans in 1769 and eventually planted at all of the missions. The "Mission cactus," as it became known, was cultivated at the missions and ranchos for its edible fruit and for its mucilage that was used as glue in making adobe bricks. Indian-fig cactus probably originated in central Mexico, but its exact native habitat is unknown because humans have transplanted this cactus so widely.

Indian-fig cactus is the most economically important cactus in the world and is today grown in numerous countries on five continents. Fruits of Indian-fig cactus, the "figs," are also known as "cactus apples," "cactus pears," or *tunas*. They are high in fiber, vitamin C, fructose, and other sugars and are used in an amazing array of food and medicinal products. The fruits are consumed raw or dried, after brushing off the glochids. They are also juiced and/or pressed and then cooked to make jam, syrup, candy, or a fermented drink called *colonche*. An extract from Indian-fig cactus fruits has recently shown promise in tests as a treatment for certain symptoms of alcohol hangover because of its anti-inflammatory properties. Some spineless Indian-fig cultivars, known as *nopales* or *nopalitos*, are especially valued for their pads, which are utilized in countless ways, ranging from ingredients in gourmet salads to disposable lunch "plates" by field laborers.

Indian-fig cactus grows in cismontane California from Santa Cruz County south into Mexico and on Santa Cruz, Santa Catalina, and San Clemente islands; it is not found in Nevada. In California, Indian-fig cactus is seldom seen in undisturbed native plant communities far from population centers, but it is locally common in disturbed and native habitats near historic missions and ranchos. It occurs in coastal sage scrub, chaparral, and grasslands, often in the company of other non-native species. Indian-fig cactus was once thought to hybridize with several prickly-pear species, but the only proven genetic hybrids with this cactus are crosses with brown-spined prickly-pear in a single area on the east side of the city of San Luis Obispo.

*Spanish missionaries brought Indian-fig cactus to California in the 18th century. [La Purisima Mission S.H.P]*

**Arborescent prickly-pear** *(Opuntia leucotricha)* is a large tree-like cactus that is cultivated for its sweet fruits high in vitamin C. This species grows 8 to 13 feet (2.4–4 m) tall and branches widely. The distinct roundish pads have closely spaced areoles with 1 to 3 white flexible spines and a layer of very short, fine hairs, giving the pads a velvet-like sheen. Arborescent prickly-pear is native to the highlands of central Mexico but has become naturalized in Florida and more recently in some canyons in the San Diego area.

**Bunny ears prickly-pear** *(Opuntia microdasys)* grows as a shrub to 3.3 feet (1 m) tall and up to twice as wide. Bunny ears prickly-pear is sometimes known as polka-dot cactus due to its closely spaced areoles with dense tufts of pale yellow to brown glochids. This highly adaptable and unique-looking prickly-pear is popular in cultivation despite its abundant and potentially irritating glochids, which can become airborne on a windy day. Bunny ears prickly-pear is a native of Mexico's Chihuahuan Desert but some plants have become established close to urban areas in southern California and Arizona.

**Golden torch cereus** *(Echinopsis spachiana)* is more readily identified by people as an exotic cactus since it appears more out of place in California than the naturalized prickly-pears noted above. It is a popular garden plant that produces multiple columnar golden stems approximately 2.5 inches (6 cm) wide and 3 to 6 feet (1–2 m) tall that bear beautiful white, night-blooming flowers 6 inches (15 cm) wide. Golden torch cereus can be seen in many parts of southern California, where it occasionally escapes cultivation. It is native to western Argentina and Bolivia.

**Century plant or American agave** *(Agave americana)* is frequently seen in cultivation and has naturalized in Mediterranean areas throughout the world. The common name, century plant, is also used to refer to the entire *Agave* genus and sometimes to desert agave, but this century plant is a familiar sight in populated regions of central and southern California. It is much more robust than any of our native agaves and can form a rosette up to 12 feet (3.7 m) across and 4.5 to 6.5 feet (1.5–2 m) tall. The broad, stiff, spine-margined leaves may be green or variegated with yellow or white, depending on the subspecies and cultivar. The immense flowering stalk of century plant reaches 16 to 30 feet (5–9 m) high with yellow tubular flowers emerging from horizontal branches in the upper half of the inflorescence.

*Many people mistake* Agave americana *for a California native since it is widely planted here. [San Diego Co.]*

The native subspecies and varieties of *Agave americana* are found from eastern Mexico through southern Texas to southern Arizona. There are numerous forms in cultivation, although not all of them are naturalizing. This agave is spread through dissemination of its seeds or when uprooted plants are contained in garden cuttings that are dumped near native plant communities.

*Whether in the wild or in cultivation, Mojave prickly-pear is a showy species. [Hiko Range, Lincoln Co.]*

CHAPTER FOUR

# Conservation and Cultivation

*The desert is the kingdom of the cacti, for the cacti are the special offspring of the desert... Their part is to hold the frontier that meets the Empire of Drought, and they are shaped and armed for the task... Yet, it seems as if when the matter of blossoms came up, Nature's heart relented: she could not bring herself to fashion a forbidding flower.*
—J. Smeaton Chase, *California Desert Trails*, 1919

## Conservation in Cactus Country

Over 60 different native species or varieties of cacti, agaves, and yuccas grow in California and Nevada. Some are common and widespread, such as buckhorn cholla and Mojave yucca, while others are intriguing and rare, such as Great Basin fishhook cactus and Shaw agave. These plants inhabit millions of acres within the two states, and although they look formidable and demonstrate resilience to environmental change, they are vulnerable to a wide array of impacts, ranging from habitat loss to illegal collecting.

Direct loss of habitat is usually cited as the most significant factor leading to the decline of a given plant or animal species, and this is the case for many species of cacti, agaves, and yuccas. Commercial, residential, and agricultural development, as well as mining and construction of highway and utility-line corridors are some of the causes of habitat destruction. Within existing habitat, threats to these native plants include: heavy grazing by cattle, wild burros, and horses; illegal off-highway vehicle (OHV) use; military activities; competition from invasive, exotic weeds; and illegal collecting.

Some of the most imperiled species grow in areas directly impacted by urbanization. Snake cholla, Shaw agave, and golden cereus all have populations that have been negatively affected by development in southern coastal San Diego County. Locations within commuting distance of large urban centers, such as the Antelope Valley outside of Los Angeles, have also experienced large scale loss of habitat for cacti, agaves, or yuccas. The city of Palmdale responded to rapid commercial and residential development by enacting an ordinance to protect desert vegetation in 1992. The law was written expressly to protect the Joshua tree and other native desert vegetation, "so as to retain the unique natural desert aesthetics in some areas of this city."

*This coastal prickly-pear makes an attractive garden specimen. [Santa Barbara Bot. Gar.]* PHOTO © JOHN EVARTS

The Bakersfield cactus *(Opuntia basilaris* var. *treleasei)* is currently the only species of Cactaceae or Agavaceae in our region that is listed as endangered. It has been protected under the Endangered Species Act since 1990. This species is still threatened by future housing developments, OHV use, sand and gravel mining, pesticide drift from adjacent farmland, and competition from exotic

*Mojave yucca is used here to help revegetate a new pipeline route in the Spring Mountains. [Toiyabe N.F.]*

*A small population of the endangered Bakersfield cactus is protected here at Sand Ridge Reserve. [Kern Co.]*

weeds. The recovery goal for Bakersfield cactus is to protect its habitat—especially within its five largest populations—and maintain self-sustaining populations throughout its current range.

In addition to loss of habitat, degradation of remaining habitat puts plants at risk. Grazing has a detrimental effect when domestic or feral cattle, goats, burros, and horses eat young yuccas and trample and uproot young plants. OHV travel outside of designated routes may smash seedlings and small plants. Although restricted military lands protect thousands of square miles of native plant habitats in our region, bombing and large-scale tank maneuvers on military bases can destroy vegetation over extended areas. All of these activities cause soil compaction, which makes some soils more prone to erosion and invasion by weeds.

Mitigation of deleterious effects to the habitat of these and other native plants are detailed in laws and ordinances passed by various local, state, and federal agencies. Mining, and road- and power-corridor construction projects are usually required to reduce impacts to cactus, agave, and yucca populations; this is done by salvaging plants affected by disturbance and either transplanting them to adjacent areas or holding them to be transplanted back onsite when construction is completed. Native plant society chapters or other groups often volunteer their labor and expertise for such "cactus wrangling," but the project proponent is legally responsible for the success of the transplant operation. In most cases, survival of transplants is high if it is done under the supervision of experienced botanical consultants. Plants featured in this book that are considered rare, threatened, endangered, or of special concern by either public agencies or private organizations are listed in Appendix F, "Species Rarity Status" on page 220.

## Invasive Weeds in Arid Habitats

Invasive weeds, as defined here, are non-native plants that become established in disturbed habitats and eventually spread into otherwise healthy habitats. Most of California's and Nevada's exotic weeds are from southern Europe and northern Africa; they were either brought over deliberately as cattle and sheep forage or arrived here by accident. These are not your garden-variety weeds that can be reasonably managed by pulling, spraying, or burning. These weeds are highly adaptable species—often self-pollinated or wind-pollinated—capable of producing thousands of seeds that germinate early and grow rapidly, out-competing natives for available moisture and living space. The spread of invasive weeds into native plant habitats throughout the United States is having increasingly destructive consequences, and many public land managers now consider this problem to be a biological emergency.

The most aggressive and damaging invasive weeds in our region are annual plants. The list of top offenders includes: cheatgrass, red brome or foxtail chess, ripgut brome, red-stemmed filaree, Russian thistle or tumbleweed, fountain grasses, Mediterranean grass, and Sahara mustard. In wet years, the dense growth of exotic brome grasses engulfs low-growing cacti and the lower stems of prickly-pears, which makes them more susceptible to rot. Sahara mustard—one of our region's newest and worst weeds—has spread rapidly through the low deserts of California and Nevada since the 1980s and has recently invaded coastal sage scrub communities in southern California. It now grows alongside the endangered Bakersfield cactus in central Kern County. All of these weeds reduce local biodiversity by displacing native species and altering the fire regime and plant community structure.

Winters with above-average rainfall give a huge boost to the annual weeds noted above. When these weeds die, they add fuel to the landscape, enabling wildfires to burn through desert vegetation that is not adapted to burning. Although fire is a natural event in chaparral and other Mediterranean vegetation types, fire in the deserts of California and Nevada was rare and local before the recent arrival of weeds. A lightning strike that might have ignited a lone Joshua tree will now spread through the dry weedy grasses that blanket the open ground between shrubs, carrying even into sparsely vegetated rocky areas and burning desert barrel and fishhook cacti. Annual weeds increase the severity and frequency of fires and germinate readily during the winter following a wildfire. This enables them to become even more abundant and better able to spread farther into undisturbed habitats. The vicious cycle of weed

*After a fire killed these Mojave yuccas and other plants, red brome has taken over. [Red Rock Canyon N.C.A.]*

proliferation and fire can be partially thwarted by drought, but most of these weed seeds persist in the soil for several years.

Federal and state public-land managers, non-profit organizations, and dedicated individuals have started Cooperative Weed Management Areas (WMAs) throughout the country that promote weed awareness and raise funds for eradication programs. For more information on WMAs see Appendix G, "Education, Conservation, and Cultivation Resources" on page 221.

**Illegal Harvest**

Vandalism and illegal collecting of native cacti, agaves, and yuccas are crimes that often go undetected and unpunished. Although current California and Nevada state laws prohibit the destruction or unpermitted removal of these plants from public lands, the sight of a Joshua tree or giant saguaro that has been used for target practice is a depressing reminder that these plants are difficult to protect.

California and Nevada have fewer rare and highly coveted cactus species than Mexico, Arizona, Texas, or Utah. Nevertheless, wild collecting threatens local populations of desirable *Coryphantha, Ferocactus, Mammillaria,* and *Sclerocactus* species in our region. In the 1920s it was not uncommon for Hollywood producers and Los Angeles residents with "Saguaro Fever" to harvest saguaros from California's few populations along the Colorado River for use on movie sets and in landscaping. California's only known population of saguaros today numbers around 100 adult specimens, making it one of the state's rarest cacti.

Numerous nurseries propagate and sell cacti, agaves, and yuccas, so there is no justification for abducting plants from the wild. One good way to help conserve these desirable plants and lessen the demand for wild-collected plants is by supporting nurseries that do not trade in illegally collected plants, but legally and responsibly propagate their own. For a list of nurseries that may carry some of the plants in this book, see Appendix G, "Education, Conservation, and Cultivation Resources" on page 221.

**Cultivation**

A key characteristic of cacti, agaves, and yuccas is their tolerance of drought. Their adaptability to dry growing conditions makes them excellent choices for "xeriscaping," which is a type of landscaping that uses xeric (drought-tolerant) plants. Since water is a limited resource in most of California and Nevada, it makes good economic and environmental sense for residents of these states to grow plants that can thrive on local rainfall. Our native cacti, agaves, and yuccas need the right conditions to thrive in a garden or container, but once they are established, many of them require little or no supplemental water.

Before growing these plants outdoors, it is important to find out how well a given species will

*Shotgun shells litter the ground near a truncated Joshua tree that was used for target practice. [Clark Co.]*

*A Joshua tree is a showpiece in this private garden that combines several desert plants. [Palm Desert, CA]*

do in a specific climate zone. For instance, Shaw agave will thrive from San Diego to San Francisco, but would probably not survive the high summer temperature and aridity of Las Vegas, a city better suited for growing desert agave. Some plants, such as beehive cactus, have a wide geographic scope and can tolerate a broad range of temperatures and soil types. Others, such as the limestone-dwelling Utah agave, are more narrowly distributed and are more specific in their cultivation requirements.

## Growing Plants in Containers

Growing small cacti, agaves, and yuccas in containers has many advantages. It offers more control over growing conditions and allows for specialized soil mixtures and watering regimes. Plants in pots are also transportable; they can be moved indoors to avoid frost damage or placed under protective shade to reduce excess summer heat. Agaves and yuccas are especially amenable to container cultivation because their roots tolerate crowding. Growing plants in containers, however, can be labor intensive. Potted plants need to be repotted every few years and require more attention to watering and fertilizing than plants grown in the ground. Plants in containers will dry out more quickly, and if placed outdoors, they will experience wider temperature swings than those planted in the ground or kept indoors.

In general, cacti, agaves, and yuccas cope better when under-potted, because an over-sized pot encourages over-watering, which can lead to rot. A deep pot that provides adequate room for roots is preferable to one that is too shallow. Soil mixtures in porous clay pots dry out more rapidly than those in plastic pots. Repotting with new mix rejuvenates the root system and assures that your plant is not root-bound. A layer of rocks, a paper towel, or a piece of window screen placed in the bottom of the pot work well for retaining the mix while allowing water to pass through the pot's drainage holes. Before re-potting, loosen the plant's root ball. Cut back any damaged or dead roots and allow them to dry for a day or two; this will stimulate growth of their fine feeder roots. Agaves and yuccas should be potted a bit high to avoid crown rot. Place them so that their lowest leaves are above the edge of the pot and where their crowns are unlikely to subside below the soil level. A top-dressing of clean gravel or colorful rocks aids in reducing moisture, helps keep soil in the pot when you water, and adds a finishing touch.

Most cacti, agaves, and yuccas need excellent drainage, whether they are potted and grown on a windowsill or planted outside in a garden. Roots require air as well as water, and a soil that holds water to the exclusion of air will suffocate the roots. The easiest and often best choice for potted plants is a general commercial cactus and succulent mix with adequate organic material, perlite, and vermiculite; this combination will help to trap air, hold water, and prevent soil compaction. Many cactus and succulent growers make their own soilless mix with one part porous materials, such as perlite, vermiculite, or pumice, and one part organic materials, such as pine or fir bark, coconut

*Many cacti, agaves, and yuccas thrive in pots, like these two specimens of desert barrel cactus. [Mono Co.]*

*Desert agave (center) may be carried at specialty nurseries. [Santa Barbara Bot. Gar.]* PHOTO © JOHN EVARTS

fiber (coir), or composted peanut shells. Another recipe recommends one part commercial potting mix, one part pumice, and one part decomposed granite.

The right amount of water is critical to the survival of potted cacti, agaves, and yuccas. Provide water only when necessary. This may seem obvious, but giving too much water too frequently is easy to do and will surely lead to the premature death of your native succulent. Watering should be thorough, but allow the soil to dry out before the next watering. Our region's native plants are most active from the late winter to mid-summer months, and they require more water during this growing and flowering season than when resting or dormant. Their roots will still grow during the fall and winter, as long as some water is provided. However, avoid watering unless the soil is completely dry in the root zone. Since the watering regime depends on how often a plant dries out, relevant factors such as light, temperature, soil mix, and container size and type will also help dictate watering needs. In general, providing water every 5 to 10 days during active growth, and every 4 to 6 weeks during dormancy, should be adequate in most situations.

Your plants will benefit from a light monthly fertilizing beginning in the early spring and through the summer. Dilute liquid fertilizers to approximately one-quarter of the label's recommended strength. Most fertilizers for soilless mixes contain numerous trace elements as well as three main components—nitrogen (N), phosphorus (P), and potassium (K). Nitrogen is used by plants for building cells and tissues that make up leaves and stems; phosphorus is necessary for flower and seed production and for a healthy root system; and potassium is crucial for plant metabolic processes and for maintaining proper cellular water content. A fertilizer with more phosphorus than the other minerals, such as an N-P-K content of 5-10-5 or 5-10-6, is best for these plants. Our native cacti, agaves, and yuccas do not need any fertilizer during their winter resting season.

Most container-grown cacti, agaves, and yuccas will flourish in a location where you can maximize their sun exposure without scorching them. In the hotter climates zones, they generally do best with some partial shade that protects them from excessive summer heat. Newly potted plants should be gradually acclimated if they are being moved into a spot that receives full sun. For indoor plants, a good location is a south or southeast-facing window, as long as it is not too hot and ventilation is good.

## Growing Plants in the Garden

It is essential that garden-grown cacti, agaves, and yuccas have good drainage, so their roots do not remain wet and become prone to rot during cold, damp weather. If your garden soil has too much clay to provide adequate drainage, you will need to create a raised bed or mound using a commercial succulent mix. Adding large-grain sand, pumice, or clean gravel to your existing soil may be feasible for small areas, such as raised beds or mounds, and will help with aeration and drainage. Native succulents in the garden, like their counterparts in containers, should be watered more during the spring and summer. However, when compared to container-grown specimens, plants in the garden require less watering throughout the year and will dry out more slowly after each irrigation. Garden plants will also better withstand cold weather if the soil is not too damp.

Planting outdoors should be done in the spring for areas with cool to cold winters, such as the Great Basin and northern Mojave deserts, so that roots can become established during the spring and summer growing season. New plants that are set out in a hot, southern exposure in the garden need shading until they become established and acclimated to these new conditions, especially if they are planted in the spring. For regions with very hot and dry summers and more mild winters, such as the Colorado and southern Mojave deserts, it is best to transplant outdoors after the summer heat has passed. If the plant's roots can become established during the winter, then the plant will not be as prone to heat stress during the following summer. For areas with more moderate winters and summers, such as coastal southern California, the seasonal timing for outdoor planting is not as critical.

When planting agaves or stemless yuccas outside, follow the same advice used to avoid crown rot in containers; raise the center of the hole slightly so that the crown of the plant does not sink below what will be the eventual soil line when the soil inevitably settles. A mulch of rocks or gravel around your cactus, agave, or yucca serves several functions. It will keep soil temperatures near the root zone from getting too hot in the summer, offer some winter insulation, help retain moisture, and minimize weeds.

## Propagating from Seeds and Cuttings

Starting a plant from seed and nurturing the seedling until it is a mature, flowering specimen is a rewarding experience. To raise cacti, yuccas, and agaves from seed, it is best to sow their seeds in the spring. Start by filling 2-inch pots or a 2- to 3-inch-deep flat with a mix that is 2 parts potting soil amended with 1 part pumice, perlite, or decomposed granite to increase drainage. Alternatively, you can use commercial cactus and succulent mix and add a small amount of potting soil to help retain water. Water the mix thoroughly and allow

*These Shaw agave offsets are ready for replanting. [Santa Barbara Bot. Gar.]* PHOTO © JOHN EVARTS

the water to drain completely. The seeds should be sown evenly about 1 inch apart on top of the mix and covered lightly with coarse sand. Keep the surface of the seeded mix warm and moist but not saturated (using a water-sprayer is ideal), and place the flat or small pots in bright, indirect light. Seedlings need more water than older plants, but they can succumb to damping-off (a disease caused by soil fungi) if kept too wet. Covering your container(s) with clear plastic will create a warm and humid microclimate, but be careful

*This demonstration garden features snake cholla, golden cereus, Shaw agave, and dudleyas. [Imperial Beach]*

*Snake cholla is vegetatively propagated in one-gallon pots at Recon Native Plant Nursery. [Imperial Beach]*

not to over-heat. A cover is not necessary once the seeds have germinated and grown for a week or two. Most seeds will germinate within three weeks. When the seedlings become crowded—after 2 months for most agaves and yuccas and 6 to 12 months for cacti—they can be transplanted into individual containers filled with cactus and succulent mix. As their size increases over time, transplant them into bigger pots as needed.

As with sowing seeds, spring is also the best time to propagate with cuttings. Segmented cacti, such as chollas and prickly-pears, are the easiest to propagate from cuttings. To start a cutting, use a sterile sharp knife or clippers, or simply break off a new, but mature, pad or stem-joint. Fungi and bacteria can infect the fresh wound on a cut cactus. To avoid this, keep the cutting in a warm, dry, shaded place for one to two weeks until a callus has formed, but before the stem starts to greatly shrivel. Bury the cut end just deep enough into standard cactus mix for the cutting to stand upright. Water or spray it lightly, and keep it humid and in bright indirect light. Eventually new roots will grow from the buried areoles to produce a self-supporting clone of the original cholla or prickly-pear.

The easiest way to vegetatively propagate agaves and chaparral yucca is to separate their offsets, or pups, from the mother plant. It is illegal to dig up any native plant on public lands, but taking offsets from a garden plant is a convenient way to start a new colony somewhere else. Offsets can be removed simply by digging them out. They usually pull free from the mother plant with some prodding, although not always easily. If they need to be cut, let the roots dry and callus over for a week or two before planting. Separating offsets is best done in the fall or spring.

**Ten Native Choices for Cultivation**
Many of our regional cacti, agaves, and yuccas have proven themselves worthy of cultivation in a container or in a garden landscape and are sure to add drama and diversity to any plant collection. Their placement in a garden landscape requires planning because of the hazards posed by spines, glochids, or spine-tipped leaves. A well-designed garden should account for proper placement of these plants away from traffic areas where unwary visitors, children, or pets will not accidentally be stuck, poked, or gouged. These plants can also be difficult to weed around, so rid the area of weeds before planting. A rock mulch around the new transplants will also minimize weeds and insulate the root zone. To help you select a species that is a good match for your area, we have included the *Sunset Western Garden Book* Climate Zones with each plant profile that follows.

In addition to the 10 species listed below, there are others that do well in cultivation and are available at some nurseries. For coastal regions of southern and central California, these include coastal prickly-pear, coastal cholla, and coast barrel cactus. Desert agave, Joshua tree, fishhook cacti, and giant saguaro all do relatively well when cultivated outdoors in our desert areas, and any of these would make a spectacular addition to most home landscapes.

*A flowering stalk rises from a clustered planting of Shaw agave. [Santa Barbara Bot. Gar.]* PHOTO © JOHN EVARTS

*Left: Utah agave thrives in warmer locales and is exceptionally cold-hardy. [Grand Canyon N.P.]*
*Right: This close-up shows the inflorescence and leaf tips of chaparral yucca. [Santa Barbara Bot. Gar.]*

**Shaw agave,** *Agave shawii* var. *shawii*
Sunset Climate Zones: 12, 16–24; hardy to 25°F (-4°C).
Light/Soil: full sun to partial shade/well-drained, loamy soils.
Uses: outdoor gardens or in containers; produces numerous offsets and can make a short but formidable barrier; its ornamental shape and colonial growth work well on a slope; blends well with cacti and other succulents; decorative form and color lends itself to container use.
Notes: its architectural form makes Shaw agave a handsome garden plant; rosette dies after flowering, but forms offsets; it is relatively adaptable and could be grown in a shaded, warm desert garden with summer irrigation, but better adapted for cooler, coastal climate; limited frost tolerance.

**Utah agave,** *Agave utahensis* varieties
Sunset Climate Zones: 2, 3, 10–12, 18–21; hardy to -10°F (-23°C).
Light/Soil: full sun/exceptionally well-drained.
Uses: outdoor gardens or in containers; produces offsets and thrives in warmer locales; its ornamental shape and small rosettes make it good as a featured plant or to add contrast.
Notes: rosette dies after flowering, but forms numerous offsets, so works best as a clump; flowers attract hummingbirds, and foliage is rabbit and deer resistant; exceptionally cold-hardy.

**Chaparral yucca,** *Hesperoyucca whipplei*
Sunset Climate Zones: 2, 3, 7–12, 14–24; hardy to 10°F (-12°C).
Light/Soil: full sun to partial shade/well-drained, loamy soils.
Uses: outdoor gardens; produces offsets and can make a formidable barrier; silhouette looks good against a wall.
Notes: its distinctive form makes chaparral yucca a dramatic garden plant for contrast; variable and

relatively adaptable; rosette flowers after 3 to 15 years; most forms produce offsets and may grow quite large, other forms require propagation from seed; sold also as *Yucca whipplei*.

**Banana yucca,** *Yucca baccata* var. *baccata*
Sunset Climate Zones: 2, 3, 7, 9–12, 14, 18–23; hardy to -20°F (-29°C).
Light/Soil: full sun to partial shade/well-drained.
Uses: outdoor gardens; its branches make a good barrier; good for native plant gardens or as transition from wild habitat to formal garden.
Notes: its extreme temperature tolerance, large flower clusters, sculptural form, and blue-green leaves make banana yucca a popular garden plant throughout the interior southwestern U.S., with different forms available; needs lots of room to grow and spread; will not tolerate cold, damp, loamy soils.

**Beehive cactus,** *Coryphantha vivipara* var. *rosea*
Sunset Climate Zones: 2, 3, 9–12, 18–23; hardy to -25°F (-32°C).
Light/Soil: full sun to partial shade/well-drained.
Uses: outdoor rock gardens or containers; bright magenta flowers and hemispherical shape make beehive cactus very attractive.
Notes: its small size could be lost in some gardens; relatively easy to grow and adaptable, but needs to be dry during cold weather; available in several forms as *Escobaria vivipara,* or "spiny star."

**Teddy-bear cholla,** *Cylindropuntia bigelovii*
Sunset Climate Zones: 11–13, 19–24; hardy to 0°F (-18°C).
Light/Soil: full sun/well-drained.
Uses: outdoor gardens; can make a formidable barrier; its golden-spined silhouette is captivating when backlit.
Notes: its dramatic, golden sculptural form, especially when backlit, makes teddy-bear cholla a bold addition to any garden; tolerant of high temperatures and needs little water; fallen stem-joints can take root, and it is easy to propagate from stem-joints; plan for freely falling, hazardous stem-joints; sold also as *Opuntia bigelovii*.

**Mojave mound cactus,** *Echinocereus mojavensis*
Sunset Climate Zones: 2, 3, 10, 11, 14, 18–24; hardy to -10°F (-23°C).
Light/Soil: full sun or partial shade/well-drained.
Uses: outdoor gardens or containers; rich claret-

*Left: Large pendant blossoms are a feature that makes banana yucca popular with gardeners. [Mojave N. Pr.]*
*Right: The diminutive beehive cactus is a good choice for rock gardens or containers. [Mojave N. Pr.]*

*Teddy-bear cholla adds a sculptural element to the landscape. [Santa Barbara Bot. Gar.]* PHOTO © JOHN EVARTS

*Left: Its gorgeous flowers are reason alone to grow Mojave mound cactus in a garden. [Joshua Tree N.P.] Right: Desert barrel cactus has many attractive qualities, such as colorful spines. [Anza-Borrego Desert S.P.]*

colored flowers and eventual tightly clustered, mounded shape make this variable cactus captivating in a garden.
Notes: quite variable with many forms available, including some with very few spines; attracts hummingbirds; recommended for experienced gardeners when grown outdoors.

**Desert barrel cactus,** *Ferocactus cylindraceus*
Sunset Climate Zones: 10–13, 18–24; hardy to 0°F (–18°C).
Light/Soil: full sun/well-drained.
Uses: outdoor gardens or containers; barrel silhouette looks good against a wall or as a contrast to shrubs and perennials; combines very well with other cacti, yuccas, and agaves.
Notes: its distinctive shape makes desert barrel cactus a unique garden plant; tolerates a broad range of temperatures; slow-growing but can reach 8 feet tall, changes from globular to columnar shape; sold also as *Ferocactus acanthodes*.

**Beavertail cactus,** *Opuntia basilaris* var. *basilaris* and var. *brachyclada*
Sunset Climate Zones: 3, 7–14, 18–24; hardy to –5°F (–20°C).
Light/Soil: full sun to partial shade/well-drained.
Uses: outdoor gardens, rock gardens, or in containers; short clumps slowly spread and produce very colorful flower display; provides color and forms a contrast with most other plants.
Notes: beavertail cactus is an adaptable and relatively fast-growing species that will bloom prolifically; easy to propagate from pads or seeds; be wary of glochids.

**Mojave prickly-pear,** *Opuntia polyacantha* var. *erinacea*
Sunset Climate Zones: 2, 3, 7, 10, 11, 18–21; hardy to –10°F (–23°C).
Light/Soil: full sun to partial shade/well-drained.
Uses: outdoor gardens or in containers; adds form and unusual texture to most gardens; its hairy silhouette, especially the long-spined, "grizzly bear" form *(ursina)*, looks dazzling when backlit.
Notes: tolerates broad range of temperatures, but needs strong light for best spine development; easy to propagate from pads or seeds; sold also as *Opuntia erinacea*.

*Above: Mojave prickly-pear's long spines develop best in settings with strong light. [Inyo N.F.] Left: Beavertail cactus is adaptable, relatively fast-growing, and will bloom prolifically. [Mojave N. Pr.]*

*Cottontop cactus survives in harsh environments like this wash in the Funeral Mountains. [Death Valley N.P.]*

CHAPTER FIVE

# Exploring the Cactus Country of California and Nevada

*You meet rough or muddy roads to vex you, and blind paths to perplex you, rocks, mountains, and steep ascents . . . The pleasures of a botanical exploration fully compensate for these miseries and dangers . . . Every step taken into the fields, groves, and hills appears to afford new enjoyments, Landscapes and Plants jointly meet in your sight. Here is an old acquaintance seen again; there a novelty, a rare plant, perhaps a new one! greets your view.*
  —Constantine Samuel Rafinesque, *New Flora of North America*, 1836

## Where to See Cacti, Agaves, and Yuccas on Public Lands

Much of the scenic and biological diversity of California and Nevada's wildlands is protected within our region's parks and preserves. The places profiled in the following pages offer some of the best opportunities for seeing our native cacti, agaves, and yuccas in their natural environment. Although this selection is not exhaustive, the chosen locations feature the major habitats where cactus, agave, and yuccas species are found in California and Nevada.

The directions provided are general, and visitors should always utilize up-to-date road maps, especially when traveling off-highway. Four-wheel-drive roads are indicated, but high-clearance is advisable on most back-country two-wheel-drive roads. Peak flowering times obviously vary with species and seasonal weather patterns, but these plants generally bloom in the Colorado Desert and other low-elevation desert areas from March through May, in the coastal sites from April through June or July, and at middle and upper elevations of the Mojave and Great Basin deserts from April through July.

For a complete list of the cacti, agaves, and yuccas found at each of the featured sites on the following pages, refer to Appendix H, "Species List For Selected Public Lands in California and Nevada" on page 222.

## CALIFORNIA
### Cabrillo National Monument
(San Diego County)

Cabrillo National Monument on Point Loma offers panoramic views of the Pacific Ocean, San Diego Bay, and the San Diego skyline. It protects a small but fine stand of coastal sage scrub, a plant

*Golden cereus grows in cool, foggy locations, such as this seaside slope on Point Loma. [Cabrillo N.M.]*

community that is increasingly rare. Because the tip of Point Loma has long been important for military defense and off-limits to real estate developers, much of its native vegetation has remained unscathed. The south end of Point Loma became a military reserve in 1852 and held strategic defense facilities during World Wars I and II. Six cactus species, Shaw agave, and Mojave yucca grow in the 668-acre Point Loma Ecological Conservation Area, which includes most of Cabrillo National Monument as well as adjacent lands owned by the U.S. Navy and others.

The Bayside Trail, the only trail in the monument, descends from near the Old Point Loma Lighthouse down an old roadway on the east side of the point and passes by coastal prickly-pear and Mojave yucca. California fishhook cactus and coast barrel cactus grow on the more open slopes above the trail. Thickets of golden cereus are visible on the west slope below the lighthouse, and large specimens of Shaw agave stand out among the other plants south of the lighthouse. Shaw agave was re-introduced here for restoration purposes, but "wild" clumps can be seen on a bluff in the northwest part of the monument and below the Bayside Trail near its northern end.

Only open for day use, Cabrillo National Monument is located at the end of Catalina Blvd., south of the Fort Rosecrans National Cemetery. Public transportation is available to the upper area of the monument from the Old Town Trolley Station. Call (619) 557-5450 or see www.nps.gov/cabr for more information.

**Torrey Pines State Reserve**
(San Diego County)
Torrey Pines State Reserve contains some of southern California's best remaining examples of coastal shrublands. Vegetation types within the reserve include coastal sage scrub, maritime succulent scrub, chaparral, and Torrey pine woodland. The reserve's varied topography, composed of coastal headlands and dramatic sandstone cliffs and canyons, provides habitat for about 300 native plant species, including 9 cacti, 2 yuccas, and Shaw agave, which was reintroduced here in the 1960s. This scenic park is the only place where coastal prickly-pear and coast barrel cactus grow together with Torrey Pine—the country's rarest pine.

The Guy Fleming Trail through the North Grove provides amazing views of the Pacific Ocean with a foreground of the reserve's most common cactus—coastal prickly-pear—and the

*Green, fleshy fruits are ripening on this Mojave yucca in coastal San Diego County. [Torrey Pines S.R.]*

rare Shaw agave. Mojave yucca and chaparral yucca, as well as coastal cholla, are plentiful on the aptly named Yucca Point. Trails out to the point pass by tall prickly-pear, coast barrel cactus, and California fishhook cactus.

The visitor center at the Reserve Headquarters and the native plant garden at the head of the Parry Grove Trail each have labeled examples of the reserve's cactus, agave, and yucca species. The 1750-acre reserve offers nearly a dozen trails and is open for day-use only. Its entrance is located on Pacific Coast Highway (County Road S-21) between Del Mar and La Jolla, approximately 1.5 miles south of Del Mar. Call (858) 755-2063 or see www.parks.ca.gov for more information.

## Anza-Borrego Desert State Park

(San Diego, Imperial, and Riverside counties) Anza-Borrego Desert State Park is the official showcase for the Colorado Desert—California's portion of the species-rich Sonoran Desert. Encompassing 600,000 acres, it is California's largest state park and features 500 miles of dirt roads and over 100 miles of hiking trails. The park and immediately adjacent lands contain the greatest cactus diversity in the state; rocky mountain slopes, sandy washes, and boulder-strewn bajadas provide varied habitats for at least 18 cactus species, 1 agave, 2 yuccas, 2 nolinas, and ocotillo. Although a few of the Anza-Borrego Desert species listed in Appendix H (page 226) occur near the edges of the park's boundaries and are more abundant outside the park, most of the species found here are relatively common and easy to encounter. It is actually difficult to avoid seeing chollas, barrel cactus, or the ubiquitous desert agave, except on the most barren badlands where only a few extremely hardy plants survive.

*A desert agave blooms among flowering ocotillo in California's biggest state park. [Anza-Borrego Desert S.P.]*

The best route for viewing the most cactus species in the shortest time is probably the drive between Ocotillo (beyond the southern edge of the park at Interstate 8) and Tamarisk Grove Campground, which follows—from south to north—County Road S-2, Highway 78, and County Road S-3. The locally common but range-restricted Wolf cholla grows about ½ mile up Mortero Canyon Road, a four-wheel-drive route that heads west from S-2 just north of the park's southern boundary. Anza-Borrego's most abundant cholla—Gander cholla—as well as Mason Valley cholla and its close relative, teddy-bear cholla (see "Cholla Hybrids" on page 55) are all common along most of the S-2 corridor from the Carrizo Valley area north to Mason Valley, just south of Box Canyon. In Mason Valley, 2 miles north of the Butterfield Ranch RV Park, the slopes east of a roadside parking area (dubbed "Mason Valley Cactus Gardens" on some maps) have good stands of these three chollas in addition to California fishhook cactus, Engelmann hedgehog, brown-spined prickly-pear, desert barrel cactus, desert agave, and ocotillo.

The Cactus Loop Trail, across from Tamarisk Grove Campground on County Road S-3, is a good place to see a rich variety of cactus species, including California fishhook cactus, which blooms in March or early April. East of Tamarisk Grove, a broad alluvial apron at the base of the Pinyon Mountains, known as Mescal Bajada, has expansive stands of desert agave, or mescal. From Tamarisk Grove, take Highway 78 east 2.5 miles to the turnoff (south side) for Mine Wash Road and continue 1.6 miles on this dirt road to reach the Mine Canyon Indian Village Site, where there is nearby evidence of agave-roasting pits that were once used by the Kumeyaay Indians. In a good year, the agave bloom here runs from March until June.

There are countless other places worth visiting to see cacti, agaves, and yuccas in the Anza-Borrego Desert State Park region, and camping is available in many areas. The park's excellent visitor center has a native plant garden and is located near the entrance to Borrego Palm Canyon. The Anza-Borrego Natural History Association bookstore and information center is found nearby in downtown Borrego Springs. Call (760) 767-5311 or visit www.parks.ca.gov or www.anzaborrego.statepark.org for more information.

## Joshua Tree National Park
(San Bernardino and Riverside counties)
Joshua Tree National Park stands out in many ways and has the distinction of being the only national park named in honor of a woody monocot. It is also unique because it embraces significant portions of two different deserts—the Colorado Desert to the southeast and the Mojave Desert to the northwest. The confluence of these two desert ecosystems and the park's large size (nearly 800,000 acres) account for the presence of 15 cactus species, 2 yuccas, 2 nolinas, and ocotillo within the park's boundaries.

While many of the one million or more annual visitors come to admire or climb the weathered granite outcrops and boulders that make Joshua Tree National Park so distinctive, others are drawn by the picturesque "tree yuccas" and the expansive Joshua tree woodlands. Some of the largest and oldest known Joshua trees grow in Queen Valley, Lost Horse Valley, and Upper Covington Flat. These broad expanses are also home to silver cholla and beavertail cactus, as well as the less frequently seen Parish club-cholla; in nearby rockier sites, look for common fishhook cactus. Upper Covington Flat and the section of the Little San Bernardino Mountains near Keys View provide good habitat for Mojave mound cactus and Parry nolina, including some especially impressive nolina specimens along the upper road to Keys View. Parry nolina is also widespread in the Wonderland of Rocks, along with pancake prickly-pear, brown-spined prickly-pear, and hybrids between Engelmann and brown-spined prickly-pear.

The transitional zone between the Mojave and Colorado deserts is where cushion foxtail cactus makes its home. This California endemic occurs most commonly at elevations between 3200 and 4200 feet. Look for it from the Jumbo Rocks area southeast throughout the lower slopes of the Hexie Mountains, as well as in other areas. Cholla Cactus Garden, on Pinto Basin Road in the same part of the park, features a very dense stand of teddy-bear cholla that superbly illustrates the colonial nature of this asexual species.

Joshua Tree National Park has three main entrances, three visitor centers, and eight campgrounds. The Cottonwood Visitor Center is near the south entrance, approximately 8 miles north of Interstate 10; the Oasis Visitor Center is near the north entrance in Twentynine Palms; and the Joshua Tree Visitor Center is near the west entrance on Park Blvd. just south of Highway 62 in Joshua Tree. Call (760) 367-5500 or see www.nps.gov/jotr or www.joshuatree.org for more information.

## Mojave National Preserve
(San Bernardino County)
The 1.6 million-acre Mojave National Preserve contains limestone cliffs and caverns, mountain ranges reaching above 6000 feet, vast alluvial valleys, sand dunes, springs, lava beds, and a rich cornucopia of cactus, agave, and yucca species. Located

*Upper Covington Flat in the Little San Bernardino Mountains is known for large Joshua trees. [Joshua Tree N.P.]*

*Buckhorn cholla and desert paintbrush glow in early-morning light at the Granite Mountains. [Mojave N. Pr.]*

between the Great Basin Desert to the north, the Colorado Plateau to the east, the Colorado Desert to the south, and the Mojave Desert to the west, the preserve forms a crossroads for different plant communities and species. Several species found here are at the edge of their geographic ranges. For instance, desert agave reaches its northernmost extent and Utah agave has its southernmost distribution in the Ivanpah Mountains, south of Interstate 15.

The Mojave National Preserve's immense size and great geomorphological variation provide habitat for 18 cactus species, 2 agaves, and 3 yuccas, as well as nearly 900 other plant species. Cima Dome—a symmetrical, 75-square-mile area of granite that appears as a vast bulge when viewed from a distance—is blanketed by what is arguably the densest and most extensive stand of Joshua tree woodland found anywhere. At least nine cactus species can be seen along the Teutonia Peak Trail (on Cima Road, 6.3 miles north of Cima or 11 miles south of I-15), including beehive cactus, Parish club-cholla, and fine examples of pancake prickly-pear.

Another cactus-rich Mojave landscape is found at Providence Mountains State Recreation Area, a 5900-acre unit of the California State Park system within the Mojave National Preserve. Located about 16 miles north of Interstate 40 via Essex Road, the recreation area's namesake range supports brown-spined, Engelmann, and Mojave prickly-pear cactus. Simple desert agave grows in the canyon just above the Mitchell Caverns Visitor Center in Providence Mountains SRA.

The Mojave National Preserve spans the desert between I-40 in the south and I-15 in the north, with a separate portion north of I-15 that includes most of the Clark Mountains. There are visitor centers and campgrounds at Mitchell Caverns Natural Preserve and Hole-in-the-Wall (the world's tallest Mojave yucca grows near this visitor center). The Mid-Hills Campground in the Providence Mountains offers a cooler climate at 5600 feet elevation. Other primitive backcountry camping options are available in many parts of the preserve. The historic Kelso Depot, located at the junction of Kelbaker and Kelso-Cima roads, now serves as a visitor center and museum. Call (760) 252-6100 or see www.nps.gov/moja for more information.

## Death Valley National Park and the Northern Mojave Desert

(San Bernardino, Inyo, and Mono counties)
The northwestern edge of California's cactus country can be found in the region stretching from the northern Mojave Desert west to the eastern Sierra Nevada and northwest to the White-Inyo Range. From eastern California's sedimentary Nopah Range through the mountains and valleys of Death Valley National Park and to the eastern slopes of the Sierra Nevada, the assortment of vegetation types containing cacti, agaves, and yuccas ranges from creosote bush scrub at lower elevations through Joshua tree woodland at mid-elevations and up higher into pinyon-juniper woodland.

*In the Inyo Mountains' Mazourka Canyon, a cottontop cactus displays its habit of forming clusters. [Inyo Co.]*

Within this vast region of basin and range topography, there are at least 14 cactus species, 1 agave, 1 yucca, and 1 nolina.

Death Valley National Park forms the heart of the northern Mojave Desert and includes 3.3 million acres of some of the least hospitable but most beautiful parts of North America. Cacti that can endure the extreme heat and aridity at park elevations below 3500 feet include silver cholla and beavertail, cottontop, and Johnson pineapple cacti. Beavertail cactus creates brilliant springtime displays on alluvial fans at elevations from 1000 to 4000 feet in Death Valley, Saline Valley, and Eureka Valley; cottontop cactus nestles on rocky slopes at similar elevations throughout the national park.

Joshua tree woodlands occur at elevations roughly between 3500 and 5500 feet on flats and basins in the mountains of the northern Mojave. Two of the largest Joshua tree woodlands are found at Joshua Flats, along the Big Pine-Death Valley Road in the Inyo Mountains west of Eureka Valley, and at Lee Flat, north of Highway 190 in the southern Inyo Mountains. Mojave prickly-pear and silver cholla are both very widespread in this region and are commonly found in Joshua tree woodlands.

Sagebrush scrub and pinyon-juniper woodlands are generally found at elevations above 5500 feet, and these vegetation types harbor the lovely and uncommon Mojave fishhook cactus. Mojave fishhook cactus extends down to 4000 feet in this region and is scattered throughout the Panamint, Last Chance, and Inyo mountains. The lower and middle sections of Mazourka Canyon in the Inyo Mountains (just east of Independence) have healthy stands of cottontop cactus, Engelmann hedgehog, and beavertail cactus. Pinyon-juniper woodlands in the area's tallest ranges are also home to California's two highest-elevation cactus species; the Mojave mound cactus grows here in locations up to nearly 10,000 feet, and Mojave prickly-pear ranges to 10,400 feet.

Of the 17 species of interest noted above, all but 3—ivory-spined agave, porcupine prickly-pear, and Parry nolina—are found within Death Valley National Park. Ivory-spined agave is restricted

*Porcupine prickly-pear grows near Convict Lake where the Great Basin meets the Sierra Nevada. [Inyo N.F.]*

in California to the Nopah Range. Porcupine prickly-pear (as well as its hybrids with Mojave prickly-pear) can be found at elevations between 6000 to 9200 feet in the eastern Sierra Nevada, most commonly from Big Pine Canyon north to Convict Lake Basin. Parry nolina reaches its northwestern extension in floristically rich Short Canyon, west of Ridgecrest in the southern Sierra (Kern County).

The mountains and valleys of this enormous and lightly populated part of California are crisscrossed with countless dirt roads offering many places to explore. Park visitors can view exhibits and get maps, books, and travel advice at the Furnace Creek Visitor Center. For more information about Death Valley call (760) 786-3200 or visit the park's website at www.nps.gov/deva or www.dvnha.org. The Shoshone Museum in Shoshone (760) 852-4414, the Maturango Museum in Ridgecrest (760) 375-6900, and the InterAgency Visitor Center in Lone Pine (760) 876-6222 all have books as well as information about camping, lodging, and other services for visitors in Death Valley National Park, the Northern Mojave, and the Eastern Sierra region.

## Whipple Mountains Wilderness
(San Bernardino County)

The Whipple Mountains, which are climatically and floristically more like western Arizona than California, are the only place in the Golden State where saguaros and Graham fishhook cacti are native. The heart of the Whipple Mountains is rugged country. The range is punctuated by deep canyons, eroded spires, and volcanic domes in the east and covered with rolling hills and broad desert washes in the west. Ten cactus species, desert agave, Bigelow nolina, and ocotillo reside within the Whipple Mountains Wilderness. The most common cacti of the creosote bush scrub here are beavertail cactus, buckhorn cholla, and teddy-bear cholla.

Widely scattered saguaros on the lower eastern slopes of the Whipple Mountains are visible from Parker Dam Road. The best access to Whipple Wash and the 76,000-acre Whipple Mountains Wilderness area is along the four-wheel-drive powerline road that forms 8 miles of the northeastern boundary of the wilderness. To get to the powerline road, take Black Meadow Landing Road

*Giant saguaro and nine other species of cacti are found in the Whipple Mountains. [San Bernardino Co.]*

Exploring the Cactus Country of California and Nevada   209

from just south of Parker Dam and go 6 miles to the dirt road to Havasu Palms. Follow this dirt road for 2 miles and turn west onto the powerline road. From here, the four-wheel-drive powerline road winds through the northeastern Whipple Mountains and joins the paved Havasu Lake Road in Chemehuevi Valley, some 20 miles to the east.

The Whipple Mountains are approximately 50 miles south of Needles and adjacent to the southwest shore of Lake Havasu. Maps and other information can be found at the BLM Field Offices in Needles (760) 326-7000 or at the following website: www.blm.gov/ca/pa/wilderness/wa/areas/whipple_mountains.html.

## NEVADA

### Desert National Wildlife Refuge

(Clark, Lincoln, and Nye counties)
The Desert National Wildlife Refuge (DNWR), like the Mojave National Preserve, is vast and varied; it serves as a transition between different deserts, and its rich flora reflects this. Part of the National Wildlife Refuge System, the DNWR encompasses 1.6 million acres of valleys, washes, cliffs, and slopes in six separate mountain ranges and spans elevations from 2500 to nearly 10,000 feet. The DNWR was established in 1936 by President Franklin Roosevelt to protect desert bighorn sheep, but it also secures habitat for 18 cacti, 1 agave, and 3 yuccas, in addition to nearly 750 other plant species. Nellis Air Force Base and the Nellis Test and Training Range (now known as the Nevada Test and Training Range) were superimposed on part of the refuge during World War II, and much of the DNWR is closed to the public.

Situated in the northeastern Mojave Desert, the DNWR is transitional to the Great Basin Desert to the north and shares some species with the Colorado Plateau to the east as well. Four cacti here are at the northern edge of their distribution: desert barrel cactus, Parish club-cholla, common fishhook cactus, and Blue Diamond cholla. Whipple cholla in the DNWR is at the western edge of its range.

The four-wheel-drive Mormon Well Road,

*Whipple cholla grows in a Joshua tree woodland at Yucca Valley. [Desert N.W.R.]*

between Corn Creek Field Station in the southwest and U.S. Highway 93 in the northeast, provides the best access into the heart of the Sheep and Las Vegas ranges. Near the southern edge of the DNWR, Blue Diamond cholla grows on the north slope of Gass Peak in the Las Vegas Range. Northeast of the turnoff to Gass Peak Road, Mormon Well Road passes through Yucca Forest Valley, where three yucca species occur together in an immense Joshua tree woodland that covers approximately 25 square miles between the Sheep Range and the Las Vegas Range. Whipple cholla is found in Yucca Forest Valley along Pine Nut Road (about 2.6 miles from its junction with Mormon Well Road) and also in Peek-a-boo Canyon farther east along Mormon Well Road. Ivory-spined agaves cling to the steep limestone slopes of Peek-a-boo Canyon, not far from where this variety was first discovered. A population of the unusual magenta-flowered Mojave prickly-pear grows with silver cholla and Engelmann hedgehog along the northeastern section of Mormon Well Road in the northern Elbow Range.

Corn Creek Field Station, 4 miles east of U.S. Highway 95 and approximately 23 miles north of Las Vegas, is the most common route into the refuge. Alamo Road, which goes north from Corn Creek, gives access to the broad western slopes of the Sheep Range, where colorful beavertail cacti and other desert shrubs and wildflowers bloom in the late spring. Camping is permitted in most areas of the DNWR, but no water or facilities are available beyond Corn Creek. Call (702) 879-6110 or see www.fws.gov/desertcomplex/desertrange for more information.

## Lake Mead National Recreation Area and the Gold Butte Region
(Clark County)

Lake Mead was created with the completion of Hoover Dam in 1935. The dam harnessed the flow of the Colorado River for hydroelectric power, and the lake became a source of future water supplies and lacustrine recreational opportunities. Lake Mead National Recreation Area is far more popular among boaters and bathers than among cactus and yucca enthusiasts, but in the mountains and bajadas surrounding the immense reservoirs of Lake Mead and Lake Mohave, there is plenty to satisfy those who love desert plants. The Black Mountains, Eldorado Hills, and Newberry Mountains all reach elevations over 5000 feet, and upland habitats account for 87% of the 1.5 million-acre Lake Mead NRA. This piece of the southeastern Mojave Desert holds 15 cactus species, 1 agave, 3 yuccas, ocotillo, and Bigelow nolina.

In Nevada, Lake Mead NRA stretches from the Newberry Mountains northwest of Laughlin in the south to just east of Valley of Fire State Park near Overton in the north. The NRA extends east into Arizona, where it adjoins both Grand Canyon National Park and Grand Canyon-Parashant National Monument.

The Newberry Mountains are one of the most scenic and accessible mountain areas of the NRA and the only place in Nevada to find Bigelow nolina. Christmas Tree Pass Road between State Highway 163 and U.S. Highway 95 passes through creosote bush scrub below Grapevine Canyon and continues up into pinyon-juniper woodland around Christmas Tree Pass. Buckhorn cholla, beavertail cactus, Mojave yucca, and Bigelow nolina are all abundant throughout the east slope of the Newberry Mountains—Nevada's southernmost named mountain range.

Limestone ridges and rocky bajadas offer the best habitats for cacti along the Northshore Road (east of Las Vegas on State Highway 167), and silver cholla, beavertail cactus, and Johnson pineapple cactus are the most commonly seen species. Beavertail cactus is especially abundant—and impossible to miss during its March to April bloom—along the Northshore Road between Roger's Spring and the road to Echo Bay. Hiking on one of the trails from the Northshore Road or taking a cross-country jaunt is the best way to really learn about and appreciate some of the area's cacti and yuccas. Hundreds of miles of roads leading into the hills and mountains of Lake Mead NRA also offer numerous opportunities to explore the eastern Mojave Desert on foot.

Additional information about Lake Mead NRA is available at the Alan Bible Visitor Center

*On slopes near Lake Mead, beavertail cacti bloom amidst Mojavean creosote bush scrub. [Lake Mead N.R.A.]*

between Boulder City and Hoover Dam on U.S. Highway 93. In addition to exhibits, maps, and books, this visitor center also has a native plant garden. For more information call (702) 293-8990 or see www.nps.gov/lame.

The Gold Butte region lies between Lake Mead NRA's Overton Arm and the Nevada-Arizona state line in an area extending south from the Virgin Mountains to Bonelli Peak. Gold Butte offers expansive and varied Mojave Desert scenery, several Wilderness Study Areas, and a network of backcountry roads. At Whitney Pockets, Joshua tree and desert barrel cactus grow among rich, red sandstone formations and rock outcrops, and Utah yucca flourishes in sandy areas. Whitney Pockets is located on the New Gold Butte Road at the junction with Pakoon Springs Road, 21 miles south of Riverside Road (State Highway 170). Open Joshua tree woodland extends southeast from Whitney Pockets to the Mud Hills and Black Wash. This area, a few miles west of the Arizona state line, is the only known Nevada location where Grand Canyon cottontop cactus grows. Utah agave and desert barrel cactus can be found on the limestone ridges and upper slopes of Tramp Ridge and Lime Ridge. A dense and diverse Joshua tree woodland, containing Mojave yucca and Mojave mound cactus, is found around the old mining camp of Gold Butte near 4000 feet, but recent fires have taken a toll on the native vegetation here. For more information about the Gold Butte region call the Las Vegas BLM Field Office at (702) 515-5000.

## The Spring Mountains National Recreation Area and Red Rock Canyon National Conservation Area

(Clark and Nye counties)

The Spring Mountain Range towers above the eastern Mojave Desert. This tallest of Mojave Desert ranges includes 11,918-foot-high Mount Charleston and stretches north-south for some 50 miles along the western edge of Las Vegas Valley. It supports several distinct climate zones and vegetation types and an amazingly rich flora of 1100 plant taxa. The Spring Mountains National Recreation Area consists of 316,000 acres of Humboldt-Toiyabe National Forest land centered around the Mount Charleston area, Lee Canyon, and the upper part of Kyle Canyon. The Red Rock Canyon National Conservation Area encompasses 196,000 acres just beyond the western edge of Las Vegas. Together, these two regions of the Spring Mountains are a welcome recreational refuge from the city and safeguard important plant habitats.

From creosote bush scrub at 3000 feet elevation to the lower reaches of ponderosa pine forest at 8000 feet, the Spring Mountains NRA offers many habitats for cacti, agaves, and yuccas. The NRA, in combination with Red Rock Canyon (see below), contains 18 cactus species, 3 varieties of Utah agave, and 3 yucca species. Mojave mound cactus and what appear to be hybrids between Mojave and porcupine prickly-pears can be found among the pinyon and ponderosa pines of upper Kyle Canyon. The one-time presumed endemic *Opuntia charlestonensis* collected in ponderosa pine forest near Fletcher Canyon has not gained acceptance as a new species and appears instead to be Engelmann prickly-pear. The limestone foothills of Lee Canyon support ivory-spined agave, and the expansive alluvial slope along Lee Canyon Road provides habitat for Nevada's three yuccas and numerous cacti, including silver cholla, diamond cholla, Engelmann hedgehog, beavertail cactus, Mojave prickly-pear, and others. Blue Diamond cholla is known from the eastern end of La Madre Mountain, south of Kyle Canyon.

Gorgeous red cliffs of Aztec sandstone and gray limestone loom above a mosaic of Mojave

*The parklands west of Las Vegas are rich in desert plants, including Mojave yucca. [Red Rock Canyon N.C.A.]*

Desert plant communities in Red Rock Canyon NCA on the east side of the Spring Mountains (south of Kyle Canyon). The Joshua trees of Red Rock Canyon NCA are especially short-leaved and short-statured (as var. *jaegeriana*) compared to those from the western Mojave. Two other yuccas—Mojave and banana yucca—as well as buckhorn cholla are also common on the lower slopes and flats of Red Rock Canyon NCA and can be seen from Scenic Drive or along the trail to Oak Creek Canyon. Numerous large specimens of Clark Mountain agave cling to the red and white sandstone rocks above an ancient agave-roasting pit near the White Rock parking area (just beyond the High Point Overlook of the Scenic Drive loop). Numerous trails from Scenic Drive lead into canyons and offer opportunities to see brown-spined prickly-pear, beehive cactus, desert pincushion cactus, and others.

Call (702) 515-5400 or see www.fs.fed.us/r4/htnf/districts/smnra.shtml for more information about the Spring Mountains NRA. The Kyle Guard and Information Station in upper Kyle Canyon provides trail information and maps. Campgrounds are available in upper Kyle Canyon and Lee Canyon and also 2 miles east of the Red Rock Visitor Center. For more information call the Red Rock Visitor Center at (702) 515-5350 or the Las Vegas BLM Field Office at (702) 515-5000, or see www.redrockcanyonlv.org or www.nv.blm.gov/redrockcanyon

## Valley of Fire State Park
(Clark County)

Spectacular, multicolored sandstone formations are the main draw to Valley of Fire State Park. Domes, arches, tanks, and other unusual geological features abound throughout the 34,880 acres that make up Nevada's oldest state park. The reddish Aztec sandstone here was formed from ancient sand dunes over 150 million years ago, and today the park's pink sands support the growth of Utah yucca, an elegant plant that looks especially dramatic during its spring bloom in April and May. Mojave yucca and seven species of cactus also grow in this low-elevation Mojave Desert park, which lies at 2000 to 2600 feet.

*Utah yucca thrives in the sandy soils of Nevada's oldest and largest state park. [Valley of Fire S.P.]*

Most of the plants of interest (i.e., the spiny ones) are visible from the park's roads and short trails. The road from Rainbow Vista north to White Domes has a few parking sites where visitors can observe the two most common cacti here—silver cholla and beavertail cactus—along with Utah yucca, which inhabits sites with loose sand. The 1.25-mile White Domes Loop Trail offers close-up views of Utah yucca, a few huge Mojave yuccas in a wash west of the trail, and the common beavertail cactus. Hikers off-trail should be careful to avoid crushing the fragile cryptobiotic soil crusts and delicate sandstone.

Valley of Fire State Park is located approximately 50 miles northeast of Las Vegas and 15 miles south of Overton. The park's eastern edge adjoins Lake Mead National Recreation Area. Two campsites are available, and a visitor center with a non-native cactus garden offers exhibits, books, and other information. Call (702) 397-2088 or see www.parks.nv.gov/vf.htm for more information.

# Appendix A: Cactus, Agave, and Yucca Species of California and Nevada

**Key:** Endemic to the state denoted by ★
Regions where found: m for Mojave Desert, gb for Great Basin Desert, c for Colorado Desert, and cs for cismontane California

| Genus/Species | Common Name | State/Region |
|---|---|---|
| **Cactaceae** | | |
| *Bergerocactus emoryi* | golden cereus | CA/cs |
| *Carnegiea gigantea* | giant saguaro | CA/c |
| *Coryphantha alversonii* | cushion foxtail cactus | CA★/m, c |
| *Coryphantha chlorantha* | desert pincushion cactus | CA NV/m, gb |
| *Coryphantha vivipara* var. *rosea* | beehive cactus | CA NV/m, gb |
| *Cylindropuntia acanthocarpa* var. *acanthocarpa* | buckhorn cholla | CA NV/m, c |
| *Cylindropuntia bigelovii* | teddy-bear cholla | CA NV/m, c |
| *Cylindropuntia californica* var. *californica* | snake cholla | CA/cs |
| *Cylindropuntia californica* var. *parkeri* | cane cholla | CA/cs |
| *Cylindropuntia chuckwallensis* | Chuckwalla cholla | CA★/c |
| *Cylindropuntia echinocarpa* | silver cholla | CA NV/m, gb, c |
| *Cylindropuntia fosbergii* | Mason Valley cholla | CA★/c |
| *Cylindropuntia ganderi* | Gander cholla | CA/c |
| *Cylindropuntia multigeniculata* | Blue Diamond cholla | NV/m |
| *Cylindropuntia munzii* | Munz cholla | CA/c |
| *Cylindropuntia prolifera* | coastal cholla | CA/cs |
| *Cylindropuntia ramosissima* | diamond cholla | CA NV/m, c |
| *Cylindropuntia whipplei* | Whipple cholla | NV/m, gb |
| *Cylindropuntia wolfii* | Wolf cholla | CA/c |
| *Echinocactus polycephalus* var. *polycephalus* | cottontop cactus | CA NV/m, c |
| *Echinocactus polycephalus* var. *xeranthemoides* | Grand Canyon cottontop | NV/m |
| *Echinocereus engelmannii* | Engelmann hedgehog | CA NV/m, gb, c |
| *Echinocereus mojavensis* | Mojave mound cactus | CA NV/m, gb |
| *Ferocactus cylindraceus* | desert barrel cactus | CA NV/m, c |
| *Ferocactus viridescens* | coast barrel cactus | CA/cs |
| *Grusonia parishii* | Parish club-cholla | CA NV/m, gb |
| *Grusonia pulchella* | sand-cholla | CA NV/gb |
| *Mammillaria dioica* | California fishhook cactus | CA/c, cs |
| *Mammillaria grahamii* var. *grahamii* | Graham fishhook cactus | CA/c |
| *Mammillaria tetrancistra* | common fishhook cactus | CA NV/m, c |
| *Opuntia basilaris* var. *basilaris* | beavertail cactus | CA NV/m, gb, c |
| *Opuntia basilaris* var. *brachyclada* | short-joint beavertail | CA★/m, cs |
| *Opuntia basilaris* var. *treleasei* | Bakersfield cactus | CA★/cs |
| *Opuntia chlorotica* | pancake prickly-pear | CA NV/m, c |
| *Opuntia* X*curvispina* | curve-spined prickly-pear | CA NV/m |
| *Opuntia engelmannii* var. *engelmannii* | Engelmann prickly-pear | CA NV/m, c |
| *Opuntia fragilis* | little prickly-pear | CA[1] |
| *Opuntia littoralis* | coastal prickly-pear | CA/cs |
| *Opuntia* X*occidentalis* | western prickly-pear | CA/cs |

| Genus/Species | Common Name | State/Region |
|---|---|---|
| *Opuntia oricola* | tall prickly-pear | CA/cs |
| *Opuntia phaeacantha* | brown-spined prickly-pear | CA NV/m, c, cs |
| *Opuntia polyacantha* var. *erinacea* | Mojave prickly-pear | CA NV/m, gb |
| *Opuntia polyacantha* var. *hystricina* | porcupine prickly-pear | CA NV/m, gb |
| *Opuntia polyacantha* var. *polyacantha* | Plains prickly-pear | NV/gb |
| *Opuntia Xvaseyi* | Vasey prickly-pear | CA/cs |
| *Pediocactus simpsonii* | mountain cactus | NV/gb |
| *Sclerocactus blainei* | Blaine fishhook cactus | NV/gb |
| *Sclerocactus johnsonii* | Johnson pineapple cactus | CA NV/m |
| *Sclerocactus nyensis* | Tonopah fishhook cactus | NV★/m, gb |
| *Sclerocactus polyancistrus* | Mojave fishhook cactus | CA NV/m, gb |
| *Sclerocactus pubispinus* | Great Basin fishhook cactus | NV/gb |

### AGAVACEAE

| Genus/Species | Common Name | State/Region |
|---|---|---|
| *Agave deserti* var. *deserti* | desert agave | CA/c |
| *Agave deserti* var. *simplex* | simple desert agave | CA/m |
| *Agave shawii* var. *shawii* | Shaw agave | CA/cs |
| *Agave utahensis* var. *eborispina* | ivory-spined agave | CA NV/m, gb |
| *Agave utahensis* var. *nevadensis* | Clark Mountain agave | CA NV/m, gb |
| *Agave utahensis* var. *utahensis* | Utah agave | NV/m, gb |
| *Hesperoyucca whipplei* | chaparral yucca | CA/cs |
| *Yucca baccata* var. *baccata* | banana yucca | CA NV/m, gb |
| *Yucca brevifolia* | Joshua tree | CA NV/m, gb |
| *Yucca harrimaniae* | Harriman yucca | NV/gb |
| *Yucca schidigera* | Mojave yucca | CA NV/m, gb, c, cs |
| *Yucca utahensis* | Utah yucca | NV/m |

### NOLINAS AND OCOTILLO

| Genus/Species | Common Name | State/Region |
|---|---|---|
| *Nolina bigelovii* | Bigelow nolina | CA NV/c |
| *Nolina cismontana* | chaparral nolina | CA★/cs |
| *Nolina interrata* | Dehesa nolina | CA/cs |
| *Nolina parryi* | Parry nolina | CA★/m, c |
| *Fouquieria splendens* ssp. *splendens* | ocotillo | CA NV/m, c |

[1] Found primarily in the Pacific Northwest, Great Plains, and Rocky Mountains

# Appendix B: Major Vegetation Types and Habitats for Cacti, Agaves, and Yuccas

The "Distribution/Elevation" sections of this appendix summarize the areas of each major vegetation type where cacti, agaves, and yuccas may be found. These descriptions do not include areas within a vegetation type where cacti, agaves, and yuccas are absent, such as chaparral in California's North Coast Ranges.

## CISMONTANE/COASTAL CALIFORNIA

### Coastal Sage Scrub
(Includes Maritime Succulent Scrub)
**Distribution/Elevation:** Channel Islands, coastal strip, and sea bluffs; from sea level to 3000 feet.
**General Characteristics:** Dominant plants are soft-leaved, shrubby species 1 to 6 feet tall, forming dense to open stands. Herbs are well-developed in open areas. Common shrub species include black sage, California sagebrush, coyote brush, and buckwheat. Maritime influence is strong, with fog, cool, wet winters, and mild, dry summers. Average rainfall is 10 to 20 inches.
**Cactaceae Species:** California fishhook cactus, coast barrel cactus, coastal cholla, coastal prickly-pear, golden cereus, snake cholla, tall prickly-pear, Vasey prickly-pear, western prickly-pear.
**Agavaceae Species:** chaparral yucca, Mojave yucca, Shaw agave.

### Chaparral
**Distribution/Elevation:** Channel Islands, lower slopes of the South Coast Ranges, lower, western slopes of the Sierra Nevada and Transverse and Peninsular ranges, as well as upper eastern slopes of the Peninsular Ranges; from near sea level to 4000 feet.
**General Characteristics:** Dominant plants are evergreen, hard-leaved, shrubby species 3 to 10 feet tall, forming dense stands. Common species include chamise, toyon, and numerous ceanothus and manzanita species. Maritime influence is weak to strong, with cool, wet winters and hot, dry summers. Average rainfall is 15 to 25 inches.
**Cactaceae Species:** brown-spined prickly-pear, California fishhook cactus, cane cholla, coast barrel cactus, coastal cholla, coastal prickly-pear, Gander cholla, short-joint beavertail, snake cholla, tall prickly-pear, Vasey prickly-pear, western prickly-pear.
**Agavaceae Species:** chaparral yucca, Mojave yucca.

### Valley and Foothill Woodland
**Distribution/Elevation:** Eastern slopes of the South Coast Ranges, inland valleys, mid-level western slopes of the Sierra Nevada and Transverse and South Coast ranges, mid-level elevations of Peninsular Ranges; from 300 to 5000 feet.
**General Characteristics:** Dominant plants include scattered to dense trees with an understory of grasses or low shrubs; highly variable depending on slope aspect and rainfall. Common species include oaks, gray pine, chaparral shrubs, and numerous grasses. Maritime influence is absent with cold, moist winters and hot, dry summers. Average rainfall is 6 to 25 inches.
**Cactaceae Species:** Bakersfield cactus, beavertail cactus, brown-spined prickly-pear, cane cholla, coastal prickly-pear, Gander cholla, Vasey prickly-pear, western prickly-pear.
**Agavaceae Species:** chaparral yucca, Mojave yucca.

### Valley Grassland
**Distribution/Elevation:** Central Valley and small valleys of the South Coast, Transverse and Peninsular ranges; from 100 to 1200 feet.
**General Characteristics:** Dominant plants include native perennial grasses and invasive, exotic, perennial and annual grasses. Common species include needle grasses, brome grasses, and many annual wildflowers. Maritime influence is weak to absent with cold, moist winters and hot, dry summers. Average rainfall is 6 to 20 inches.
**Cactaceae Species:** Bakersfield cactus (in saltbush scrub plant communities within Valley Grassland vegetation).
**Agavaceae Species:** chaparral yucca, Joshua tree.

# MONTANE AND TRANSMONTANE/ INLAND CALIFORNIA AND NEVADA

## Montane Chaparral and Montane Coniferous Forest

**Distribution/Elevation:** Mid-level slopes of the eastern Sierra Nevada and Great Basin mountain ranges of Nevada; from 7000 to 10,500 feet.
**General Characteristics:** Dominant plants include low, moderate to dense cover of shrubs with scattered Jeffrey and pinyon pines. Higher, wetter areas have forests of lodgepole, whitebark, or limber pine. Common shrubs include mountain mahogany, manzanita species, and ceanothus species. Cold, snowy winters and warm, dry summers. Average precipitation is 10 to 30 inches, with at least half the total falling as snow.
**Cactaceae Species:** Beavertail, Mojave prickly-pear, mountain cactus, porcupine prickly-pear.

## Pinyon-Juniper Woodland

**Distribution/Elevation:** Mid-level slopes of the eastern Sierra Nevada from 6000 to 8000 feet, mountain ranges in the Mojave and Great Basin deserts from 4500 to 8000 feet, and Transverse and Peninsular ranges from 4000 to 7000 feet.
**General Characteristics:** Dominant plants include scattered to dense cover of pinyon pines and/or junipers, with moderate to sparse understory of shrubs. Common shrub species include bitterbrush, sagebrush, and mountain mahogany. Cold, wet winters and warm, dry summers. Average precipitation is 12 to 20 inches, with part of the total falling as snow.
**Cactaceae Species:** beavertail cactus, beehive cactus, brown-spined prickly-pear, desert barrel cactus, desert pincushion, Great Basin fishhook cactus, little prickly-pear, Mojave fishhook cactus, Mojave mound cactus, Mojave prickly-pear, mountain cactus, Plains prickly-pear, porcupine prickly-pear, short-joint beavertail, Whipple cholla.
**Agavaceae Species:** banana yucca, Clark Mountain agave, Harriman yucca, ivory-spined agave, Joshua tree, Utah agave.

## Sagebrush Scrub

**Distribution/Elevation:** Mid-level slopes of the eastern Sierra Nevada, the northern and eastern Mojave Desert mountain ranges, and the north slopes of the Transverse Ranges and Great Basin ranges; from 4000 to 7000 feet.
**General Characteristics:** Dominant plants include dense to moderate cover of sagebrush, frequently with bitterbrush. Other common plants include rabbitbrush, ephedra, native bunch grasses and cheat grass. Cold, wet winters and hot, dry summers. Average precipitation is 8 to 15 inches with part of the total falling as snow.
**Cactaceae Species:** beavertail cactus, beehive cactus, Blue Diamond cholla, Great Basin fishhook cactus, Mojave fishhook cactus, Mojave mound cactus, Mojave prickly-pear, mountain cactus, porcupine prickly-pear, sand-cholla, short-joint beavertail, silver cholla, Tonopah fishhook cactus, Whipple cholla.
**Agavaceae Species:** banana yucca, Clark Mountain agave, Harriman yucca, ivory-spined agave, Utah agave.

## Shadscale Scrub

**Distribution/Elevation:** Tablelands and valleys of the northern and central Mojave and Great Basin deserts; from 3000 to 6000 feet.
**General Characteristics:** Dominant plants include moderate to sparse cover of shadscale and other shrubs less than 3 feet tall. Other common shrub species include spiny hop-sage, winterfat, and blackbush. Soil is relatively alkaline. Cold, dry winters and hot, dry summers. Average precipitation is 3 to 7 inches with occasional snow.
**Cactaceae Species:** beavertail cactus, Blaine fishhook cactus, Johnson pineapple cactus, Mojave fishhook cactus, Parish club-cholla, sand-cholla, silver cholla, Tonopah fishhook cactus.
**Agavaceae Species:** Harriman yucca, Joshua tree.

## MONTANE AND TRANSMONTANE/ INLAND CALIFORNIA AND NEVADA
(continued)

### Joshua Tree Woodland
(includes Blackbush Scrub)

**Distribution/Elevation:** Well-drained slopes and tablelands of the Mojave Desert; from 2000 to 6000 feet.

**General Characteristics:** Dominant plants include sparse to dense stands of Joshua trees, often with junipers, and a diverse understory of shrubs, cacti and other yuccas. Other common plants include blackbush, bitterbrush, Great Basin blue sage, and spiny hop-sage. Cool, moist winters and hot, dry summers. Average precipitation is 6 to 15 inches, with occasional snow.

**Cactaceae Species:** beavertail cactus, beehive cactus, Blue Diamond cholla, brown-spined prickly-pear, buckhorn cholla, cottontop cactus, curve-spined prickly-pear, desert barrel cactus, desert pincushion, diamond cholla, silver cholla, Engelmann hedgehog, Engelmann prickly-pear, Johnson pineapple cactus, Mojave fishhook cactus, Mojave mound cactus, Mojave prickly-pear, pancake prickly-pear, Parish club-cholla, sand-cholla, silver cholla, Whipple cholla.

**Agavaceae Species:** banana yucca, Clark Mountain agave, ivory-spined agave, Joshua tree, Mojave yucca, simple desert agave, Utah agave.

### Mojavean Creosote Bush Scrub

**Distribution/Elevation:** Lower slopes, alluvial fans, and valleys throughout the Mojave Desert, below 4000 feet in the west but up to 5000 feet in the northeastern Mojave.

**General Characteristics:** Dominant plants include evenly spaced creosote and burrobush. Other common plants include brittlebush, cheesebush, and red brome. Cool, sporadically wet winters and hot, dry summers. Average rainfall is 2 to 8 inches.

**Cactaceae Species:** beavertail cactus, beehive cactus, Blue Diamond cholla, brown-spined prickly-pear, buckhorn cholla, common fishhook cactus, cottontop cactus, cushion foxtail cactus, desert barrel cactus, diamond cholla, Engelmann hedgehog, Engelmann prickly-pear, Grand Canyon cottontop, Johnson pineapple cactus, Mojave mound cactus, Mojave prickly-pear, Mojave fishhook cactus, pancake prickly-pear, Parish club-cholla, silver cholla, teddy-bear cholla.

**Agavaceae Species:** Clark Mountain agave, ivory-spined agave, Joshua tree, Mojave yucca, Utah agave, Utah yucca.

### Sonoran Creosote Bush Scrub
(includes Wash Woodland)

**Distribution/Elevation:** Lower slopes, alluvial fans, valleys, and washes throughout the Colorado Desert; below 3000 feet.

**General Characteristics:** Dominant plants include evenly spaced creosote and burrobush. Other common plants include brittlebush, ocotillo, and desert agave. Wash woodland plants include desert ironwood, palo verde, smoke tree, catclaw acacia, and others. Mild, sporadically wet winters and very hot, dry summers with occasional thunderstorms. Average rainfall is 2 to 8 inches.

**Cactaceae Species:** beavertail cactus, brown-spined prickly-pear, buckhorn cholla, California fishhook cactus, Chuckwalla cholla, common fishhook cactus, cottontop cactus, cushion foxtail cactus, desert barrel cactus, diamond cholla, Engelmann hedgehog cactus, Engelmann prickly-pear, Gander cholla, giant saguaro, Graham fishhook cactus, Mason Valley cholla, Munz cholla, pancake prickly-pear, silver cholla, teddy-bear cholla, Wolf cholla.

**Agavaceae Species:** desert agave, Mojave yucca.

# Appendix C: Scientific Names for Non-featured Species

## PLANTS
acacia *(Acacia greggii)*
bitterbrush *(Purshia tridentata)*
black sage *(Salvia mellifera)*
blackbrush *(Coleogyne ramosissima)*
badderpod *(Isomeris arborea)*
brittlebush *(Encelia farinosa)*
brome grasses *(Bromus* spp.*)*
buckwheat *(Eriogonum* spp.*)*
burrobush *(Ambrosia dumosa)*
California sagebrush *(Artemisia californica)*
catclaw acacia *(Acacia greggii)*
ceanothus *(Ceanothus* spp.*)*
chamise *(Adenostoma fasciculatum)*
cheatgrass *(Bromus tectorum)*
cheesebush *(Hymenoclea salsola)*
coyote brush *(Baccharis pilularis)*
creosote *(Larrea tridentata)*
desert ironwood *(Olneya tesota)*
desert senna *(Senna armata)*
Engelmann fishhook cactus *(Sclerocactus spinosior)*
ephedra *(Ephedra* spp.*)*
palo verde *(Cercidium floridum)*
fountain grasses *(Pennisetum* spp.*)*
giant horsetail plant *(Equisetum giganteum)*
gray pine *(Pinus sabiniana)*
Great Basin blue sage *(Salvia dorrii)*
Jeffrey pine *(Pinus jeffreyi)*
junipers *(Juniperus occidentalis, J. osteosperma)*
limber pine *(Pinus flexilis)*
lodgepole pine *(Pinus contorta* ssp. *murrayana)*
manzanita *(Arctostaphylos* spp.*)*
Mediterranean grass *(Schismus barbatus)*
mountain mahogany *(Cercocarpus ledifolius)*
needle grasses *(Achnatherum* spp.*)*
oaks *(Quercus* spp.*)*
phacelia *(Phacelia* spp.*)*
pinyon pine *(Pinus monophylla)*
rabbitbrush *(Chrysothamnus nauseosus)*
red brome or foxtail chess *(Bromus madritensis* ssp. *rubens)*
red-stemmed filaree *(Erodium cicutarium)*
ripgut brome *(Bromus diandrus)*
Russian thistle or tumbleweed *(Salsola tragus)*
sagebrush *(Artemisia tridentata)*
Sahara mustard *(Brassica tournefortii)*
Schlesser pincushion *(Sclerocactus schlesseri)*
shadscale *(Atriplex confertifolia)*
smoke tree *(Psorothamnus spinosus)*
spiny hopsage *(Grayia spinosa)*
toyon *(Heteromeles arbutifolia)*
whitebark pine *(Pinus albicaulis)*
winterfat *(Krascheninnikovia lanata)*

## ANIMALS
acrobat ants *(Crematogaster* spp.*)*
banana yucca moths *(Tegeticula baccatella)*
cactus bug *(Chelinidea vittiger)*
cactus fruit midge *(Asplondylia opuntiae)*
Cactus longhorn beetle *(Moneilema semipunctata)*
Cactus wren *(Campylorhynchus brunneicapillus)*
carpenter bee *(Xylocopa califonica)*
desert night lizard *(Xantusia vigilis)*
desert packrat *(Neotoma lepida)*
European honey bee *(Apis mellifera)*
ground-nesting cactus bees *(Diadasia* spp.*)*
high plains yucca moth *(Tegeticula altiplanella)*
hooded oriole *(Icterus cucullatus)*
loggerhead shrike *(Lanius ludovicianus)*
night snake *(Hypsiglena torquata)*
Sap beetles *(Nitidulidae)*
Scott's oriole *(Icterus parisorum)*
woodrat or packrat *(Neotoma* spp.*)*
Yucca moths specific to Joshua trees *(Tegeticula antithetica* and *Tegeticula synthetica)*

## Appendix D: Cholla Species Comparison [table reads across to facing page]

| SCIENTIFIC NAME | COMMON NAME | STEM-JOINTS (length) | STEM-JOINTS (diameter) | SPINES (#/areole) | SPINES (length) |
|---|---|---|---|---|---|
| *Cylindropuntia* | | | | | |
| *C. acanthocarpa* var. *acanthocarpa* | buckhorn cholla | 4-12 in. (10-30 cm) | 0.8-1.25 in. (2-3 cm) | 18-30 | 0.5-1.2 in. (12-30 mm) |
| *C. bigelovii* | teddy-bear cholla | 1.5-5.1 in. (4-13 cm) | 1.5-2.4 in. (4-6 cm) | 10-15 | 0.6-1 in. (15-25 mm) |
| *C. californica* var. *californica* | snake cholla | 2.4-12 in. (6-30 cm) | 0.6-1 in. (1.5-2.5 cm) | 7-13 | 0.4-1.2 in. (10-30 mm) |
| *C. californica* var. *parkeri* | cane cholla | 2.4-12 in. (6-30 cm) | 0.6-1 in. (1.5-2.5 cm) | 7-13 | 0.4-1.2 in. (10-30 mm) |
| *C. chuckwallensis* | Chuckwalla cholla | 1.2-4 in. (3-10 cm) | 0.7-1.1 in. (1.7-2.9 cm) | 10-21 | 0.3-1.6 in. (0.8-4 cm) |
| *C. echinocarpa* | silver cholla | < 4.7 in. (< 12 cm) | 0.4-1 in. (1-2.5 cm) | 6-22 | 0.8-1.8 in. (20-45 mm) |
| *C. fosbergii* | Mason Valley cholla | < 7 in. (< 18 cm) | 1.6-2.4 in. (4-6 cm) | 7-10 | 0.6-1 in. (15-25 mm) |
| *C. ganderi* | Gander cholla | 4-10 in. (10-26 cm) | 1-1.6 in. (2.5-4 cm) | 11-28 | 0.4-1.4 in. (10-35 mm) |
| *C. multigeniculata* | Blue Diamond cholla | 0.8-2.8 in. (2-7 cm) | 0.6-0.8 in. (1.5-2 cm) | 10-14 | 0.4-0.8 in. (10-20 mm) |
| *C. munzii* | Munz cholla | 1.6-6.3 in. (4-16 cm) | 0.8-2 in. (2-5 cm) | 7-14 | 0.5-1.2 in. (12-30 mm) |
| *C. prolifera* | coastal cholla | 1.6-6 in. (4-15 cm) | 1.4-2 in. (3.5-5 cm) | 6-12 | 0.6-0.8 in. (15-20 mm) |
| *C. ramosissima* | diamond cholla | < 4 in. (2-10 cm) | < 0.4 in. (0.4-1 cm) | 0-5 | 0.8-2.4 in. (20-60 mm) |
| *C. whipplei* | Whipple cholla | 1.2-6 in. (3-15 cm) | 0.2-0.6 in. (0.5-1.5 cm) | 3-8 | 0.2-1.6 in. (5-40 mm) |
| *C. wolfii* | Wolf cholla | 2.4-15.7 in. (6-40 cm) | 1-1.6 in. (2.5-4 cm) | 12-30 | 0.4-1.2 in. (10-30 mm) |

## Appendix D: [continued]

| SPINES (notes) | FLOWERS (tepal color) | FLOWERS (filament color) | MATURE FRUITS (notes) |
|---|---|---|---|
| yellow to brown | yellow to dark orange | dark red | tan, densely spiny |
| obscuring stem | pale yellowish green | green | yellow, strongly tuberculate, mostly spineless |
| spines about equal length | yellow with reddish tips | greenish yellow | tan, tuberculate, mostly spineless |
| central spines longer | yellow to orange with reddish tips | greenish yellow | tan, tuberculate, mostly spineless |
| dense, translucent white | variable; dark red-purple, orange, or yellow | red to pink | densely spiny, thin-walled and dry |
| obscuring stem | yellowish green | green to yellowish green | tan, densely spiny or bur-like |
| tan to pink | pale yellowish green | green | tan, tuberculate, mostly spineless |
| white to pale yellow | yellow to greenish yellow | green to yellowish green | tan, densely spiny or bur-like |
| white, extremely crowded | bright yellow to greenish yellow | green to yellow | yellow, tuberculate, usually spineless |
| yellowish white | dull green suffused with red | green | yellow, tuberculate, with long glochids |
| pale red to dark brown | red | yellowish green | green, fleshy, prolific |
| sheaths baggy, yellow-tipped | variable; greenish yellow, orange, or pale red | green | tan, densely spiny or bur-like |
| central spines longer, spreading | bright greenish yellow | green to yellow | yellow to green, tuberculate, spineless, |
| gold to pale brown | variable; dark reddish bronze, red, or pale yellow | red | gray to tan, tuberculate, densely spiny |

# Appendix E: Prickly-Pear Species Comparison [table reads across to facing page]

| SCIENTIFIC NAME | COMMON NAME | PADS (length) | PADS (width) | SPINES areoles per diagonal row/ spines per areole | SPINES (length) |
|---|---|---|---|---|---|
| *Opuntia* | | | | | |
| *O. basilaris* var. *basilaris* | beavertail cactus | 2.8-13.8 in. (7-35 cm) | 2.6-6.3 in (6.5-16 cm) | 8-19/0 | |
| *O. basilaris* var. *brachyclada* | short-joint beavertail | 2-5.1 in. (5-13 cm) | 0.6-2 in. (1.5-5 cm) | 4-6/0 | |
| *O. basilaris* var. *treleasei* | Bakersfield cactus | 3.5-8 in. (9-20 cm) | 2-3 in. (5-7.5 cm) | 7-8/2-8 | 0.3-1 in. (7-26 mm) |
| *O. chlorotica* | pancake prickly-pear | 5-8.3 in. (13-21 cm) | 4.5-7.5 in. (11.5-19 cm) | 7-10/0-7 | 1-1.8 in. (25-45 mm) |
| *O.* X*curvispina* | curve-spined prickly-pear | 4.7-8.7 in. (12-22 cm) | 5-8 in. (12.5-20 cm) | 6-8/4-8 | 1.6-2.4 in. (40-60 mm) |
| *O. engelmannii* var. *engelmannii* | Englemann prickly-pear | 6-12 in. (15-30 cm) | 4.7-7.9 in. (12-20 cm) | 5-8/0-12 | 0.8-2 in. (20-50 mm) |
| *O. ficus-indica* | Indian-fig cactus | 8-24 in. (20-60 cm) | 4-10 in. (10-25 cm) | 7-11/0-6 | < 1.6 in. (1-40 mm) |
| *O. fragilis* | little prickly-pear | 0.6-2.2 in. (1.5-5.5 cm) | 0.6-1.2 in. (1.5-3 cm) | 3-5/3-8 | < 1 in. (8-24 mm) |
| *O. littoralis* | coastal prickly-pear | 6-12 in. (15-30 cm) | 2.6-5.5 in. (6.5-14 cm) | 5-7/4-11 | 0.8-1.6 in. (20-40 mm) |
| *O.* X*occidentalis* | western prickly-pear | 7.5-13.8 in. (19-35 cm) | 5.5-7 in. (14-18 cm) | 5-8/3-6 | 0.8-2 in. (20-50 mm) |
| *O. oricola* | tall prickly-pear | 6-10 in. (15-25 cm) | 4.7-7.5 in. (12-19 cm) | 8-10/5-13 | 0.8-1.6 in. (20-40 mm) |
| *O. phaeacantha* | brown-spined prickly-pear | 4-10 in. (10-25 cm) | 2.8-8 in. (7-20 cm) | 5-7/0-8 | 1-3 in. (25-80 mm) |
| *O. polyacantha* var. *erinacea* | Mojave prickly-pear | 4-8 in. (10-20 cm) | 2-4 in. (5-10 cm) | 8-14/1-18 | 1.6-7 in. (40-180 mm) |
| *O. polyacantha* var. *hystricina* | porcupine prickly-pear | 3.2-4 in. (8-10 cm) | 2-3.2 in. (5-8 cm) | 8-10/0-6 | 2-3.2 in. (50-80 mm) |
| *O. polyacantha* var. *polyacantha* | Plains prickly-pear | 1.6-4.7 in. (4-12 cm) | 4.6-4.3 in. (4-11 cm) | 6-11/0-6 | 0.8-1.6 in. (20-40 mm) |
| *O.* X*vaseyi* | Vasey prickly-pear | 2.8-8.7 in. (7-22 cm) | 2-4.7 in. (5-12 cm) | 5-7/0-6 | 0.8-1.9 in. (20-48 mm) |

## APPENDIX E: [CONTINUED]

| SPINES (notes) | FLOWERS (tepal color) | FLOWERS (filament color) | MATURE FRUITS (notes) |
|---|---|---|---|
| glochids conspicuous | pale pink to bright magenta | red | purplish green drying to tan, spineless |
| glochids conspicuous | pale pink to bright magenta | red | purplish green drying to tan, spineless |
| yellowish, sraight | pale pink to bright magenta | red | few pale yellow spines |
| yellow, deflexed | yellow, may be suffused with reddish orange | white to pale yellow | purplish red, fleshy, spineless |
| brown and yellow, curved and straight | pale yellow | yellow | dull red, green inside, fleshy, spineless |
| yellow to white, some with reddish bases | yellow, may be suffused with reddish orange | white to pale yellow | purplish red throughout, fleshy, spineless |
| white to brown, flattened basally | yellow to orange | yellow | orange to purple, fleshy, usually spineless |
| gray with darker tips, finely barbed | pale greenish yellow to pale orange | orange to red | tan, spiny near tip |
| white, aging dark gray | dark yellow | yellow | dark reddish purple throughout, fleshy, spineless |
| pale yellow to white, angularly flattened | yellow to pink, sometimes darker basally | yellow to white | reddish purple throughout, fleshy, spineless |
| yellow to white, generally curved and deflexed | yellow | yellow to orangish yellow | dark red, yellowish inside, fleshy, spineless |
| yellow to white with brown bases | yellow, often with orange basal portions | green bases and yellowish tips | purplish red outside, greenish inside, fleshy, spineless |
| brown to pale gray, becoming very long and wavy | pale yellow to orange, or pink | yellow in yellow flowers, red in pink flowers | tan, very spiny with 20-33 areoles |
| yellow, tan or brown, mostly stiff | pale yellow to orange, or pink | yellow | tan, spiny with 11-21 areoles |
| minor spines white, deflexed, major spines gray to pale brown | pale yellow to orange, or pink | yellow in yellow flowers, red in pink flowers | tan, spiny with 12-28 areoles |
| white with yellow bases | yellow, orange, or red | orange to red | reddish purple throughout, fleshy, spineless |

# Appendix F: Species Rarity Status

*Agave shawii* var. *shawii*/**shaw agave**—CA; CRPR: 2B.1

*Agave utahensis* var. *eborispina*/**ivory-spined agave**—CA, NV; NV Harvest Regulated; CRPR: 1B.3

*Agave utahensis* var. *nevadensis*/**Clark Mountain agave**—CA, NV; NV Harvest Regulated; CRPR: 4.2

*Bergerocactus emoryi*/**golden cereus**—CA; CRPR: 2B.2

*Carnegiea gigantea*/**giant saguaro**—CA; CRPR: 2B.2

*Coryphantha alversonii*/**cushion foxtail cactus**—CA endemic; CRPR: 4.3

*Coryphantha chlorantha*/**desert pincushion**—CA, NV; NV Harvest Regulated; CRPR: 2B.1

*Coryphantha vivipara* var. *rosea*/**beehive cactus**—CA, NV; NV Harvest Regulated; CRPR: 2B.2

*Cylindropuntia californica* var. *californica*/**snake cholla**—CA; CRPR: 1B.1

*Cylindropuntia fosbergii*/**Mason Valley cholla**—CA Endemic; CA; CRPR: 1B.3

*Cylindropuntia multigeniculata*/**Blue Diamond cholla**—NV; NNHP: Sensitive; NV Fully Protected; BLM:State Listed; NNPS:Threatened

*Cylindropuntia munzii*/**Munz cholla**—CA; CRPR: 1B.3

*Cylindropuntia wolfii*/**Wolf cholla**—CA; CRPR: 4.3

*Ferocactus viridescens*/**coast barrel cactus**—CA; CRPR: 2B.1

*Grusonia parishii*/**Parish club-cholla**—CA, NV; NV Harvest Regulated; CRPR: 2B.2

*Grusonia pulchella*/**sand-cholla**—CA, NV; NNHP: Sensitive; NV Harvest Regulated; CRPR: 2B.2

*Nolina cismontana*/**chaparral nolina**—CA Endemic; CRPR: 1B.2

*Nolina interrata*/**Dehesa nolina**—CA; CITES: Appendix I; CA Endangered; CRPR: 1B.1

*Opuntia basilaris* var. *brachyclada*/**short-joint beavertail**—CA Endemic; CRPR: 1B.2

*Opuntia basilaris* var. *treleasei*/**Bakersfield cactus**—CA Endemic; USFWS/ESA: U.S. Endangered; CA Endangered; CRPR: 1B.1

*Opuntia fragilis*/**little prickly-pear**—CA; CRPR: 2B.1

*Opuntia* X*curvispina*/**curve-spined prickly-pear**—CA, NV; NV Harvest Regulated; CRPR: 2B.2

*Sclerocactus blainei*/**Blaine fishhook cactus**—NV; USFWS/ESA: Species of Concern; NNHP: Sensitive; NV Harvest Regulated; BLM: Sensitive; NNPS:Watch List

*Sclerocactus johnsonii*/**Johnson pineapple cactus**—CA, NV; NV Harvest Regulated; CRPR: 2B.2

*Sclerocactus nyensis*/**Tonopah fishhook cactus**—NV Endemic; CITES: Appendix I; NNHP: Sensitive; NV Harvest Regulated; BLM: Sensitive; NNPS:Watch List

*Sclerocactus polyancistrus*/**Mojave fishhook cactus**—CA, NV; NNHP: Sensitive; NV Harvest Regulated; BLM: Sensitive; CRPR: List 4.2; Inyo National Forest Watch List

*Sclerocactus pubispinus*/**Great Basin fishhook cactus**—NV; CITES: Appendix I; NNHP: Watch List; NNPS: Watch List; NV Harvest Regulated

## Abbreviations
USFWS/ESA: United States Fish & Wildlife Servies/Endangered Species Act
CITES Conventon on International Trade in Endangered Species of Wild Fauna and Flora*
NNHP Nevada Natural Heritage Program
BLM Bureau of Land Management
CRPR California Rare Plant Rank**
NNPS Nevada Native Plant Society

## *CITES Definitions
Appendix I: Species threatened with extinction that are or may be affected by trade. Trade in Appendix-I specimens may only take place in exceptional circumstances.
Appendix II: Species that are not presently threatened with extinction, but may become so if their trade is not regulated. All Cactaceae are included in Appendix II.

## **CRPR Definitions
CRPR 1B: Plants rare, threatened, or endangerd in CA and elsewhere.
CRPR 2B: Plants rare, threatened, or endangered in CA, but more common elsewhere.
CRPR 4: Plants of limited distribution-A Watch List.
Threat codes are appended to rare plant ranks and are defined below:
1: seriously threatened in CA (over 80% of occurrences threatened/high degree and immediacy of threat).
2: moderately threatened in CA (20-80% of occurrences threatened/moderate degree and immediacy of threat).
3: not very endangered in CA (less than 20% of occurrences threatened/low degree and immediacy of threat or no current threats known).

# Appendix G: Education, Conservation, and Cultivation Resources

## EDUCATION AND CONSERVATION

**Cactus and Succulent Society of America** (CSSA)
An international organization dedicated to the education and preservation of cacti and succulents worldwide. There are at least 20 regional chapters in California, and one in Las Vegas, NV. The CSSA publishes bimonthly *The Cactus and Succulent Journal* and a scientific journal *Haseltonia,* once a year.
http://www.cssainc.org/

**California Native Plant Society**
2707 K Street, Suite 1, Sacramento, CA 95816-5113. (916) 447-2677, www.cnps.org

**Huntington Botanical Gardens**
1151 Oxford Road, San Marino, CA 91108
(626) 405-3500, www.huntington.org

**Maturango Museum**
100 E. Las Flores Ave., Ridgecrest, CA 93555
(760) 375-6900, www.maturango.org

**Nevada Native Plant Society**
P.O. Box 8965, Reno, NV 89507-8965
http://heritage.nv.gov/nnps.htm

**Nevada Natural Heritage Program**
901 South Stewart St., Suite 5002, Carson City, NV 89701-5245, (775) 684-2900
http://heritage.nv.gov/index.htm

**Rancho Santa Ana Botanic Garden**
1500 North College Ave., Claremont, CA 91711-3157, (909) 625-8767, www.rsabg.org

**Santa Barbara Botanic Garden**
1212 Mission Canyon Road, Santa Barbara, CA 93105, (805) 682-4726, www.sbbg.org

**Springs Preserve**
333 S. Valley View Blvd. (at I-95), Las Vegas, NV 89107, (702) 822-7700
http://www.springspreserve.org/html/home.html

## LINKS TO WEBSITES ON WEED MANAGEMENT

**California Department of Food and Agriculture**
Integrated Pest Control/Weed Management Areas
http://www.cdfa.ca.gov/phpps/ipc/weedmgtareas wma_index_hp.htm

**California Invasive Plant Council**
Cal-IPC: http://www.cal-ipc.org

**Center for Invasive Plant Management**
http://www.weedcenter.org

**Nevada Department of Agriculture**
http://agri.nv.gov/nwac/PLANT_NoxWeeds_index.htm

**Western U.S. Cooperative Weed Management Areas (CWMAs)**
http://www.weedcenter.org/weed_mgmt_areas/wma_overview.html

## HORTICULTURAL RESOURCES

**Cactus Canyon Succulent Nursery**
33439 Couser Canyon Road, Valley Center, CA 92082, (760) 742-1308
http://www.cactus-canyon.com/index.html

**Cactus Jungle**
1509 Fourth Street, Berkeley, CA 94710
(510) 558-8650
http://www.cactusjungle.com/index.html

**El Nativo Growers, Inc.**
200 S. Peckham Road, Azusa, CA 91702
(626) 969-8449
http://www.elnativogrowers.com/Natives.htm

**Grigsby Cactus Gardens**
2326-2354 Bella Vista Drive, Vista, CA 92084-7836
(760) 727-1323
http://www.cactus-mall.com/grigsby/index.html

**High Country Gardens**
2902 Rufina Street, Santa Fe, NM 87507-2929
1-800-925-9387
http://www.highcountrygardens.com

**Living Stones Nursery & Plants for the Southwest**
50 E. Blacklidge (Nursery), 2936 N. Stone Avenue (Mailing), Tucson, AZ 85705, (520) 628-8773
http://www.lithops.net/

**Poot's House of Cactus**
17229 E. Highway 120, Ripon, CA, (209) 599-7241

**The Cactus and Succulent Plant Mall**
An internet resource with hundreds of links to nurseries, bookstores, cactus and succulent organizations, and other information.
http://www.cactus-mall.com/

**Turner-Greenhouse Cactus and Succulent Nursery**
4455 Quadrel Street, Las Vegas, NV 89129
(702) 645-2032
http://www.turner-greenhouse.com/

## Appendix H: Species List for Selected Public Lands in Califorina and Nevada [table reads across to facing page]

| SCIENTIFIC NAME | COMMON NAME | CHANNEL ISLANDS | CABRILLO NATL. MON. | TORREY PINES ST. RESERVE | ANZA-BORREGO DESERT ST. PARK |
|---|---|---|---|---|---|
| **CALIFORINA** | | | | | |
| **Cactaceae** | | | | | |
| *Bergerocactus emoryi* | golden cereus | • | • | • | |
| *Carnegiea gigantea* | giant saguaro | | | | |
| *Coryphantha alversonii* | cushion foxtail cactus | | | | |
| *Coryphantha vivipara* var. *rosea* | beehive cactus | | | | |
| *Coryphantha chlorantha* | desert pincushion cactus | | | | |
| *Cylindropuntia acanthocarpa* var. *acanthocarpa* | buckhorn cholla | | | | |
| *Cylindropuntia bigelovii* | teddy-bear cholla | | | | • |
| *Cylindropuntia californica* var. *californica* | snake cholla | | • | • | |
| *Cylindropuntia californica* var. *parkeri* | cane cholla | | | | • |
| *Cylindropuntia chuckwallensis* | Chuckwalla cholla | | | | |
| *Cylindropuntia echinocarpa* | silver cholla | | | | • |
| *Cylindropuntia fosbergii* | Mason Valley cholla | | | | • |
| *Cylindropuntia ganderi* | Gander cholla | | | | • |
| *Cylindropuntia munzii* | Munz cholla | | | | |
| *Cylindropuntia prolifera* | coastal cholla | • | • | • | |
| *Cylindropuntia ramosissima* | diamond cholla | | | | • |
| *Cylindropuntia wolfii* | Wolf cholla | | | | • |
| *Echinocactus polycephalus* var. *polycephalus* | cottontop cactus | | | | • |
| *Echinocereus engelmannii* | Engelmann hedgehog | | | | • |
| *Echinocereus mojavensis* | Mojave mound cactus | | | | |
| *Ferocactus cylindraceus* | desert barrel cactus | | | | • |
| *Ferocactus viridescens* | coast barrel cactus | | • | • | |
| *Grusonia parishii* | Parish club-cholla | | | | |
| *Grusonia pulchella* | sand-cholla | | | | |
| *Mammillaria dioica* | California fishhook | | • | • | • |
| *Mammillaria grahamii* | Graham fishhook | | | | |
| *Mammillaria tetrancistra* | common fishhook | | | | • |
| *Opuntia basilaris* var. *basilaris* | beavertail cactus | | | | • |
| *Opuntia basilaris* var. *brachyclada* | short-joint beavertail | | | | |
| *Opuntia basilaris* var. *treleasei* | Bakersfield cactus | | | | |
| *Opuntia chlorotica* | pancake prickly-pear | | | | • |
| *Opuntia Xcurvispina* | curve-spined prickly-pear | | | | |
| *Opuntia engelmannii* var. *engelmannii* | Engelmann prickly-pear | | | | • |
| *Opuntia ficus-indica* | Indian-fig prickly-pear | • | | • | |
| *Opuntia fragilis* | little prickly-pear | | | | |
| *Opuntia littoralis* | coastal prickly-pear | • | • | • | |
| *Opuntia Xoccidentalis* | western prickly-pear | • | | • | |
| *Opuntia oricola* | tall prickly-pear | • | | • | |

# Appendix H: [continued]

| JOSHUA TREE NATL. PARK | DEATH VALLEY NATL. PARK TO E. SIERRA | MOJAVE NATL. PRESERVE | WHIPPLE MOUNTAINS WILDERNESS AREA | OTHER |
|---|---|---|---|---|
|  |  |  |  |  |
|  |  |  |  |  |
|  |  |  |  | Border Field State Park |
|  |  |  | • |  |
| • |  |  |  |  |
|  |  | • |  |  |
|  | • | • |  |  |
|  |  | • | • |  |
| • |  | • | • |  |
|  |  |  |  |  |
|  |  |  |  |  |
| • |  |  |  |  |
| • | • | • | • |  |
|  |  |  |  |  |
|  |  |  |  |  |
|  |  |  |  | Imperial and Riverside counties only |
|  |  |  |  |  |
| • | • | • | • |  |
|  |  |  |  |  |
| • | • | • |  |  |
| • | • | • | • |  |
| • | • | • |  |  |
| • | • | • | • |  |
|  |  |  |  |  |
| • |  | • |  |  |
|  |  |  |  | northeastern Inyo County only |
|  |  |  |  |  |
|  |  |  | • |  |
| • | • | • | • |  |
| • | • | • | • |  |
|  |  |  |  | San Bernardino County only |
|  |  |  |  | Kern County only |
| • |  | • |  |  |
|  |  | • |  |  |
|  |  | • |  |  |
|  |  |  |  |  |
|  |  |  |  | Siskiyou County only |
|  |  |  |  |  |
|  |  |  |  |  |
|  |  |  |  |  |

# Appendix H: Species List for Selected Public Lands in Califorina and Nevada [table reads across to facing page]

| SCIENTIFIC NAME | COMMON NAME | CHANNEL ISLANDS | CABRILLO NATL. MON. | TORREY PINES ST. RESERVE | ANZA-BORREGO DESERT ST. PARK |
|---|---|---|---|---|---|
| **CALIFORINA** [CONTINUED] | | | | | |
| **Cactaceae** | | | | | |
| *Opuntia phaeacantha* | brown-spined prickly-pear | | | | • |
| *Opuntia polyacantha* var. *erinacea* | Mojave prickly-pear | | | | • |
| *Opuntia polyacantha* var. *hystricina* | porcupine prickly-pear | | | | |
| *Opuntia Xvaseyi* | Vasey prickly-pear | | | | |
| *Sclerocactus johnsonii* | Johnson pineapple cactus | | | | |
| *Sclerocactus polyancistrus* | Mojave fishhook cactus | | | | |
| **Agavaceae** | | | | | |
| *Agave deserti* var. *deserti* | desert agave | | | | • |
| *Agave deserti* var. *simplex* | simple desert agave | | | | |
| *Agave shawii* var. *shawii* | Shaw agave | | • | • | |
| *Agave utahensis* var. *eborispina* | ivory-spined agave | | | | |
| *Agave utahensis* var. *nevadensis* | Clark Mountain agave | | | | |
| *Hesperoyucca whipplei* | chaparral yucca | | | • | • |
| *Yucca baccata* var. *baccata* | banana yucca | | | | |
| *Yucca brevifolia* | Joshua tree | | | | |
| *Yucca schidigera* | Mojave yucca | | • | • | • |
| **Nolinas & Ocotillo** | | | | | |
| *Nolina bigelovii* | Bigelow nolina | | | | • |
| *Nolina cismontana* | chaparral nolina | | | | |
| *Nolina interrata* | Dehesa nolina | | | | |
| *Nolina parryi* | Parry nolina | | | | • |
| *Fouquieria splendens* ssp. *splendens* | ocotillo | | | | • |

## Appendix H: [continued]

| JOSHUA TREE NATL. PARK | DEATH VALLEY NATL. PARK TO E. SIERRA | MOJAVE NATL. PRESERVE | WHIPPLE MOUNTAINS WILDERNESS AREA | OTHER |
|---|---|---|---|---|
|  |  |  |  |  |
|  |  |  |  |  |
| • |  | • |  |  |
| • | • | • |  |  |
|  | • | • |  |  |
|  |  |  |  | Los Angeles, Orange, Riverside, and San Bernardino counties. only |
|  | • |  |  |  |
|  | • |  |  |  |
|  |  |  |  |  |
|  |  |  |  |  |
|  |  | • | • |  |
|  |  |  |  | Border Field State Park |
|  |  |  |  | eastern Inyo County only |
|  |  | • |  |  |
|  |  |  |  |  |
|  |  | • |  |  |
| • | • | • |  |  |
| • |  | • |  |  |
|  |  |  |  |  |
| • |  |  | • |  |
|  |  |  |  | Ventura County to San Diego County only |
|  |  |  |  | San Diego County only |
| • |  |  |  |  |
| • |  |  | • |  |

## Appendix H: Species List for Selected Public Lands in Califorina and Nevada [continued, table reads across to facing page]

| SCIENTIFIC NAME | COMMON NAME | DESERT NATL. WILDLIFE REFUGE | LAKE MEAD NATL. REC. AREA/GOLD BUTTE AREA |
|---|---|---|---|
| **Nevada** | | | |
| **Cactaceae** | | | |
| *Coryphantha vivipara* var. *rosea* | beehive cactus | • | |
| *Coryphantha chlorantha* | desert pincushion cactus | • | |
| *Cylindropuntia acanthocarpa* var. *acanthocarpa* | buckhorn cholla | • | • |
| *Cylindropuntia bigelovii* | teddy-bear cholla | | • |
| *Cylindropuntia echinocarpa* | silver cholla | • | |
| *Cylindropuntia ramosissima* | diamond cholla | • | • |
| *Cylindropuntia multigeniculata* | Blue Diamond cholla | • | • |
| *Cylindropuntia whipplei* | Whipple cholla | • | |
| *Echinocactus polycephalus* var. *polycephalus* | cottontop cactus | • | • |
| *Echinocactus polycephalus* var. *xeranthemoides* | Grand Canyon cottontop | | • |
| *Echinocereus engelmannii* | Engelmann hedgehog | • | • |
| *Echinocereus mojavensis* | Mojave mound cactus | • | • |
| *Ferocactus cylindraceus* | desert barrel cactus | • | • |
| *Grusonia parishii* | Parish club-cholla | • | • |
| *Grusonia pulchella* | sand-cholla | | |
| *Mammillaria tetrancistra* | common fishhook | • | • |
| *Opuntia basilaris* var. *basilaris* | beavertail cactus | • | • |
| *Opuntia chlorotica* | pancake prickly-pear | | • |
| *Opuntia Xcurvispina* | curve-spined prickly-pear | | |
| *Opuntia engelmannii* var. *engelmannii* | Engelmann prickly-pear | | |
| *Opuntia phaeacantha* | brown-spined prickly-pear | • | • |
| *Opuntia polyacantha* var. *erinacea* | Mojave prickly-pear | • | • |
| *Opuntia polyacantha* var. *hystricina* | porcupine prickly-pear | • | |
| *Opuntia polyacantha* var. *polyacantha* | Plains prickly-pear | • | |
| *Pediocactus simpsonii* | mountain cactus | | |
| *Sclerocactus blainei* | Blaine fishhook cactus | | |
| *Sclerocactus johnsonii* | Johnson pineapple cactus | • | • |
| *Sclerocactus nyensis* | Nye fishhook cactus | | |
| *Sclerocactus polyancistrus* | Mojave fishhook cactus | | |
| *Sclerocactus pubispinus* | Great Basin fishhook cactus | | |
| **Agavaceae** | | | |
| *Agave utahensis* var. *eborispina* | ivory-spined agave | • | |
| *Agave utahensis* var. *nevadensis* | Clark Mountain agave | | • |
| *Agave utahensis* var. *utahensis* | Utah agave | | • |
| *Yucca baccata* var. *baccata* | banana yucca | • | |
| *Yucca brevifolia* | Joshua tree | • | • |
| *Yucca harrimaniae* | Harriman yucca | | |
| *Yucca schidigera* | Mojave yucca | • | • |
| *Yucca utahensis* | Utah yucca | | • |
| **Nolinas & Ocotillo** | | | |
| *Nolina bigelovii* | Bigelow nolina | | • |
| *Fouquieria* ssp. *splendens* | ocotillo | | • |

# Appendix H: [continued]

| SPRING MOUNTAINS NRA AND RED ROCK CANYON NCA | VALLEY OF FIRE STATE PARK | OTHER |
|---|---|---|
|  |  |  |
|  |  |  |
| • |  |  |
| • |  |  |
| • | • |  |
|  |  |  |
| • | • |  |
| • |  |  |
| • |  |  |
|  |  |  |
| • |  |  |
|  |  |  |
| • | • |  |
| • |  |  |
| • | • |  |
| • |  |  |
|  |  | most counties of central NV |
| • |  |  |
| • | • |  |
| • |  |  |
|  |  | southwestern Clark County only |
| • |  |  |
| • |  |  |
| • | • |  |
| • |  |  |
| • |  |  |
|  |  | northern Lincoln County to Humboldt County and east |
|  |  | Nye and Lincoln counties only |
|  | • |  |
|  |  | Nye and Esmeralda counties only |
|  |  | Nye and Esmeralda counties only |
|  |  | eastern Lincoln, White Pine, and Elko counties only |
|  |  |  |
| • |  |  |
| • |  |  |
| • |  |  |
| • |  |  |
| • |  |  |
|  |  | Lincoln, White Pine, and Elko counties only |
| • | • |  |
|  | • |  |
|  |  |  |
|  |  |  |
|  |  |  |

## Key to the Genera of Agavaceae and Cactaceae, Including *Nolina* (Nolinaceae) and *Fouquieria* (Fouquieriaceae)

1. Leaves forming a rosette; spines, if present, on leaf tips or margins; flowers borne on an inflorescence greater than 1 foot long; flowers yellow or whitish, with 6 stamens.
    2. Leaves not succulent, strap-shaped, flexible, not spine-tipped; flowers much shorter than 1 inch .................................................................... *Nolina*
    2'. Leaves succulent or semi-succulent, usually rounded on underside, sharply spine-tipped; flowers longer than 1 inch .................................................. 3. Agavaceae
        3. Leaves rigid, inflexible, with marginal teeth or spines; flowers yellow with inferior ovary ................................................................. *Agave*
        3'. Leaves rigid to flexible, margins without spines, but may be finely serrate; flowers whitish with superior ovary ................................................. 4
            4. Rosettes without a trunk; leaves semi-succulent, sharply spine-tipped, without marginal fibers; rosettes monocarpic ....................... *Hesperoyucca*
            4'. Rosettes with or without a trunk; leaves succulent, spine-tipped, sometimes with whitish marginal fibers; each rosette or tree-like plant capable of flowering numerous times .............................................................. *Yucca*
1'. Leaves not forming a rosette; spines usually present on stems; flowers borne singly or on an inflorescence less than 1 foot long; flowers red, orange, yellow, green, or pink, with more than 6 stamens. ............. 5
    5. Plants not succulent, stems mostly brown to gray, cane-like, leafless or with clusters of small green leaves; flowers in short inflorescences at branch tips, tubular ..................... *Fouquieria*
    5'. Plants succulent, stems green, columnar, barrel-shaped, or branched into cylindrical joints or flattened pads; flowers borne singly, vase-or bowl-shaped .......................... 6. Cactaceae
        6. Plants mat-like, shrubby or tree-like, with discrete, jointed stem segments; glochids present ................................................................. 7
            7. Jointed stem segments flattened into discrete pads .............. *Opuntia*
            7'. Jointed stem segments cylindrical or club-shaped .................... 8
                8. Plants low-growing, shrubby, or tree-like; spines round in cross-section, with deciduous sheaths covering entire spine ........ *Cylindropuntia*
                8'. Plants low-growing, forming clumps or mats; some spines flattened, with deciduous sheath at spine tip only ................... *Grusonia*
        6'. Plants columnar, barrel-shaped, cylindrical, or globular; stems not jointed; glochids absent ................................................................. 9
            9. Stems columnar, ascending, branched or not; generally at least 3 feet tall; plants not widespread, found only in either lower Colorado River Basin or coastal San Diego County ...................................................... 10
                10. Plants massive, branching above 5 feet only; lower Colorado River Basin .......................................................... *Carnegiea*
                10'. Plants slender, branching at base; coastal San Diego County ...... ................................................................. *Bergerocactus*
            9'. Stems barrel-shaped, cylindrical or globular, not narrowly columnar; less than 6 feet tall; plants widespread, of Mojave, Great Basin or Colorado deserts, or coastal southern California ........................................... 11
                11. Stems with prominent tubercles; ribs absent; generally less than 12 inches tall .................................................... 12

12. Areoles with some central spines hooked;
>13. Spines no more than 1 inch long, not flattened; flowers produced in a ring near the stem tips . . . . . . . . . . . . . . . . . . . . . . . . . . . . . . . . . . . . . . . . . *Mammillaria*
>13'. Spines up to 3 inches long, some flat and ribbon-like; flowers not forming a ring . . . . . . . . . . . . . . . . . . . . . . . . . . . . . . . . . . . . . . . . . . . . . . . . *Sclerocactus* (in part)

12'. Areoles without any hooked spines; flowers produced at stem tips . . . . . . . . . . . . . . . . . . . . . . . . . . . . . . . . . . . . . . . 14
>14. Flower-bearing portion of areole separate from spine-bearing portion, with flower and fruit standing apart from spine cluster; ripe fruit fleshy, indehiscent; plants of southern California or Nevada. . . . . . . . . . . . . . . . . . . . . . . . . . . . . . . . . . . . . . . *Coryphantha*
>14'. Flower-bearing portion of areole adjacent to spine-bearing portion, with flower and fruit crowded against the spine cluster; ripe fruit dry, splitting along the side; plants of central and northern Nevada. . . . . . . . . . . . . . . . . . . . . . . . . . . . . . . . . . . . . *Pediocactus*

11'. Stems prominently to weakly ribbed; 4 inches to 6 feet tall . . . . 15
>15. Stems generally clustered . . . . . . . . . . . . . . . . . . . . . . . . 16
>>16. Stems barrel-shaped or rounded; mature plants greater than 6 inches in diameter; fruits dry, white-woolly; flowers yellow . . . . . . . . . . . . . . . *Echinocactus*
>>16'. Stems cylindrical to globular; mature plants less than 6 inches in diameter; fruits juicy; flowers pink to red . . . . . . . . . . . . . . . . . . . . . . . . . . . *Echinocereus*

>15'. Stems generally solitary, or only rarely branched . . . . . 17
>>17. Stems prominently ribbed; spines straight to curved, not hooked; mature plants greater than 6 inches in diameter . . . . . . . . . . . . . . . . . . *Ferocactus*
>>17'. Stems weakly ribbed, lower between tubercles; spines straight, curved, ribbon-like or hooked; mature plants usually less than 6 inches in diameter. . . . . . . . . . . . . . . . . . . . . . . . . . . . . . . . . . . *Sclerocactus* (in part)

# Glossary

**androecium.** The male reproductive parts of a flower; the stamens collectively.
**areole.** A specialized spot on cactus stems that produce spines, leaves, roots, flower buds, or new stems.
**asexual.** Mode of reproduction that does not involve seed fertilization; vegetative reproduction.
**basal.** Relating to a base; the lower portion of a plant, or plant part.
**bract.** A reduced, modified leaf subtending a flower or inflorescence.
**calyx.** The collective term for sepals, the outermost series of flower parts.
**central spines.** Spines that arise from the center of an areole, usually surrounded by radial spines (see spines).
**chlorophyll.** The green photosynthetic pigment within plant cells.
**chromosome.** A large cellular molecule composed of DNA, self-duplicating, usually present in pairs in all plant cells other than reproductive cells.
**cismontane.** Situated on "this side" (west) of the mountains, i.e. west of the Sierra Nevada and Peninsular Ranges (see transmontane).
**cryptobiotic.** Soil crusts formed from cyanobacteria filaments, lichens, and mosses.
**decumbent.** Growth habit that is reclining except for an upward-growing tip.
**deflexed.** Turned or bent downward.
**dicotyledon.** Class of plants having two cotyledons or seed leaves; eudicot.
**dimorphic.** Having two different shapes or forms.
**dioecious.** Having male (staminate) and female (pistillate) flowers on separate plants of a species.
**diploid.** Having two sets (2n) of chromosomes per cell, the typical case for sexually-reproducing plants.
**endemic.** Native and restricted to a certain geographic area.
**epidermis.** The outer layer of cells on a plant.
**epiphyte.** A plant that grows entirely upon another plant (usually a tree) and relies on it for mechanical but not nutritional support.
**filament.** The thread-like stalk of an anther; part of a flower's androecium.
**filiferous.** Bearing thread-like fibers, used to characterize yucca leaves.
**floral remnant.** The dried remains of a withered flower following fertilization of the ovary (fruit development).
**flora.** All plant species of a particular region or time period.
**genetic.** That which is inherited; the science of genes and the variation of organisms.
**geophyte.** A perennial plant with an underground storage organ, such as a tuber.
**glaucous.** Pertaining to stems or leaves having a bluish or whitish waxy coating that is easily rubbed off.
**glochid.** A tiny, deciduous, barbed spine, characteristic of cactus subfamily Opuntioideae, (chollas and prickly-pears).
**gynodioecious.** A plant having both perfect (male and female) flowers and female, or pistillate, flowers.
**habit.** The general appearance or growth form of a plant.
**habitat.** The type of locality or ecological conditions in which a plant or animal is naturally found.
**hybrid.** Progeny resulting from a cross between two or more different taxa.
**indehiscent.** A plant fruit that does not open via splits or pores to release its seeds.
**inferior ovary.** An ovary attached below the point of attachment of the perianth and androecium.
**inflorescence.** The flowering segment of a plant; also the arrangement of flowers on a stem.
**intergrade.** To show characters intermediate between two parent plant species because of shared genes; hybridize.
**lanceolate.** Lance-shaped, narrow, tapered at the tip and broadest at or below the middle.
**linear.** Long and narrow, generally eight or more times longer than wide.
**monoecious.** Having flowers of one sex only, either male (staminate) or female (pistillate) on the same plant.

**monocarpic.** A plant with a rosette that dies after flowering.

**monocotyledon.** Class of plants having one cotyledon, or seed leaf; monocot.

**monotypic.** Of one type, usually referring to a genus with only one species.

**obovate.** Egg-shaped in outline, with the broadest part above the middle.

**outcrossing.** Sexual reproduction that involves genetic exchange with other plants or populations, which serves to increase genetic diversity.

**ovary.** Lower, swollen section of the pistil; female flower part that contains ovules which become seeds.

**ovate.** Egg-shaped in outline, with the broadest part below the middle.

**ovoid.** Egg-shaped, three-dimensional.

**pad.** Flattened stem section or branch of a prickly-pear (*Opuntia* spp.).

**panicle.** A branched (compound) inflorescence with the flowers on the outermost branchlets.

**perianth.** The collective term for petals, sepals, or tepals.

**petiole.** The stalk of a leaf that supports the blade.

**ploidy.** The number of paired chromosome sets in the cells of an organism.

**polyploidy.** Having multiple sets of chromosomes, rather than the usual two sets for diploid plants.

**protandrous.** Relating to a flower that produces pollen before the stigma is receptive.

**pubescent.** Covered with fine, soft, downy hairs; or hairy in a general sense (exhibiting pubescence).

**raceme.** An unbranched, elongating flowering stalk.

**radial spines.** Outer spines that surround one or more central spines (see spine).

**rhizome.** A horizontal, underground stem from which leaves emerge.

**rosette.** A radiating, circular cluster of leaves.

**spine.** A sharp-pointed leaf or portion of a leaf.

**stem-joint.** Cylindrical stem section or branch of a cholla (*Cylindropuntia* spp.).

**succulent.** Having fleshy plant parts that store and conserve water *(adj.)*; A plant with succulent leaves or stems *(noun)*.

**superior ovary.** An ovary that is attached above the attachment of the perianth and androecium.

**taxon.** A taxonomic unit or category of any rank; plural, **taxa.**

**taxonomy.** The science or principles of hierarchical classification.

**tepal.** A term used for sepals and petals when they are very similar or indistinguishable from each other.

**thorn.** A sharp-pointed section of a stem.

**transmontane.** Situated on the "other side" (east) of the mountains, i.e. east of the Sierra Nevada and Peninsular Ranges (see cismontane).

**tubercle.** "Little swelling;" a small prominence or stem protrusion in some cacti.

**umbilicus.** In cacti, the depression at the top of a fruit where the flower was seated.

# BIBLIOGRAPHY

Ackerman, Thomas L. 2003. A Flora of the Desert National Wildlife Range, Nevada. *Mentzelia* 7:1-90.

Adams, W.W. III, S. D. Smith, and C.B. Osmond. 1987. Photoinhibition of the CAM succulent *Opuntia basilaris* growing in Death Valley: Evidence from 77K fluorescence and quantum yield. *Oecologia* 71:221-228.

Anderson, Edward F. 2001. *The Cactus Family.* Portland, OR: Timber Press.

APG. 2003. An update of the angiosperm phylogeny group classification for the orders and families of flowering plants: APG II. *Botanical Journal of the Linnean Society* 141:399-436.

Armstrong, Wayne P. 2000. The yucca and its moth. *Wayne's Word* Vol. 9, no. 2 (Summer 2000). http://waynesword.palomar.edu/ww0902a.htm

Asher, Jerry. 1998. The Spread of Invasive Weeds in Western Wildlands: A state of biological emergency. Paper presented at the Governor's Idaho Weed Summit, May 1998. http://www.blm.gov/weeds/BOISUMMI.WPD.html

Bair, Janet, and Arnold Tiehm. 2003. Pages 1-16 in Ackerman, Thomas L. 2003. A Flora of the Desert National Wildlife Range, Nevada. *Mentzelia* 7:1-90.

Baker, Herbert G. 1986. Yuccas and Yucca Moths—A Historical Commentary. *Annals of the Missouri Botanical Garden* 73:556-564.

Baker, Marc A. 2005. Current knowledge and conservation of *Cylindropuntia multigeniculata* (Cactaceae), the Blue Diamond cholla. Reno: U.S. Fish and Wildlife Service, Nevada State Office.

Baker, Marc A. and Michelle A. Cloud-Hughes. 2014. *Cylindropuntia chuckwallensis* (Cactaceae), a new species from Riverside and Imperial Counties, California. *Madroño* 61:231-243.

Baker, Marc, Bruce D. Parfitt & Jon Rebman 2016. *Cylindropuntia chuckwallensis*, in Jepson Flora Project (eds.) *Jepson eFlora,* http://ucjeps.berkeley.edu/cgi-bin/get_IJM.pl?tid=99695.

Baker, Marc, Bruce D. Parfitt & Jon Rebman 2016. *Cylindropuntia fosbergii,* in Jepson Flora Project (eds.) *Jepson eFlora,* http://ucjeps.berkeley.edu/cgi-bin/get_IJM.pl?tid=80396.

Baldwin, B.G., D.H. Goldman, D.J. Keil, R. Patterson, T.J. Rosatti, and D.H. Wilken, eds. 2012. *The Jepson Manual: Vascular Plants of California,* second edition. Berkeley: University of California Press.

Barbour, Michael G., and Valerie Whitworth. 1994. California's living landscape. *Fremontia* 22:3-13.

Baxter, Edgar M. 1935. *California Cactus: A Complete and Scientific Record of the Cacti Native in California.* Los Angeles: Abbey San Encino Press.

Beatley, Janice C. 1976. Vascular plants of the Nevada Test Site and central-southern Nevada: Ecologic and geographic distributions. TID-26881, Prepared for the Division of Biomedical and Environmental Research. Washington, D.C.: Technical Information Center, Energy Research and Development Administration.

Benson, Lyman. 1969. *The Native Cacti of California.* Stanford: Stanford University Press.

Benson, Lyman. 1982. *The Cacti of the United States and Canada.* Stanford: Stanford University Press.

Betancourt, Julio L., Thomas R. Van Devender, and Paul S. Martin, eds. 1990. *Packrat Middens: The Last 40,000 Years of Biotic Change.* Tucson: The University of Arizona Press.

Bogler, David J., John L. Neff, and Beryl B. Simpson. 1995. Multiple origins of the yucca-yucca moth association. *Proceedings of the National Academy of Sciences, USA* 92:6864-6867.

Bogler, David J., and Beryl B. Simpson. 1996. Phylogeny of Agavaceae based on ITS rDNA sequence variation. *American Journal of Botany* 83:1225-1235.

Bornstein, Carol, David Fross, and Bart O'Brien. 2005. *California Native Plants for the Garden.* Los Olivos, CA: Cachuma Press.

Bowers, Janice E. 1996. More flowers or new cladodes? Environmental correlates and biological consequences of sexual reproduction in a Sonoran Desert prickly pear cactus, *Opuntia engelmannii*. *Bulletin of the Torrey Botanical Club* 123:34-40.

Bowers, Janice E. 2002. Flowering patterns and reproductive ecology of *Mammillaria grahamii* (Cactaceae), a common, small cactus in the Sonoran Desert. *Madroño* 49:201-206.

Bowers, Janice E. 2004. Temporal variation in longevity of *Opuntia engelmannii* (Cactaceae) flowers. *Madroño* 51:280-286.

Brenzel, Kathleen Norris, ed. 2005. *Gardening in the Southwest.* Menlo Park: Sunset Publishing Corporation.

Brewer, William Henry, Sereno Watson, and Asa Gray. 1876. *Botany of California, Volume 1.* Second (Revised) Edition. Boston: Little Brown and Company. Accessed at: http://books.google.com/books?vid=OCLC05436856&id=p6FgQDviH2cC&pg=RA2-PA1&lpg=RA2-PA1&dq=Botany+of+California

Britton, Nathaniel L., and Joseph N. Rose. 1919-1923. *The Cactaceae.* 4 volumes. Carnegie Institution of Washington, DC, 248 (1-4).

Brown, James H., and Arthur C. Gibson. 1983. *Biogeography.* St. Louis: The C.V. Mosby Company.

Brum, Gilbert D. 1973. Ecology of the saguaro (*Carnegiea gigantea*): Phenology and establishment in marginal populations. *Madroño* 22:195-204.

Burleigh, Malcom. 2004. *Mammillaria tetrancistra* and *M. guelzowiana:* Care, culture and hybridization. *Cactus and Succulent Journal* 76:114-118.

California Native Plant Society (CNPS). 2017. *Inventory of Rare and Endangered Plants* (online edition, v8-02). Sacramento: California Native Plant Society. http://www.rareplants.cnps.org.

Chamberland, Michael. 1997. Systematics of the *Echinocactus polycephalus* complex (Cactaceae). *Systematic Botany* 22:303-313.

Cheeke, P.R. 2000. Actual and potential applications of *Yucca schidigera* and *Quillaja saponaria* saponins in human and animal nutrition. *Proceedings of the American Society of Animal Science, 1999:* 1-10. http://www.asas.org/symposia/proceedings/0909.pdf

CITES. 2007. Convention on International Trade in Endangered Species of Wild Fauna and Flora. Appendices I, II, and III (May 3, 2007). http://www.cites.org/eng/app/appendices.shtml

Clary, Karen H. 2001. The genus *Hesperoyucca* (Agavaceae) in the western United States and Mexico: New nomenclatural combinations. *Sida* 19:839-847.

Clary, Karen H. 2002. *Hesperoyucca.* In: Flora of North America Editorial Committee, eds. 1993+. *Flora of North America North of Mexico.* 12+ vols. 26:439-441. New York and Oxford.

Cochrane, Susan. 1979. Status of endangered and threatened plant species on Nevada Test Site – A Survey, Parts 1 and 2, Appendix C: Collection records for the taxa considered. March 1979. Prepared for the Nevada Operations Office of the Department of Energy. Goleta, CA: EG&G Inc.

Cornet, Bruce. 2006. When Did Angiosperms First Evolve? http://www.sunstar-solutions.com/sunstar/Why02/why.htm

Cornett, James W. 1995. *Indian Uses of Desert Plants.* Palm Springs: Palm Springs Desert Museum.

Cornett, James W. 1999. *The Joshua Tree.* Palm Springs: Nature Trails Press.

Cota, J. Hugo. 1993. Pollination syndromes in the genus *Echinocereus:* A review. *Cactus and Succulent Journal* 65:19-26.

Cota, Hugo J. 1996. A review of *Ferocactus* Britton and Rose, pages 35-77 In: George Lindsay, *The taxonomy and ecology of the Genus Ferocactus: Explorations in the USA and Mexico.* Escondido, CA: Tireless Termites Press.

Cronquist, Arthur, Noel H. Holmgren, James L. Reveal, and Patricia K. Holmgren. 1977. *Intermountain Flora Vol. 6: The Monocotyledons.* Bronx, NY: New York Botanical Garden Press.

Cseh, Tom. 2006. Cacti and succulents in Pre-Colombian symbology. *To the Point,* Supplement to the *Cactus and Succulent Journal.* 78:16-21.

Cullman, Willy, Erich Götz, and Gerhard Gröner. 1986. *The Encyclopedia of Cacti.* English edition. Portland, OR: Timber Press.

Darwin, Charles. 1859. *On The Origin of Species.* (Reprinted 1952). Chicago: Encyclopedia Britannica, Inc.

Dawson, E. Yale. 1966. *The Cacti of California.* Berkeley: University of California Press.

DeDecker, Mary. 1984. *Flora of the Northern Mojave Desert, California.* Sacramento: California Native Plant Society.

DeDecker, Mary. 2000. *Mary DeDecker's Specimen Card Collection: Taxonomic, Distribution, and Cultural Information on Plants of the Eastern Sierra, Owens Valley, White-Inyo Mountains, and Northern Mojave Desert.* Scanned and compiled by Larry

Blakely, Bristlecone Chapter, California Native Plant Society. Unpublished CD's.

De Groot, Sarah J. 2007. The "nose" of California: An important part of the state's plant diversity. *Fremontia* 35(1):2-6.

Drezner, Teri D. 2004. Saguaros and their nurses in the Sonoran Desert: A review. *Desert Plants* 20:3-10.

Drezner, Teri D. 2004. Saguaro patterns and ecology over Arizona: A closer look at rainfall. *Desert Plants* 20:24-32.

Edwards, Erika J., and Michael J. Donaghue. 2006. *Pereskia* and the origin of the cactus life-form. *American Naturalist* 167:777-793.

Edwards, Erika J., Reto Nyfeller, and Michael J. Donaghue. 2005. Basal cactus phylogeny: Implications of *Pereskia* (Cactaceae) paraphyly for the transition to the cactus life form. *American Journal of Botany* 92:1177-1188.

Elias, Thomas S. 1983. Extraflora nectaries: Their structure and distribution. In: *The Biology of Nectaries*. B.L. Bentley and T.S. Elias, eds. New York: Columbia University Press.

Emming, Jan. 2005. Nevadagascar? The threat that invasive weeds and wildfires pose to our North American desert biomes, Part 1: The Mojave Desert and Joshua tree woodlands. *Cactus and Succulent Journal* 77:302-312.

Emming, Jan. 2006. The threat that invasive weeds and wildfires pose to our North American desert biomes, Part 2: The Sonoran saguaros. *Cactus and Succulent Journal* 78:15-21, 43.

Eppele, David L. 1990. *On the Desert: Essays of the American Deserts.* Arizona: Tortilla Press.

Esque, Todd C., Dustin F. Haines, Lesley A. DeFalco, Jane E. Rodgers, Kimberley A. Goodwin, and Sara J. Scoles. 2003. Mortality of adult Joshua Trees *(Yucca brevifolia)* due to small mammal herbivory at Joshua Tree National Park, California. USGS Report TA#J8R07020011. Reno: University of Nevada.

Esque, Todd C., C.R. Schwalbe, Dustin F. Haines, and William L. Halvorson. 2004. Saguaros under siege: Invasive species and fire. *Desert Plants* 20:49-55.

Evarts, Bill. 1994. *Torrey Pines: Landscape and Legacy.* La Jolla, CA: Torrey Pines Association.

Ferguson, David J. 1989. Revision of the U.S. members of the *Echinocereus triglochidiatus* group. *Cactus and Succulent Journal* 61:217-224.

Foster, Lynne. 1987. *Adventuring in the California Desert.* San Francisco: Sierra Club Books.

Ganders, Fred A., and Helen Kennedy. 1978. Gynodioecy in *Mammillaria dioica* (Cactaceae). *Madroño* 25:234.

Gentry, Howard Scott. 1982. *Agaves of Continental North America.* Tucson: The University of Arizona Press.

Gibson, Arthur C. 2003. *Bergerocactus.* In: Flora of North America Editorial Committee, eds. 1993+. *Flora of North America North of Mexico.* 12+ vols. 4:181-182. New York and Oxford.

Gibson, Arthur C. 2003. *Carnegiea.* In: Flora of North America Editorial Committee, eds. 1993+. *Flora of North America North of Mexico.* 12+ vols. 4:184-185. New York and Oxford.

Gibson, Arthur C., and Park S. Nobel. 1986. *The Cactus Primer.* Cambridge: Harvard University Press.

Gibson, Arthur C., Kevin C. Spencer, Renu Bajaj, and Jerry L. McLaughlin. 1986. The ever-changing landscape of cactus systematics. *Annals of the Missouri Botanical Garden* 73:532-555.

Good-Avila, Sara V., Valeria Souza, Brandon S. Gaut, and Luis E. Eguiarte. 2006. Timing and rate of speciation in *Agave* (Agavaceae). *Proceedings of the National Academy of Sciences, Evolution* 103:9124-9129.

Grant, Verne, and Walter A. Connell. 1979. The association between *Carpophilus* beetles and cactus flowers. *Plant Systematics and Evolution* 133:99-102.

Grantham, Keith, and Paul Klaassen. 1999. *The Plantfinder's Guide to Cacti & Other Succulents.* Portland, OR: Timber Press.

Hancock, Ken. 2003. Hail to Canada's hardy cacti. *Ottowa Valley Rock Garden and Horticultural Newsletter,* reprinted in 2005 at: http://www3.sympatico.ca/lycacti/hail.html

Harlow, Nora, and Kristin Jakob, eds. 2003. *Wild Lilies, Irises, and Grasses: Gardening With California Monocots.* Berkeley and Los Angeles: University of California Press.

Heil, Kenneth D., and J. Mark Porter. 1994. *Sclerocactus* (Cactaceae): A revision. *Haseltonia*

2:20-46.

Heil, Kenneth D., and J. Mark Porter. 2003a. *Sclerocactus.* In: Flora of North America Editorial Committee, eds. 1993+. *Flora of North America North of Mexico.* 12+ vols. 4:197-207. New York and Oxford.

Heil, Kenneth D., and J. Mark Porter. 2003b. *Pediocactus.* In: Flora of North America Editorial Committee, eds. 1993+. *Flora of North America North of Mexico.* 12+ vols. 4:211-216. New York and Oxford.

Hershkovitz, Mark A., and Elizabeth A. Zimmer. 1997. On the evolutionary origins of the cacti. *Taxon* 46:217-232.

Hess, William J. 2002. *Nolina.* In: Flora of North America Editorial Committee, eds. 1993+. *Flora of North America North of Mexico.* 12+ vols. 26:415-421. New York and Oxford.

Hess, William J., and R. Laurie Robbins. 2002. *Yucca.* In: Flora of North America Editorial Committee, eds. 1993+. *Flora of North America North of Mexico.* 12+ vols. 26:423-439. New York and Oxford.

Heywood, Vernon H., ed. 1985. *Flowering Plants of the World.* Englewood Cliffs, NJ: Prentice-Hall, Inc.

Hochstätter, Fritz. 1993. *The Genus Sclerocactus, Cactaceae-Revised.* Published by the author, Mannheim, Germany. [English translation by Chris Holland.]

Hodgson, Wendy. 1999. Agavaceae, Agave Family, Part 1. *Journal of the Arizona-Nevada Acacdemy of Sciences.* 32:1-21.

Houk, Rose. 1996. *Wild Cactus.* New York: Workman Publishing Company, Inc.

Humphreys, Anna, and Susan Lowell. 2002. *Saguaro: The Desert Giant.* Tucson: Rio Nuevo Publishers.

Irish, Mary, and Gary Irish. 2000. *Agaves, Yuccas, and Related Plants: A Gardener's Guide.* Portland, OR: Timber Press.

Jaeger, Edmund C. 1933 (Revised edition, 1938). *The California Deserts: A Visitor's Handbook.* Stanford, CA: Stanford University Press.

Jaeger, Edmund C. 1940 (Revised edition, 1969). *Desert Wild Flowers.* Stanford, CA: Stanford University Press.

Jordan, Peter W., and Park S. Nobel. 1979. Infrequent establishment of seedlings of *Agave deserti* (Agavaceae) in the northwestern Sonoran Desert. *American Journal of Botany* 66:1079-1084.

Junak, Steve, Tina Ayers, Randy Scott, Dieter Wilken, and David Young. 1995. *Flora of Santa Cruz Island.* Santa Barbara: Santa Barbara Botanic Garden; Sacramento: California Native Plant Society.

Keator, Glenn. 1994. *Complete Garden Guide to the Native Shrubs of California.* San Francisco: Chronicle Books.

Kemp, Paul R., and Pietra E. Gardetto. 1982. Photosynthetic pathway types of evergreen rosette plants (Liliaceae) of the Chihuahuan Desert. *Oecologia* 55:149-156.

Knut, Adrienne. 1991. *Plants of the East Mojave.* Cima, CA: Wide Horizons Press.

Kolendo, Jan. 1998. The Agave: A plant and its story, part 1. http://www.desert-tropicals.com/Articles/Agave/

Krutch, Joseph Wood. 1951. *The Desert Year.* New York: The Viking Press, Inc.

Leebens-Mack, Jim, Olle Pellmyr, and Marcus Brock. 1998. Host specificity and the genetic structure of two yucca moth species in a yucca hybrid zone. *Evolution* 52:1376-1382.

Lenz, Lee W. 1977. Rancho Santa Ana Botanic Garden: The First Fifty Years, 1927-1977. *Aliso* 9:1-156.

Lewis, Meriwether, William Clark, et al. July 15, 1805. *The Journals of the Lewis and Clark Expedition,* ed. Gary Moulton. (Lincoln, NE: University of Nebraska Press / University of Nebraska-Lincoln Libraries-Electronic Text Center, 2005), http://lewisandclarkjournals.unl.edu.

Lightner, James. 2004. *San Diego County Native Plants.* San Diego: San Diego Flora.

Lindsay, George. 1996. *The taxonomy and ecology of the Genus Ferocactus, Explorations in the USA and Mexico.* Escondido, CA: Tireless Termites Press

Loik, Michael E., and Park S. Nobel. 1993. Freezing tolerance and water relations of *Opuntia fragilis* from Canada and the United States. *Ecology* 74:1722-1732.

MacKay, Pam. 2003. *Mojave Desert Wildflowers.* Guilford: The Globe Pequot Press.

Magallón, Susana, and Michael J. Sanderson. 2001. Absolute diversification rates in angiosperm clades. *Evolution* 55:1762-1780.

Masilko, Todd. 2007. Border Field State Park: A unique habitat for succulent plants at the US-Mexico border. *Cactus and Succulent Journal* 79:63-71.

Mauseth, James D. 1990. Continental drift, climate and the evolution of cacti. *Cactus and Succulent Journal* 62:302-308.

Mauseth, James D. 2004. *Mauseth Research: Cacti.* http://www.sbs.utexas.edu/mauseth/ResearchOnCacti/Flowers.htm

May, Richard W. 1982. Distribution and status of *Sclerocactus polyancistrus* on the Naval Weapons Center — A survey. China Lake: Naval Weapons Center, CA

May, Richard W. 1988. Interrelationships between two new taxa within the genus *Sclerocactus* (Cactaceae). *Cactus and Succulent Journal* 60:35-45.

May, Richard W. 1994. The ecology of *Sclerocactus polyancistrus* (Cactaceae) in California and Nevada. *Desert Plants* 11:6-22.

Mayer, Michael S., Anastasia Gromova, Kristen Hasenstab-Lehman, Molly Lippitt, Mia Barnett, and Jon P. Rebman. 2011. Is *Cylindropuntia Xfosbergii* (Cactaceae) a hybrid? *Madroño* 58:106-112.

Mayer, Michael S., Laura L. Williams, and Jon P. Rebman. 2000. Molecular evidence for the hybrid origin of *Opuntia prolifera* (Cactaceae). *Madroño* 47:109-115.

McCarten, Naill F. 1981. Fossil cacti and other succulents from the late Pleistocene. *Cactus and Succulent Journal* 53:122-123.

McIntosh, Margrit E. 2002. Flowering phenology and reproductive output in two sister species of *Ferocactus* (Cactaceae). *Plant Ecology* 159:1-13.

McIntosh, Margrit E. 2005. Pollination of two species of Ferocactus: Interactions between cactus-specialist bees and their host plants. *Functional Ecology* 19:727-734.

McKelvey, Susan Delano. 1956. *Botanical Exploration of the Trans-Mississippi West, 1790-1850.* Jamaica Plain, MA: Arnold Arboretum of Harvard University. (1991 Reprint, Introduction by Stephen Dow Beckham, Corvallis: Oregon State University Press.)

McKinney, John. 2004. *Day Hiker's Guide to California's State Parks.* Santa Barbara: Olympus Press.

McLeod, Malcolm. 1975. A new hybrid fleshy-fruited prickly-pear. *Madroño* 23:96-98.

Mead, F.W., and J.L. Herring. 2001-2005. Cactus bug, *Chelinidea vittiger aequoris* McAtee (Insecta: Hemiptera:Coreidae). *University of Florida, IFAS Extension.* Publication EENY-208. http://edis.ifas.ufl.edu/pdffiles/IN/IN36500.pdf

Menzies, Archibald. Menzies' Journal of Vancouver's Voyage, April to October, 1792. Edited, with Botanical and Ethnological Notes, by C.F. Newcombe, M.D., and a Biographical Note by J. Forsyth. Madison: Wisconsin Historical Society, 2003. http://content.wisconsinhistory.org/cgi-bin/docviewer.exe?CISOROOT=/aj&CISOPTR=7725&CISOSHOW=7162

Mills, Anne H. 1996. The splendid ocotillo. *Fremontia* 24:3-7.

Morefield, James D., ed. 2001. *Nevada Rare Plant Atlas,* compiled by the Nevada Natural Heritage Program. Reno, NV and Portland, OR: U.S. Department of the Interior, Fish and Wildlife Service. http://heritage.nv.gov/atlas/atlas.html

Morhardt, Sia, and Emil Morhardt. 2004. *California Desert Flowers.* Berkeley and Los Angeles: University of California Press.

Mozingo, Hugh N. and Margaret Williams. 1969. *Yucca gilbertiana* in central Nevada. *Cactus and Succulent Journal* 41:242-244.

Munz, Philip A. 1974. *A Flora of Southern California.* Berkeley: University of California Press.

Nabhan, Gary Paul. 1989. *Enduring Seeds: Native American Agriculture and Wild Plant Conservation.* New York: North Point Press.

Niles, Wesley E., and Patrick J. Leary. 2007. Annotated checklist of the vascular plants of the Spring Mountains, Clark and Nye Counties, Nevada. *Mentzelia* 8:1-72.

Nilsson, Karen B. 1994. *A Wild Flower By Any Other Name: Sketches of Pioneer Naturalists Who Named Our Western Plants.* Yosemite: Yosemite Association.

Nobel, Park S. 1981. Influences of photosynthetically active radiation on cladode orientation, stem tilting, and height of cacti. *Ecology* 62:982-990.

Nobel, Park S. 1994. *Remarkable Agaves and Cacti.* Oxford: Oxford University Press.

Nyfeller, Reto. 2002. Phylogenetic relationships in the cactus family (Cactaceae) based on evidence from *trnK/ matK* and *trnL-trnF* sequences. *American Journal of Botany* 89:312-326.

Ornduff, Robert, Phyllis M. Faber, and Todd Keeler-Wolf. 2003. *Introduction to California Plant Life,* Revised edition. Berkeley and Los Angeles: University of California Press.

Osborn, Martha M., Peter G. Kevan, and Meredith A. Lane. 1988. Pollination biology of *Opuntia polyacantha* and *Opuntia phaeacantha* (Cactaceae) in southern Colorado. *Plant Systematics and Evolution* 159:85-94.

Parfitt, Bruce D. 1985. Dioecy in North American Cacataceae: A review. *Sida* 11:200-206.

Parfitt, Bruce D. 1991. Biosystematics of the *Opuntia polyacantha* complex (Cactaceae) of western North America. Ph.D. dissertation, Arizona State University.

Parfitt, Bruce D., and Arthur C. Gibson. 2003. Cactaceae In: Flora of North America Editorial Committee, eds. 1993+. *Flora of North America North of Mexico.* 12+ vols. 4:92-99. New York and Oxford.

Parfitt, Bruce D., and Charles H. Pickett. 1980. Insect pollination of prickly-pears (*Opuntia*: Cactaceae). *Southwestern Naturalist* 25:104-107.

Parfitt, Bruce D., and Donald J. Pinkava. 1988. Nomenclatural and systematic reassessment of *Opuntia engelmannii* and *O. lindheimeri* (Cactaceae). *Madroño* 35:342-349.

Pellmyr, Olle. 1999. Systematic revision of the yucca moths in the *Tegeticula yuccasella* complex (Lepidoptera: Prodoxidae) north of Mexico. *Systematic Entomology* 24:243-271.

Pellmyr, Olle. 2003. Yuccas, yucca moths, and coevolution: A review. *Annals of the Missouri Botanical Garden* 90:35-55.

Pellmyr, Olle, James Leebens-Mack, and C.J. Huth. 1996. Non-mutualistic yucca moths and their evolutionary consequences. *Nature* 380:256-257.

Pellmyr, Olle, and James Leebens-Mack. 1999. Forty million years of mutualism: Evidence for Eocene origin of the yucca-yucca moth association. *Proceedings of the National Academy of Sciences, Evolution.* 96:9178-9183.

Pellmyr, Olle and Kari A. Segraves. 2003. Pollinator divergence within an obligate mutualism: Two yucca moth species (Lepidoptera; Prodoxidae: *Tegeticula*) on the Joshua tree (*Yucca brevifolia;* Agavaceae). *Entomological Society of America* 96:716-722.

Pellmyr, Olle, John N. Thompson, Jonathan M. Brown, and Richard G. Harrison. 1996. Evolution of pollination and mutualism in the yucca moth lineage. *American Naturalist* 148:827-847.

Philbrick, Ralph N. 1963. Biosystematic studies of two Pacific Coast Opuntias. Ph.D. dissertation, Cornell University.

Pickett, Charles H. and W. Dennis Clark. 1979. The function of extrafloral nectaries in *Opuntia acanthocarpa* (Cactaceae). *American Journal of Botany* 66:618-625.

Pinkava, Donald. J. 2002. On the evolution of the continental North American Opuntioideae (Cactaceae). *Succulent Plant Research* 6:59-98.

Pinkava, Donald J. 2003a. *Cylindropuntia.* In: Flora of North America Editorial Committee, eds. 1993+. *Flora of North America North of Mexico.* 12+ vols. 4:103-118. New York and Oxford.

Pinkava, Donald J. 2003b. *Grusonia.* In: Flora of North America Editorial Committee, eds. 1993+. *Flora of North America North of Mexico.* 12+ vols. 4:118-123. New York and Oxford.

Pinkava, Donald J. 2003c. *Opuntia.* In: Flora of North America Editorial Committee, eds. 1993+. *Flora of North America North of Mexico.* 12+ vols. 4:123-148. New York and Oxford.

Porter, J. Mark, Michael S. Kinney, and Kenneth D. Heil. 2000. Relationships between *Sclerocactus* and *Toumeya* (Cactaceae) based on chloroplast TRNL-TRNF sequences. *Haseltonia* 7:7-23.

Powell, Jerry A. 1989. Synchronized, mass-emergences of a yucca moth, *Prodoxus Y-inversus* (Lepidoptera: Prodoxidae) after 16 and 17 years in diapause. *Oecologia* 81:490-493.

Powell, Jerry A. 1992. Interrelationships of Yuccas and Yucca Moths. *Trends in Ecology and Evolution* 7:10-15.

Powell, Jerry A., and Richard A. Mackie. 1966. *Biological interrelationships of moths and* Yucca whipplei. University of California Publications in Entomology 42:1-59. Berkeley: University of California Press.

Powell, Jerry A. and Charles L. Hogue. 1979. *Califor-*

*nia Insects.* Berkeley: University of California Press.

Qiu, Yin-Long, Jungho Lee, Fabiana Bernasconi-Quadroni, Douglas E. Soltis, Pamela E. Soltis, Michael Zanis, Elizabeth A. Zimmer, Zhuiduan Chen, Vincent Savolalnen, and Mark W. Chase. 1999. The earliest angiosperms: Evidence from mitochondrial, plastid and nuclcar genomes. *Nature* 42:404-407.

Raphael, Deborah O., and Park S. Nobel. 1986. Growth and survivorship of ramets and seedlings of *Agave deserti:* Influences of parent-ramet connections. *Botanical Gazette* 147:78-83.

Raven, Peter H., and Daniel I. Axelrod. 1978. Origin and relationships of the California flora. *University of California publications in Botany* 72:1-134.

Rebman, Jon P. 1994. Stamen aberration in *Opuntia prolifera* Engelmann (Cactaceae). *Haseltonia* 2:103-108.

Rebman, Jon P. 2001. Succulent diversity in Lower California, Mexico. *Cactus and Succulent Journal* 73:131-138.

Rebman, Jon P. 2005. Gander's cholla: Our common but barely known cactus. *The Sand Paper: Anza-Borrego Desert Natural History Association Newsletter* vol. XXXIV, Winter 2005-2006:3-4.

Rebman, Jon P., and Donald J. Pinkava. 2001. *Opuntia* Cacti of North America - An Overview. *Florida Entomologist* 84(4):474-483.

Reveal, James L., and Wendy C. Hodgson. 2002. Agave. In: Flora of North America Editorial Committee, eds. 1993+. *Flora of North America North of Mexico.* 12+ vols. 4:442-461. New York and Oxford.

Rhoads, William A., Susan A. Cochrane, and Michael P. Williams. 1978. Status of endangered and threatened plant species on Tonopah Test Site – A Survey. Part 2: Threatened species, May 1978. Prepared for the Nevada Operations Office of the Department of Energy. Goleta, CA: EG&G Inc.

Rhoads, William A., Susan A. Cochrane, and Michael P. Williams. 1979. Status of endangered and threatened plant species on Tonopah Test Range – A Survey, October, 1979. Prepared for the Nevada Operations Office of the Department of Energy. Goleta, CA: EG&G Inc.

Rocha, Martha, Sara V. Good-Ávila, Francisco Molina-Freaner, Héctor T. Arita, Amanda Castillo, Abisaí García-Mendoza, Arturo Silva-Montellano, Brandon S. Gaut, Valeria Souza, and Luis E. Eguiarte. 2006. Pollination biology and adaptive radiation of Agavaceae, with special emphasis on the genus *Agave. Aliso* 22:329-344.

Ruffner, George A., and W. Dennis Clark. 1986. Extrafloral nectar of *Ferocactus acanthodes* (Cactaceae): Composition and its importance to ants. *American Journal of Botany* 73:185-189.

Schad, Jerry. 1988. *California Deserts.* Helena: Falcon Publishing, Inc.

Schoenherr, Allan A. 1992. *A Natural History of California.* Berkeley: University of California Press.

Sivarajan, V.V. 1991. *Introduction to the Principles of Plant Taxonomy.* 2nd ed. Cambridge (UK): Cambridge University Press.

Smith, Stanley D., Terry L. Hartsock, and Park S. Nobel. 1983. Ecophysiology of *Yucca brevifolia,* an arborescent monocot of the Mojave Desert. *Oecologia* 60:10-17.

Smith, Stanley D., Brigette Didden-Zopfy, and Park S. Nobel. 1984. High-temperature responses of North American cacti. *Ecology* 65:643-651.

Soltis, Pam, Doug Soltis, and Christine Edwards. 2005. Angiosperms. Flowering Plants. Version 03 June 2005. http://tolweb.org/Angiosperms/20646/2005.06.03 in The Tree of Life Web Project, http://tolweb.org/

Spiers, Dale. 1989. The Opuntias of Alberta, Canada (both of them). *Cactus and Succulent Journal* 61:235-236.

Stevens, Peter F. 2006. Angiosperm Phylogeny Website. Version 7, May 2006. http://www.mobot.org/MOBOT/research/APweb/

Stuppy, Wolfgang. 2002. Seed characters and the generic classification of the Opuntioideae (Cactaceae). *Succulent Plant Research* 6:25-58.

Sullender, Barry. 1998. A natural history of extrafloral nectar-collecting ants in the Sonoran Desert. http://www.ruf.rice.edu/~bws/efns.html

Taylor, Nigel P. 1985. *The Genus Echinocereus.* Kew: Royal Botanic Gardens.

Thorne, Robert F. 1986. A historical sketch of the vegetation of the Mojave and Colorado Deserts of the American Southwest. *Annals of the Missouri Botanical Garden* 73:642-651.

Tidwell, William D. and Lee R. Parker. 1990. *Protoyucca shadishii* gen. et sp. nov., an arborescent monocotyledon with secondary growth from the middle Miocene of northwestern Nevada, USA. *Review of Paleobotany and Palynology* 62:79-95.

Torres, John K. 1980. *The Audubon Society Encyclopedia of North American Birds.* New York: Alfred A. Knopf.

Trelease, William. 1902. The Yucceae. *Missouri Botanical Garden Annual Report.* 1902:27-133.

Turner, Raymond M., Janice E. Bowers, and Tony L. Burgess. 1995. *Sonoran Desert Plants: An Ecological Atlas.* Tucson: The University of Arizona Press.

Tweed, William C. and Lauren Davis. 2003. *Death Valley and the Northern Mojave: A Visitor's Guide.* Los Olivos, CA: Cachuma Press.

U.S. Fish and Wildlife Service. 1998. Recovery Plan for Upland Species of the San Joaquin Valley, California. Region 1, Portland, OR.

United States War Dept. 1856. *Reports of explorations and surveys, to ascertain the most practicable and economical route for a railroad from the Mississippi River to the Pacific Ocean. Route near the thirty-fifth parallel, explored by Lieutenant W.W. Whipple, Topographical Engineer, in 1853 and 1854. Part V. Report on the Botany of the Expedition.* Washington, D.C. http://quod.lib.umich.edu/cgi/t/text/text-idx?c=moa&idno=AFK4383.0004.003

Verhoek, Susan, and William J. Hess. 2003. Agavaceae. In: Flora of North America Editorial Committee, eds. *Flora of North America North of Mexico* 26:413-415. New York and Oxford.

Wallace, Robert S., and Steven L. Dickie. 2002. Systematic implications of chloroplast DNA sequence variation in subfam. Opuntioideae (Cactaceae). *Succulent Plant Research* 6:9-24.

Wallace, Robert S., and Arthur C. Gibson. 2002. Evolution and Systematics in P.S. Nobel, ed. *Cacti: Biology and Uses.* Berkeley: University of California Press.

Wells, Philip V., and Deborah Woodcock. 1985. Full-glacial vegetation of Death Valley, California: Juniper woodland opening to Yucca semidesert. *Madroño* 32:11-23.

Wiese, Jeff, Steve McPherson, Michelle C. Odden, and Michael G. Shlipak. 2004. Effect of *Opuntia ficus-indica* on symptoms of the alcohol hangover. *Archives of Internal Medicine* 164:1334-1340.

Wilson, Edward O. 1992. *The Diversity of Life.* New York: W.W. Norton & Company, Inc.

Wikström, Niklas, Vincent Savolainen, and Mark W. Chase. 2001. Evolution of the angiosperms: Calibrating the family tree. *Proceedings of the Royal Society of London, Biological Sciences* 268:2211-2220.

Wolfe, Kenneth H., Manolo Gouy, Yau-Wen Yang, Paul M. Sharp, and Wen-Hsiung Li. 1989. Date of the monocot-dicot divergence estimated from chloroplast DNA sequence data. *Proceedings of the National Academy of Sciences, Evolution* 86:6201-6205.

Zimmerman, Allan D., and Bruce D. Parfitt. 2003a. *Echinocereus.* In: Flora of North America Editorial Committee, eds. 1993+. *Flora of North America North of Mexico.* 12+ vols. 4:157-174. New York and Oxford.

Zimmerman, Allan D., and Bruce D. Parfitt. 2003b. *Echinocactus.* In: Flora of North America Editorial Committee, eds. 1993+. *Flora of North America North of Mexico.* 12+ vols. 4:188-191. New York and Oxford.

Zimmerman, Allan D., and Bruce D. Parfitt. 2003c. *Echinomastus.* In: Flora of North America Editorial Committee, eds. 1993+. *Flora of North America North of Mexico.* 12+ vols. 4:192-196. New York and Oxford.

Zimmerman, Allan D., and Bruce D. Parfitt. 2003d. *Coryphantha.* In: Flora of North America Editorial Committee, eds. 1993+. *Flora of North America North of Mexico.* 12+ vols. 4:220-237. New York and Oxford.

Zimmerman, Allan D., and Bruce D. Parfitt. 2003e. *Ferocactus.* In: Flora of North America Editorial Committee, eds. 1993+. *Flora of North America North of Mexico.* 12+ vols. 4:243-247. New York and Oxford.

Zimmerman, Allan D., and Bruce D. Parfitt. 2003f. *Mammillaria.* In: Flora of North America Editorial Committee, eds. 1993+. *Flora of North America North of Mexico.* 12+ vols. 4:247-257. New York and Oxford.

# Index

aborescent prickly-pear, 189
adaptations for an arid environment, 8–12, 88, 96, 104, 108–109
*Agave*, 5, 151
    *americana*, 189
    *deserti* var. *deserti*, 7, 152–155
    *deserti* var. *simplex*, 152–155
    *shawii* var. *shawii*, 156–157, 199
    *utahensis* var. *eborispina*, 158–161, 199
    *utahensis* var. *nevadensis*, 158–161, 199, 224
    *utahensis* var. *utahensis*, 158–161, 199
Agavaceae, 5
Alverson, Allen H., 40
American agave, 189
Anderson, Edward, 39
Angiosperm Phylogeny Group (APG), 7–8
Anza-Borrego Desert State Park, 205–206, 226, 228
apricot prickly-pear, 130–131

Baker, Marc, 56, 64, 73
Bakersfield cactus, 108–111, 191–192, 193, 222–223, 224
banana yucca, 168–169, 200
barrel cactus, 77, 86
Baxter, Edgar M., 88, 120
Bazell, Susan, ix
beargrass, 182
beavertail cactus, 108–111, 201, 222–223
beehive cactus, 44–45, 200, 224
Benson, Lyman, 25, 44, 53, 60, 74, 82, 122, 130, 134
Berger, Alwin, 31
*Bergerocactus*, 31
*Bergerocactus emoryi*, 30, 32–33, 224
Bigelow nolina, 182–185
Bigelow, John M., 50, 72, 144
Blaine fishhook cactus, 138–139, 224
Blue Diamond cholla, 64–65, 220–221, 224
Bowers, Janice, 114
Britton, Nathaniel, 31, 35, 87, 133, 137
brown-spined prickly-pear, 114, 122–123, 128, 130, 222–223
buckhorn cholla, 46, 48–49, 220–221
bunny ears prickly-pear, 189

Cabrillo National Monument, 203–204, 226, 228
cacti, agaves, and yuccas
    adaptations for an arid environment, 8–12, 88, 96, 104, 108–109
    animal interactions with, 17–20
    conservation of, 191–194, 224
    cultivation of, 194–201
    ecology and habitats of, 15–21
    evolutionary history of, 3–5
    flowers of, 12–13
    growing in containers, 195–196
    growing in the garden, 196–197
    heat tolerance of, 89, 101, 108
    illegal harvest of, 194
    plant relationships with, 20–21
    propagating from seeds and cuttings, 197–198
    roots of, 10
    spines of, 11–12
    succulence in, 9
    ten choices for cultivation, 198–201
    vegetation types where found, 16–17, 216–217
cactus bee, 19, 113, 114
cactus longhorn beetle, 20, 144
California fishhook cactus, 100–101
CAM photosynthesis, 9–10, 108
cane cholla, 52–54
Carnegie, Andrew, 35
*Carnegiea*, 35
*Carnegiea gigantea*, 34, 35, 36–37, 224
century plant, 151, 152, 189
chaparral nolina, 183–184, 185, 224
chaparral yucca, 162, 164–165, 199–200
cholla, 47, 220–221
cholla hydrids, 55
Chuckwalla cholla, 56–57
Clark Mountain agave, 152–155, 199, 224
Clokey, Ira, 64
Cloud-Hughes, Michelle, 56
club-cholla, 93
coast barrel cactus, 90–91, 224
coastal cholla, 68–69, 220–221
coastal prickly-pear, 118–119, 222–223
Colorado Desert, 16
common fishhook cactus, 100–101

*Coryphantha,* 39
    *alversonii,* 38, 40–41, 224
    *chlorantha,* 42–43
    *vivipara* var. *rosea,* 44–45, 200, 224
cottontop cactus, 76, 77, 78–79
Coulter, John M., 40, 41
curve-spined prickly-pear, 128–129, 131, 224
cushion foxtail cactus, 38, 40–41, 224
*Cylindropuntia,* 47
    *acanthocarpa* var. *acanthocarpa,* 48–49, 220–221
    *bigelovii,* 50–51, 200, 220–221
    *californica* var. *californica,* 52–54, 220–221, 224
    *californica* var. *parkeri,* 52–54, 220–221
    *chuckwallensis,* 56–57, 220–221
    X*deserta,* 48, 55
    *echinocarpa,* 58–59, 220–221
    *fosbergii,* 60–61, 220–221
    *ganderi,* 62–63, 220–221
    *multigeniculata,* 64–65, 220–221, 224
    *munzii,* 7, 66–67, 220–221, 224
    *prolifera,* 68–69, 220–221
    *ramosissima,* 70–71, 220–221
    *whipplei,* 72–73, 220–221
    *wolfii,* 74–75, 220–221

Darwin, Charles, 22
Dawson, Yale, 37
Death Valley National Park, 208–209, 227, 229
Dehesa nolina, 184, 185, 224
desert agave, 7, 21, 152–153
desert barrel cactus, 86, 88–89
Desert National Wildlife Refuge, 210–211, 230
desert pincushion cactus, 42–43
diamond cholla, 70–71, 220–221
Dice, James, 183

eagle-claw cactus, 137
*Echinocactus,* 77
    *polycephalus* var. *polycephalus,* 76, 78–79
    *polycephalus* var. *xeranthemoides,* 78–79
*Echinocereus,* 81
    *engelmannii,* 82–83
    *mojavensis,* 80, 84–85, 200–201
*Echinopsis spachiana,* 189
Engelmann fishhook cactus, 138, 139, 147

Engelmann hedgehog, 82–83
Engelmann prickly-pear, 114–115
Engelmann, George, 7, 31, 35, 42, 44, 47, 50, 52, 53, 72, 81, 82, 144, 146, 186
evolutionary history of cacti and agave relatives, 2
extrafloral nectary, 19–20, 88

Ferguson, David J., 84
*Ferocactus,* 86
    *cylindraceus,* 86, 88–89, 201
    *viridescens,* 90–91, 224
fishhook cactus, 137
flowers, 12–13
Fosberg, Francis Raymond, 60
*Fouquieria splendens* ssp. *splendens,* 186–187
Frémont, John C., 170

Gander cholla, 62–63, 220–221
Gentry, Howard Scott, 151, 152
giant saguaro, 16, 21, 34, 35, 36–37, 224
Gibson, Arthur, 28
Gold Butte Region, 211, 230
golden cereus, 30, 31, 32–33, 224
golden torch cereus, 189
Graham fishhook cactus, 98, 102–103, 224
Grand Canyon cottontop, 78–79
Gray, Asa, 52
Great Basin Desert, 16
Great Basin fishhook cactus, 146–147, 224
Gruson, Herman, 93
*Grusonia,* 93
    *parishii,* 92, 94–95, 224
    *pulchella,* 96–97, 224
gynodioecy, 56, 100

Harriman yucca, 174–175
Harriman, Mary Averell, 174
Haworth, Adrian, 99
hedgehog cactus, 81
Heil, Kenneth, 138
*Hesperoyucca,* 163
    *whipplei,* 162, 164–165, 199–200
Hochstätter, Fritz, 142
Hooker, Joseph, 151

Indian-fig cactus, 188, 222–223

invasive weeds in cactus habitats, 193
ivory-spined agave, 158–159, 199, 224

Jaeger Joshua tree, 171–173
Jaeger, Edmund, 19, 66
Johnson pineapple cactus, 136, 140–141, 224
Johnson, Joseph E., 140
Joshua tree, 7, 16, 20, 170–173
Joshua Tree National Park, 206, 226, 228

Lake Mead National Recreation Area, 211–212, 230
Lewis, Meriwether, 126
Linnaeus, Carolus, 151, 167
little prickly-pear, 116–117, 222–223, 224
loggerhead shrike, 19

*Mamillaria*, 99
    *dioica*, 100–101
    *grahamii* var. *grahamii*, 98, 102–103
    *tetrancistra*, 104–105
Mason Valley cholla, 55, 60–61, 220–221, 224
McKelvey, Susan Delano, 163, 178
Menzies, Archibald, 116
Mescal, 151, 154
Miller, Philip, 107
Mission cactus, 188
Mojave Desert, 16
Mojave fishhook cactus, 144–145, 224
Mojave mound cactus, 80, 84–85, 200–201
Mojave National Preserve, 206–208, 227, 229
Mojave prickly-pear, 124–125, 127, 201, 222–223
Mojave yucca, 166, 176–177
mountain cactus, 132, 134–135
Munz cholla, 7, 66–67, 220–221, 224
Munz, Carl, 183
Munz, Philip, 7, 66
Murman, Eugene O., ix

nipple cactus, 99
Nobel, Park, 50, 112, 152
nolina, 182
*Nolina*, 182
*Nolina bigelovii*, 182–183, 185
*Nolina cismontana*, 183–184, 224
*Nolina interrata*, 184–185, 224
*Nolina parryi*, 184–185

non-native species, 188–189, 193
nurse plant, 21, 36, 153
Nuttall, Thomas, 31, 44, 52

Ocotillo, 186–187
*Opuntia*, 99, 107
    *basilaris* var. *basilaris*, 108–111, 201, 222–223
    *basilaris* var. *brachyclada*, 108–111, 201, 222–223, 224
    *basilaris* var. *longiareolata*, 109
    *basilaris* var. *treleasei*, 108–111, 191–192, 222–223, 224
    *chlorotica*, 106, 112–113, 128, 222–223
    X*curvispina*, 128–129, 131, 222–223, 224
    *engelmannii* var. *engelmannii*, 114–115, 222–223
    *ficus-indica*, 107, 129, 188, 222–223
    *fragilis*, 116–117, 222–223, 224
    *leucotricha*, 189
    *littoralis*, 118–119, 129, 130, 222–223
    *microdasys*, 189
    X*occidentalis*, 120, 129–131, 222–223
    *oricola*, 120–121, 129, 222–223
    *phaeacantha*, 122–123, 128, 130, 222–223
    *polyacantha* var. *erinacea*, 124–127, 201, 222–223
    *polyacantha* var. *hystricina*, 124–125, 222–223
    *polyacantha* var. *polyacantha*, 124–127, 222–223
    X*vaseyi*, 119, 130–131, 222–223

packrat middens, 6
pancake prickly-pear, 106, 112–113, 128, 222–223
Parfitt, Bruce, 124
Parish club-cholla, 94–95, 224
Parry nolina, 184–185
Parry, Charles C., 53, 82, 140, 185
*Pediocactus*, 133
    *simpsonii*, 132, 134–135, 215
Pellmyr, Olle, 172
Philbrick, Ralph, 120
pincushion cactus, 39
pink teddy-bear cholla, 60
Pinkava, Donald, 52, 109
Pitton de Tournefort, Joseph, 107
Plains cactus, 133
Plains prickly-pear, 124–127, 215
plant classification, 7–8
pollination, 12–13, 19, 22–23

porcupine prickly-pear, 124–127, 215
Porter, Mark J., 138
prickly-pear, 107, 222–223
prickly-pear hybrids, 128–131
prickly-pear illustration, 29

Rebman, Jon, 62, 70
Red Rock Canyon National Conservation Area, 212–213, 231
roots, 10–11
Rose, Joseph 31, 35, 87, 133, 137

saguaro, 35
sand-cholla, 96–97, 224
sap beetles, 20
saponin, 176, 178, 187
*Sclerocactus*, 137
    *blainei*, 138–139, 224
    *johnsonii*, 136, 140–141, 224
    *nyensis*, 142–143 224
    *polyancistrus*, 144–145, 224
    *pubispinus*, 146–147, 224
    *spinosior*, 138
Scott's oriole, 18
Searchlight prickly-pear, 128
Segraves, Kari, 172
Shaw agave, 150, 156–157, 199
short-joint beavertail, 108–111, 201, 222–223, 224
silver cholla, 48, 62–63
simple desert agave, 152–155
snake cholla, 52–54, 220–221, 224
Sonoran Desert, 16
Spanish bayonet, 167
Spines, 11–12
Spring Mountains National Recreation Area, 212, 231
Succulence, 8

tall prickly-pear, 119, 120–121, 222–223
teddy-bear cholla, 50–51, 200, 220–221
Thorne, Kaye, 138
Tonopah fishhook cactus, 142–143, 224
Torrey Pines State Reserve, 118, 204, 226, 228
Torrey, John, 52, 168
Trelease, William, 163, 174

Utah agave, 158-161, 199
Utah yucca, 178-179

Valley of Fire State Park, 213, 231
Vasey prickly-pear, 119, 130–131, 222–223

Welsh, Stanley, 138
western prickly-pear, 129–131, 222–223
Whipple cholla, 72–73, 220–221
Whipple Mountains Wilderness, 209–210, 227, 229
Whipple, Amiel W., 72
Wolf cholla, 74–75, 220–221
Wolf, Carl B., 7, 60, 66, 74

*Yucca,* 5, 167
    *baccata* var. *baccata*, 168–169, 200
    *brevifolia*, 170–173
    *harrimaniae*, 174–175
    *schidigera*, 166, 176–177
    *utahensis*, 178–179
yuccas and yucca moths, 22–23, 165, 168, 172, 174, 176–177, 178
    cheater yucca moths, 23, 164

*Mojave mound cactus. [Joshua Tree N.P.]*